What Every Violinist
Needs to Know about the Body

What Every Violinist Needs to Know about the Body

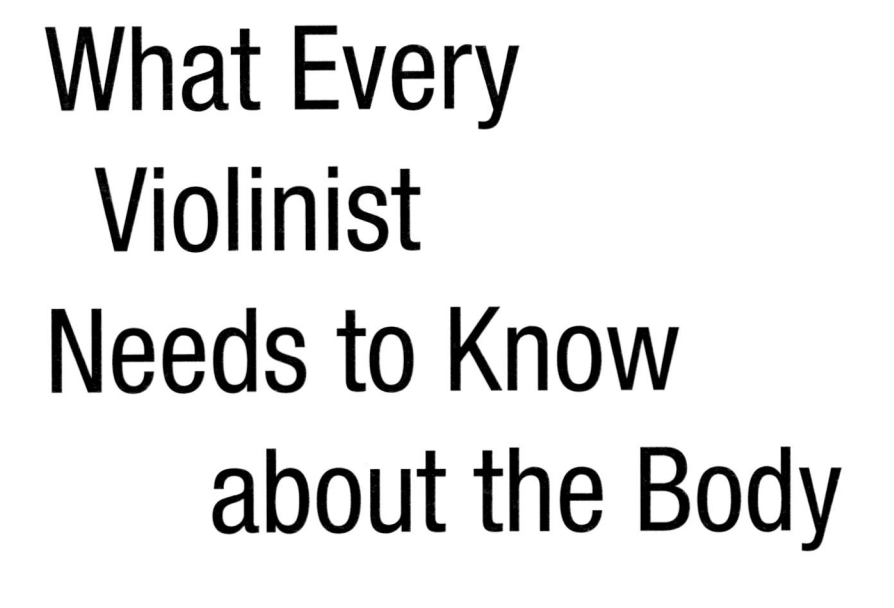

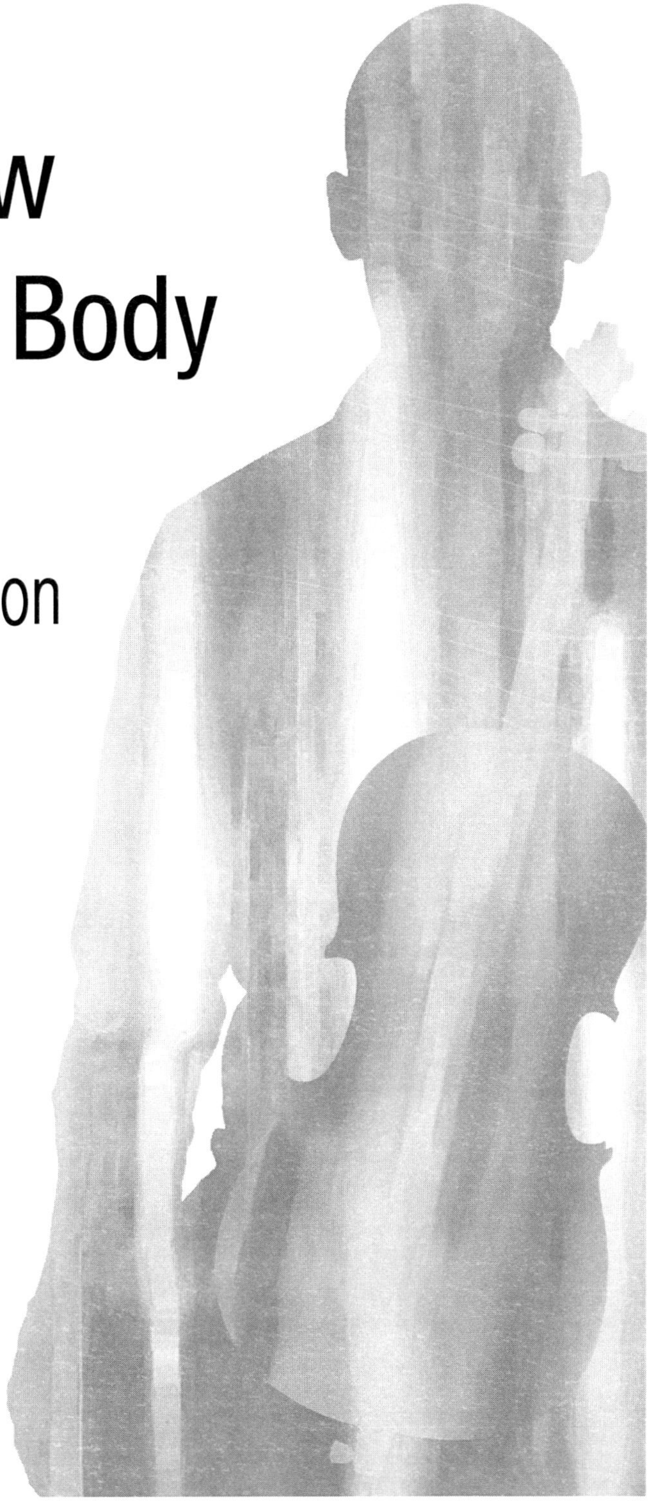

Jennifer Johnson

GIA Publications, Inc.
Chicago

What Every Violinist Needs to Know about the Body
Jennifer Johnson

G-7404
ISBN: 978-1-57999-734-2

Copyright © 2009 GIA Publications, Inc.
7404 S Mason Ave
Chicago IL 60638

www.giamusic.com

All rights reserved

Printed in the United States of America

Contents

Introduction 1

Glossary 5

Before We Start: Facts about Bones and Muscles 7
    Bones 7
    Muscles. 7

Chapter 1   Fundamental Concepts 9
    Why Does Every Violinist Need to Know about the Body?. 9
    Musicians Move for a Living. 10
    Pain 10
    Injury 11
    Limitation 11
    The Field of Somatics. 12
    Training Movement, the Senses, and Attention. 12
        Training Movement. 13
        Training the Senses 13
        Training Attention. 13
    Training Movement by Correcting Errors in the Body Map 13
        Body Mapping 16
        Process of Accessing and Changing the Body Map 16
        A Word about Drawing. 17
        A Sample Self-inquiry 17
    Training the Senses. 22
        Kinesthesia Exercise. 23
        Training Our Sense of Kinesthesia. 24
        Training Attention. 25
        Training an Inclusive Awareness 27
            Constructive Rest Exercise. 27
            Inclusive Awareness While Playing the Violin 28

Chapter 2   Balancing around the Core of the Body 31
    Balance. 31
        Experimenting with "Back and Down" 33
    The Good Posture and Relaxation Diseases 34
        The Good Posture Disease. 35
        The Relaxation Disease 36
    Core. 37

Chapter 3   Places of Balance 41
  Place of Balance 1: The A.O. Joint. 41
    Mapping the A.O. Joint too Far Back of the Central Core 42
    Mapping the A.O. Joint too Low 44
    Thought Experiment 46
    Methods for Locating the A.O. Joint 46
      Method 1: Fingers in Your Ears 46
      Method 2: Tongue Back and Up 47
      Method 3: Pivot on the Thumb 47
      Method 4: A Line at the Bottom of the Skull 47
    Mapping the Neck Muscles 48
      Finding a Free Neck 49
      Maintaining Free Neck Muscles in Movement 50
      Maintaining a Free Neck While Supporting the Violin 50
  Place of Balance 2: The Whole Arm 52
    Go Swimming 53
    Whole Arm Balance over the Torso 53
    Lateral Neutral for the Arms 54
      Lateral Neutral Exercise 54
      Finding Arm Balance from Back of Neutral 54
      Finding Arm Balance from in Front of Neutral 55
    How a Combination of the Good Posture and Relaxation Diseases Prevents
    Finding Lateral Neutral for the Arms 55
      Mapping the Coracoid Process 56
      Exploring to Locate the Front Bony Protrusion of the Shoulder Blade 56
      Exploring on the Floor to Find Release in the Front and Back Simultaneously
      to Regain a Neutral Tilt of the Shoulder Blade 57
    Vertical Neutral for the Arms 58
      Exploring to Find a Springy, Suspended Neutral 59
      Finding Arm Balance from Above Neutral 60
      Finding Arm Balance from Below Neutral 60
  Place of Balance 3: Lumbar Spine 62
    Finding Balance on the Front Half of the Lumbar Spine 62
      Rediscovering Balance around the Lumbar Core 63
    Sacrum and Coccyx 66
      Exploring the Sacrum 67
    Pelvic Arch 67
    Exploring the Rockers 69
  Place of Balance 4: Hip Joint 70
    Finding Your Halfway Point 71
    Finding Balance at the Hip Joint 74
  Place of Balance 5: Knee Joint 75
    Locating the Knee Joint 77

Three Ways to Bend at the Knee Joint 78
    Rolling 78
    Rolling on a Constant Point of Contact with the Tibia. 78
    Rolling and Gliding Forward 79
Finding Balance at the Knee Joints While Standing. 79
Finding Balance at the Knees While Bending at the Knees 80
Finding Musically Expressive Leg Movement 81
Place of Balance 6: Ankle Joint 81
Palpating the Foot 83

Chapter 4   Arms and Hands 85

The Whole Arm (Reprise) 85
Mapping the Four Arm Joints for Violin Playing 86
    Arm Joint 1: Sternoclavicular 86
        Palpating the Length of the Collarbone from One End to the Other 87
        Exercise for Maintaining a Free Neck While Bringing the Violin to Playing
        Readiness 88
    Arm Joint 2: Humeroscapular 90
        Structure of Arm Joint 2 90
        Functions of Arm Joint 2 92
        Relocating Humeral Rotation 93
        Humeroscapular Rhythm 95
        Testing Your Own Humeroscapular Rhythm 95
        Rediscovering Humeroscapular Rhythm if it Has Been Lost 96
        Humeroscapular Rhythm in Violin Playing 97
    Arm Joint 3: Elbow 98
        Structure of the Ulna and Humerus 98
        Exploring the Structure of the Ulna and Humerus 99
        Exploring the Bending Function of the Ulna with the Humerus 99
        Structure of the Radius and Humerus 101
        Function of Rotation at Arm Joint 3 101
        Exploring the Stationary Ulna and Rotating Radius 101
        Unhealthy Rotation 102
        Healthy Rotation 103
    Arm Joint 4: Wrist 105
        Locating Both Ends of the Wrist 106
        Common Wrist Mis-mappings 107
Structure of the Hand 108
    Mapping the Bones of the Hand 108
    Mapping the Location of the Finger Joints 108
        Locating FJ1 108
        Locating FJ2 110
    Functions of the Finger Joints in Violin Playing 110
        Left-hand Up-and-Down Movements from FJ1 110

Exploring Up-and-Down Movements from the Left-hand FB1. 111
Left-hand Spreading Movements from FJ1 111
Exploring Spreading Movements from the Left-hand FJ1. 111
Left-hand Forward-and-Back Movements from FJ1 112
Exploring Forward Movement from the Left-hand Fourth-finger FJ1 . . . 112
Bow-hand Forward-and-Back Movements from FJ1 112
Exploring the Bow-hand FJ1 113
Bow-hand Movements from TJ1 113
Exploring Bow-hand Movements from TJ1 for a Freer Off-the-String
Stroke. 113
Functions at FJ2, FJ3, and FJ4 115
Left-hand Co-contraction. 115
Exploring Left-hand Co-contraction 115
Bow-hand Co-contraction 116
Comparing Active and Passive Bow-hand Finger Movements. 116
Interosseous Muscles of the Hand 117
Ligaments Connecting the Fingers 118
Searching for Elastic Rebound: Rubber Mitt Exploration. 119
Spreading apart the Finger Bones 119
Stretching the Elastic Ligaments 120
Exploring How to Stretch the Hand 121
Developing Awareness along the Pinkie Side of the Arm. 121
Thumb- or Pinkie-oriented? 121
Three Examples of Pinkie Orientation in Action 123
Example 1: Breaking a Board with the Side of the Hand 123
Example 2: Hanging by One Arm 123
Example 3: Babies Crawling 123
Thumb- Versus Pinkie-orientation Movement Experiments 124
Experiment 1: Initiating Movement from the Thumb Versus the Pinkie . . 124
Experiment 2: Clumsy Versus Graceful Dancer Arms. 124
Thumb Versus Pinkie Orientation in Playing the Violin 125
Core of the Arms 126
Sources of Arm Support 127
1. Direct Support in the Sense of "Helping to Hold Up" 127
Spine, Pelvis, and Legs 127
Sternum and Surrounding Connective Tissue. 127
Suspension 127
2. Indirect Support in the Sense of "Aiding" or "Facilitating" 128
Involuntary Muscle Support 128
Gathering and Lengthening of the Spine 128
Weight Delivery of the Violinist's Left Forearm Arch 129
Balancing a Candy Cane 129
When there is too much weight delivery through the short end of the arch
and not enough through the long end 129

      When there is more weight delivery through the long end of the arch and not enough through the short end 129
      When there is no weight delivery through either end of the arch 130
      When there is a balanced weight delivery through both ends of the arch . . 130
  Weight Bearing 130
  Weight Delivery 130
  Candy Cane Exercise 131

Chapter 5   Breathing 133

Myth 1: A Violinist Needs Good Posture to Play 133
Upper-torso Breathing Structures 133
  Structure and Function of the Ribs and Sternum 133
  Rib Movement 135
  Rib Slope 136
  Sternum Slope 136
  Upper-torso Depth 137
  The Back of the Lungs 137
  Diaphragm Structure and Function 138
Lower-torso Breathing Structures 139
  Lower-torso Depth 139
  Pelvis Depth 139
  Finding Front-to-Back Pelvis Depth from the Pubic Bones to the Tailbone . . . 139
  Abdomen Depth 140
Myth 2: Violinists Must Keep the Shoulders Down 141
Myth 3: The Spine Moves Only from Front-to-Back, Side-to-Side, and into Spiral Movements 142
Observing Spinal Gathering and Lengthening as Coordinated by Breathing 142
  On the Floor 142
Observing Spinal Gathering and Lengthening with the Violin 144
Myth 4: Neck Muscles Work to Hold the Violin 146
The Pharynx 146
  Finding Your Pharyngeal Muscles 147
The Soft Palate 147
  Finding Neutral for the Soft Palate 147
The Tongue 148
  Finding Neutral for the Tongue 148
The Hyoid Bone 149
  Locating the Hyoid Bone 149
The Jaw 149
  Finding the Temporomandibular Joints 150
Face Muscles 151
Eye Muscles 152
  Finding the Point of Vision While Playing 153

Chapter 6	The Five Places of Support for the Violin	155
	The Collarbone	155
	The Head	155
	The Left Hand	155
	The Side of the Neck	155
	The Bow	156
	Interplay among the Five Places of Support	156
Chapter 7	Choices a Violinist Must Make	157
	Should I Use a Shoulder Rest?	157
	Left-hand Support: Maximal or Minimal?	158
	Points of Contact between the Jaw and Jaw-rest: Many or One?	158
	Teeth Parted with Lips Closed (Neutral); Both Slightly Parted; or Teeth Lightly Closed?	159
	Will the Bow Do All of the Moving, or Will the Violin Sometimes Move to the Bow?	159
Chapter 8	Common Mis-mappings and Myths in Violin Playing	161
	Mis-mappings Affecting the Violin Side	161
	Raising the Violin	161
	Violin-side Mis-mapping 1: Our Back Muscles Hold Us Up	161
	Violin-side Mis-mapping 2: The Kneecap Is the Knee	162
	Supporting the Violin to Play	162
	Violin-side Mis-mapping 3: The A.O. Joint Is Lower and Farther Back than It Really Is	162
	Violin-side Mis-mapping 4: The Collarbone/Shoulder-blade Unit Rests on the Ribs	163
	Violin-side Mis-mapping 5: The Ball of the Humerus Forms a Joint with Some Imagined Structure instead of the Shoulder Blade	164
	Violin-side Mis-mapping 6: The Shoulder Blade Belongs on the Back	164
	Violin-side Mis-mapping 7: The Elbow Bends an Inch Farther up the Forearm than Where the Joint Is Actually Located	164
	Violin-side Mis-mapping 8: The Hand Supinates to the String by Rotating the Ulna at the Elbow	165
	Violin-side Mis-mapping 9: The Hand Supinates to the String by Rotating at the Wrist	165
	Violin-side Mis-mapping 10: The Wrist is a Single Joint Located at the Skin Crease between the Forearm Bones and the Palm	165
	Violin-side Mis-mapping 11: A Violinist's Fingers Move apart from the Large Row of Knuckles	166
	Violin-side Mis-mapping 12: The Wrist Is at Neutral When the Back of the Hand Forms a Flat Surface with the Back of the Forearm	166
	Violin-side Mis-mapping 13: The Thumb Is a Two-jointed Digit and Joins the Hand at TJ2	166

- Depressing the Strings 167
  - Violin-side Mis-mapping 14: Most of the Bending from FJ2 to Sufficiently Depress the String Is from an Active, Muscular Flexing 167
  - Violin-side Mis-mapping 15: The Fingers Move from the Third Skin Crease Down from the Tip (as Viewed from the Palm) 168
  - Violin-side Mis-mapping 16: Active Bending or Curling at the Tip Joints (FJ3–4) Aids in Bending FJ2. 168
  - Violin-side Mis-mapping 17: Each Finger Has Only Three Joints 169
  - Violin-side Mis-mapping 18: The Only Function of the Fingers When Depressing Strings Is an Up-and-Down Movement. 169
  - Violin-side Mis-mapping 19: Only the Finger Joints Are Involved in Depressing the Strings 169
- Moving the Fingers across from the Highest to Lowest Strings 170
  - Violin-side Mis-mapping 20: It Is the Elbow That Enables the Left Hand to Move from the E to G String 170
- Shifting up the Strings into the Highest Positions. 170
  - Violin-side Mis-mapping 21: Shifting up the Strings Occurs Only by Bending at the Elbow 170
  - Violin-side Mis-mapping 22: The Wrist Has Only One Joint. 171
- Elbow Vibrato 171
  - Violin-side Mis-mapping 23: Elbow Vibrato Is Initiated by Moving the Arm 171
- Wrist Vibrato. 171
  - Violin-side Mis-mapping 24: The One-jointed Wrist Is Located at the Skin Crease between the Forearm and Palm 171
- Playing Large Intervals Such as Tenths and Fingered Octaves. 172
  - Violin-side Mis-mapping 25: Spreading Movement Must Occur at the Large Row of Knuckles because This Is Where the Fingers Begin. 172
  - Violin-side Mis-mapping 26: Fingers Can Spread While Actively Bending from FJ2 172
- Mis-mappings Affecting the Bow Side. 173
  - Supporting the Bow 173
    - Bow-side Mis-mapping 1: Finger Muscles Are Located in the Hand 173
    - Bow-side Mis-mapping 2: The Collarbone/Shoulder-blade Unit Rests on the Ribs. 173
    - Bow-side Mis-mapping 3: The Top of the Arm Is at the "Shoulder Joint" . 174
    - Bow-side Mis-mapping 4: There Is an Arm Socket at the Side Separate from the Shoulder Blade, Which Must Stay on the Back 174
    - Bow-side Mis-mapping 5: The Arm Socket Is Large Enough to Encompass the Ball of the Humerus 174
    - Bow-side Mis-mapping 6: The Ulna Turns the Hand Palm Down in Order to Pronate the Bow Hand. 175
    - Bow-side Mis-mapping 7: Pronation Happens When Both Bones Crisscross to Swap Places 175

Bow-side Mis-mapping 8: The Wrist Contributes to the
Hand's Pronation 175
Bow-side Mis-mapping 9: There Is Only One Bone Running down the
Center of the Forearm, around Which the Forearm Muscles Radiate 175
Bow-side Mis-mapping 10: The Bow Wrist Is a Hinge or Crease Found
Only at the End of the Forearm Bones 175
Bow-side Mis-mapping 11: The Thumb Has Only Two Joints 175

Playing from Frog to Tip 176
Bow-side Mis-mapping 12: A Down-bow Is Primarily an Unbending
at the Elbow 176

Playing from Tip To Frog 176
Bow-side Mis-mapping 13: The Collarbone/Shoulder-blade Unit
Rests on the Ribs 16

Crossing Strings 177
Bow-side Mis-mapping 14: The Collarbone/Shoulder-blade Unit
Rests on the Ribs 177

Playing off the String 177
Bow-side Mis-mapping 15: The Collarbone/Shoulder-blade Unit
Rests on the Ribs 177
Bow-side Mis-mapping 16: The Fingers Can Extend Only
through Muscular Effort 178

Playing over the Fingerboard 178
Bow-side Mis-mapping 17: Only the Flexion at the Wrist Joint
Provides the Necessary Suspension of the Bow 178

Playing Close to the Bridge 178
Bow-side Mis-mapping 18: The Collarbone/Shoulder-blade
Unit Is Supported by Resting on the Ribs Rather than Being
Suspended from Above 178
Bow-side Mis-mapping 19 (a Consequence of Bow-side Mis-mapping
18): The Arm Stops at the Shoulder Joint and Is Capable of "Hanging"
from Its Socket 178

Practicing and Performing 179
Practicing and Performing Mis-mapping 1: Violin Playing Requires
Movement Only from Joints in the Upper Half of the Body 179
Practicing and Performing Mis-mapping 2: The Legs Meet the Torso
at the Front, not the Sides 180
Practicing and Performing Mis-mapping 3: Removing Everything from . . . . .
Awareness Except the Task of Playing Makes the Body Freer to Perform . . 180
Practicing and Performing Mis-mapping 4: The Eyes Must
Look at What the Hands Are Doing at All Times in Order to Prevent
Distraction 180

Acknowledgements 183

Appendix A Origins and Theory of Body Mapping. 185
    by William Conable

Appendix B What to Do About Performance Anxiety 191
    by Barbara Conable

Illustration Credits. 203

Endnotes 205

About the Author. 207

Introduction

"To fully absorb the information and go beyond an intellectual understanding, it will be necessary to treat this book as both a textbook and a workbook."

There are two kinds of violinists in the world: those that have been deemed to be "natural players" and those that have not. All of us who have ever felt we have been relegated to the second category have fervently wished to find a way to overcome our limitations and graduate to the first category. And though "natural players" obviously never wish to become "unnatural," they still encounter untold frustrations when, as teachers, they try to relate to students who are experiencing pain and limitations. Despite the most earnest desire to help their students, "natural players" frequently struggle to address these kinds of problems since they are so foreign to their own experience. What Every Violinist Needs to Know about the Body has been written to help both kinds of violinists.

My own search for answers to address the restrictions I experienced as a violinist began very early in my life. Though I was fortunate enough to have some extremely insightful teachers, mentors, and friends along the way who contributed important information to my quest, it was not until I became acquainted with the work of Barbara Conable in 2004 that I knew with absolute certainty that I could get myself out of the distress I was in.

Just prior to meeting and studying with Barbara, I had spent a wonderfully intensive, fully-funded, seven-month sabbatical studying the Alexander Technique in Europe. I studied with extraordinary teachers, all of whom gave me gems of information and revelations that I continue to draw upon years later from my memories and journals. However, by the end of my studies in Europe, I still was not convinced that I knew what it meant to "let my neck be free"—that first and all-important Alexander direction necessary to lead to a freeing throughout the rest of the body. My sabbatical was nearing an end and I would be returning home to a place where there was no AT teacher within a thousand-mile radius to help me find a free neck.

As a violinist who had spent her entire student and professional life trying to muscularly hold on to the violin, my neck muscles were in a desperate state of "debauched kinesthesia," to use Alexander's words. It is certainly no reflection on my AT teachers that I still felt confused at this point; it was, however, most definitely a reflection on what I had been doing to myself for over thirty years. I so much wanted to be able to continue working independently, but frankly doubted that I would be able to if I still didn't know for certain when my neck was free and when it was not.

The last week of my sabbatical was spent in Princeton, New Jersey at Westminster Choir College, taking Barbara Conable's week-long course *What Every Musician Needs to Know about the Body*. At the end of that week I distinctly remember thinking to myself "This is the information I have been looking for all my life." I proceeded to train with Barbara to become an Andover Educator, and when she invited me to write *What Every Violinist Needs to Know about the Body* as a part of her series of books for musicians, I gratefully accepted.

The information presented here is not intended to replace any of the numerous and widely-differing violin techniques that are commonly taught. Instead, the objective of *What Every Violinist Needs to Know about the Body* (WEV) is to tell the truth about how the human body is designed to move so that there is a solid foundation on which any given technique can safely rest.

Any reader who has studied the Alexander Technique will recognize the influence that F.M. Alexander's teachings have had on Body Mapping. In particular, the emphasis put on finding a free neck will be familiar to AT students. However, it is important to emphasize that *this is not a book about the Alexander Technique.* There are many tenets pivotal to the Alexander Technique, such as *inhibition and direction,* which will not be discussed in this book.

Nearly every book ever written about the Alexander Technique states that it is impossible to actually learn the Technique from a book. This is true because an Alexander Technique (AT) teacher helps to change a student's use initially by guiding the student with the hands in order to re-educate the student's sense of kinesthesia. As lessons progress, the student develops an independence as she begins to master the Alexander directions.

By contrast, hands-on work is not used at all to teach Body Mapping unless the teacher is also a trained AT teacher or unless the music teacher has always naturally used hands-on guidance in teaching music, as some do. Body Mapping is also informed by other disciplines besides the Alexander Technique, such as anatomy and neurophysiology, and so relies heavily on the use of anatomical models and images in order to instruct. Because of the extensive use of these visual images, the information can be imparted quite successfully to the resourceful learner from the printed page. However, as with learning anything, private attention from an Andover Educator to address the body map, an AT teacher for hands-on guidance, or a Feldenkrais teacher to enhance a student's body awareness through guided movement will speed and facilitate the process of change.

In lieu of physically guiding the student into new kinesthetic experiences by a hands-on approach, Body Mapping changes the student's movement patterns by consciously training his kinesthetic sense. It is achieved in the same way that a good music teacher trains a student's auditory sense: by using modeling, verbal coaching and inquiry, and asking the student to draw on any information he can receive from all of his pertinent senses. In other words, a Body Mapping student learns to sense the difference between tension and freedom in the same way a violin student learns to hear the difference between a note that is flat and one that is in tune.

For example, when a violin student plays a note that is flat, the violin teacher will alternate modeling the correct pitch with the flat pitch and then ask the student if she can hear the difference between them. But it cannot stop there. A resourceful teacher will also require the student to employ her visual and tactile senses to play the note in tune. He will ask her to watch her finger moving back and forth between the two pitches to *see* the difference between the two places on the fingerboard. He will require her to tell him what subtle *tactile* differences along the fingerboard she notices as she moves her finger between the flat note and the in-tune note.

A good teacher recruits all of the information available from the student's other senses that are perhaps initially better developed than her auditory sense in order to instruct and improve her auditory sense. In a similar fashion, the Body Mapping instructor helps to improve a student's sense of kinesthesia by aligning it with the truth about the body as revealed through the other senses. The student will be encouraged to ask:

Am I really internally sensing what I see to be the truth in this anatomical image? Am I truly allowing these two bones to work together in the way that my exploring fingertips tell me they must? Can I hear the richer, deeper tone emerge from my violin when I go searching for a better balance around my core?

At times, Body Mapping has been criticized for only dealing in body "parts" rather than dealing with an integrated mind/body "whole." Perhaps clearing up any misunderstanding about what the word *mapping* means will be helpful in addressing this. Mapping refers to what neurophysiology sometimes calls the internal representation that we hold of ourselves in the brain. There are hundreds of maps of ourselves located in our brains, but the one that is most relevant to Body Mapping is the movement map—the part of the brain's cortex that dictates how we move our bodies. Therefore, inherent in the name Body Mapping is the undivided marriage between body and mind.

As one casually flips through *WEV,* it may initially seem that there are a great many images of parts of the body. However, upon a careful reading, the reader will notice that the *part* is always returned to the context of the *whole*. In my case, I had to know what my neck was before I could learn to free it and thus allow my whole body to move into a freer state. I needed to absorb accurate information about the *separate parts* of myself so that those parts could finally reconnect to one another according to their design, instead of according to my misconceptions, thus forming an *integrated whole.*

Having been an avid student of both the Alexander Technique and of Body Mapping, I see no conflict between the two approaches. More and more AT teachers are using Body Mapping to help speed their students' learning. If a student is fortunate enough to study with a good AT teacher while studying Body Mapping information, learning will be enhanced in both disciplines. If it is not possible to study regularly with an AT teacher, either because of financial considerations or accessibility, it is still possible for a student to begin to change harmful movement patterns by independently studying his own design and aligning his movement with the truth.

From time to time I work with a violinist who is resistant to exploring how he conceives the design of his body. He feels this line of questioning to be a waste of his time and would rather just buckle down to the business of playing the violin better. Unfortunately, he misses the point that his figurative buckling down has manifested as an actual, physical buckling down in his body and is what ultimately prevents him from experiencing the freedom and ease he craves for his violin playing. He is more interested in getting results *right now* than in his process.

In order for *WEV* to help any violinist's playing, the information must be met with a genuine interest in the *process* and a willingness to take the information past a purely intellectual understanding of anatomy and into an active application where the differences in the quality of movement can be *felt*. To fully absorb the information and go beyond an intellectual understanding, it will be necessary to treat this book as both a textbook and a workbook. As a first step, the book will need to be read and re-read as one does with a textbook to intellectually understand the information.

The second step, which is vital to absorbing the information kinesthetically, is to work with the images and suggested explorations every day with and without the violin until a change in the quality of movement is felt. The large format of *WEV* allows it to be kept open on a secondary stand next to the music stand so that the images are always in view, keeping you constantly mindful of your true design as you practice.

In your daily environment, surround yourself with images from this book or other accurate anatomical drawings so that you are immersed in the new information you wish your brain to absorb. This may seem demanding, but it is only through *absorbing* the information rather than merely understanding it that you will alter your brain's movement map and subsequently experience a practical difference in freedom of movement with the violin.

It is my hope that as you progress through this text you will embrace the information and be prepared to experiment with it over a course of weeks, months, and perhaps even years without allowing yourself to become demoralized by the length of the process. Sometimes the correction of a mis-mapping can be immediate and other times, depending on how many different mis-mappings are converging in one area of the body to create the faulty movement, the correction can take much longer. Each new discovery needs to be celebrated, since it is a step closer to *more freedom*. I stress this because there is no destination with a road sign marked "Welcome to Freedom." Once you have tasted how delicious it is to play the violin with *more freedom than yesterday,* you will never want to stop refining your search.

Happy Mapping!

Glossary

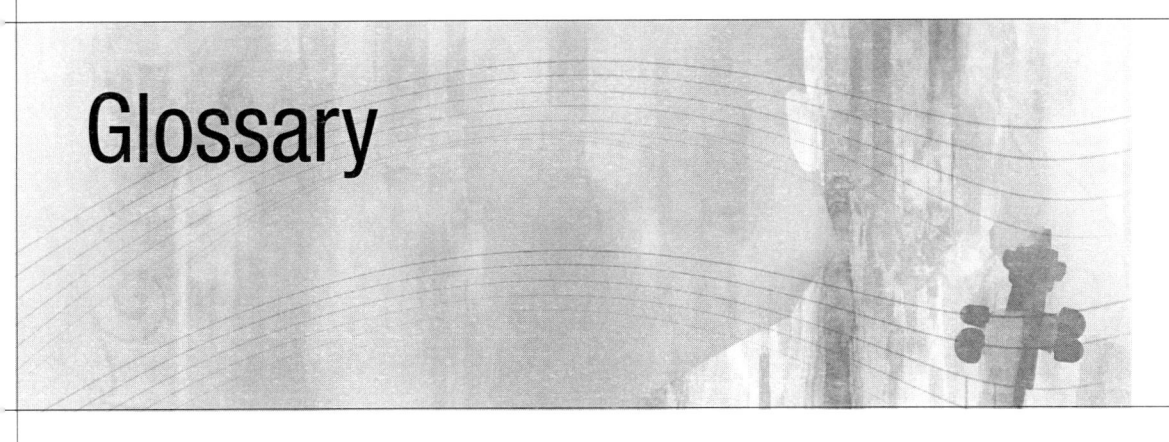

"The sense of kinesthesia informs us about our position in space as well as how and where we are moving."

Automatic Postural Patterns (APPs)

Refers to involuntary muscular activity that facilitates voluntary movement by providing the subjective experience of springiness and buoyancy.

When the bones of the body meet in right relationship to one another, APPs help to reorganize the soft tissues surrounding the bones (ligaments, tendons, fascia and muscles) so that the muscular work of both supporting and moving the body is redistributed evenly and appropriately throughout the body. This is what makes movement feel buoyant and springy.

Examples of an APP are:
1. The lengthening of the spine (which in the West was first identified by F.M. Alexander) that happens when the head is allowed to return to balance on top of the spine, allowing ease and freedom in any voluntary movement of the body;
2. The spring in the step that happens naturally to aid in locomotion when the body is integrated and free of unnecessary tension.

Back orientation

A term used to describe a person who organizes himself up the surface of the back, attempting to hold the body up with the back muscles rather than organizing himself like an apple around its core.

Body map

Sometimes called the internal representation. It is the literal, neuronal picture we have of ourselves in the brain, and dictates how we move. When the map is accurate, movement is free and healthy; when it is inaccurate, movement becomes uncoordinated and injurious.

Body Mapping

The method discovered and developed by William and Barbara Conable to access the body map and to consciously alter it when inaccuracies are found.

Connective tissue

A collective term that includes ligaments, tendons, and fascia.

Fascia

A white, stretchy, web-like connective tissue between muscles that runs through the entire body to help hold it in shape.

Joint

The space between two bones where they meet to provide movement.

Kinesthesia

The sense of kinesthesia informs us about our position in space as well as how and where we are moving. The sense receptors which inform our sense of kinesthesia are found in the connective tissue and muscles around the major joints of the body.

Ligaments

The connective tissue that attaches bone to bone.

Tendons

The connective tissue attaches muscles to bones.

Weight bearing

Experienced in the body as the support any given lower structure supplies to the structure resting above it. It is felt as an upward force.

Weight delivery

Experienced in the human body as the release of any given structure into a state of rest onto the structure directly below. It is felt as a downward force and it is the subjective sensation of gravity.

Before We Start: Facts about Bones and Muscles

"Co-contraction is set up: the two opposing muscles play tug-of-war with one another."

Bones

Our bones are designed to meet in very specific relationships to one another. When they do, they perch effortlessly, one atop the other. Discovering this right relationship of the bones triggers what neurophysiologists now call automatic postural patterns, or, for our purposes *APPs* (formerly known as "righting reflexes"). These postural patterns automatically help to reorganize the soft tissues surrounding the bones (ligaments, tendons, fascia, and muscles) so that the muscular work of both supporting and moving ourselves is redistributed evenly and appropriately throughout the body. When the bones do not stack up on balance according to design, the automatic postural patterns are not available to aid in making support and movement feel effortless. In the absence of the bony balance and the APPs, muscle groups not designed for the task at hand start compensating. This leads to all sorts of muscle discomfort and strain.

Muscles

The specific result of these muscular compensations is that muscular work becomes unevenly and inappropriately distributed throughout the body so that some muscles do jobs they were not designed to do, while other muscles do not take enough of the workload. Instead of working as one unified team to complete any given task, the muscle groups of the body work against each other. There are three ways that muscles most commonly work against each other:

1. When the superficial muscles of the body (e.g., the surface muscles of the back) which are designed to be *moving* muscles for the torso and the arms begin to do the work of *supporting* the body, they contract even before movement has begun. Movement will never feel free because these superficial muscles are trying to do the double duty of supporting and moving.

2. When the deep layer of involuntary support muscles (e.g., those around the vertebrae) are chronically shortened in contraction, the superficial moving muscles must exert excessive effort to make voluntary movements in order to overcome the excessive holding of the support muscles.

3. When two opposing muscles (e.g., biceps and triceps) contract simultaneously in a task instead of taking turns—one releasing into length while the other contracts or vice-versa—co-contraction is set up: the two opposing muscles play tug-of-war with one another.

Chapter 1
Fundamental Concepts

"Many violinists share the belief that the violin is an unnatural instrument to play."

Why Does Every Violinist Need to Know about the Body?

This book is one of a series, the first of which was written by Barbara Conable in 1998, called What Every Musician Needs to Know about the Body. *It was her wish that as more and more musicians came to understand how the body is designed to move in order to prevent pain and limitations at their instruments that there would be others who would be willing to undertake the writing of books with detailed, instrument-specific applications. And so, at the same time as I am engaged in the task of relaying this information to violinists, there are also singers as well as woodwind and brass players busily scribing away for their peers. All of us are writing about what musicians need to know about the body. However, I think for the violinist coming to this information uninitiated in any kind of body work, it is valuable to first examine why violinists need to know about the body. The following anecdotes will clearly illustrate why this information is so important for violinists.*

Several years ago I attended a master class with a world-renowned violinist who was teaching some of the local university's violinists. His own sound as he demonstrated was luscious, and his teaching advice was for the most part inspiring, save for one point. He insisted that one young student should be leaning farther backwards in his general stance as he played.

A fellow violinist friend of mine and I who had studied Alexander Technique for several years were extremely puzzled by his insistence on this point because it clearly contradicted everything we had learned about our own structural balance, both at the instrument and away from it. It never did become clear to me during the course of the master class what result this teacher was hoping to achieve with this particular piece of advice. However, moments later, in a completely unrelated context, this master violinist revealed that he suffered from chronic lower back pain and that he relied on the regular use of pain killers to cope with the problem.

Lower back pain had been one of the symptoms I had suffered with for many years but had successfully eradicated through Alexander lessons by correcting my own habitual pattern of leaning too far back of balance—the exact pattern that this great player had been advocating only moments earlier. Here was a classic example of a teacher recommending a harmful movement pattern in the mistaken belief that it contributed to artistry! Simple information about how the skeleton delivers weight centrally rather than along the back would have solved the violinist's back pain problems and protected his student. This great violinist needed to know about how his body is designed to move! So do we all.

A young solo violinist was recently heard to say, "My left hand is a half-inch longer than my right…. My shoulders are two inches different in height when I stand straight. My back has curved from doing so much of that at such a young age, and I try to do my best to go against it." And all of this because "playing the violin is, in a sense, unnatural because of the stance." This player is not alone. Many violinists share the belief that the violin is an unnatural instrument to play. Not until I gained structural balance and freedom of movement did I start to experience violin playing as a natural activity.

Musicians Move for a Living

When shown video footage of professionals performing in their chosen field, dancers and athletes immediately describe what they see with movement vocabulary. Violinists rarely do. When I teach the *What Every Violinist Needs to Know about the Body* (WEV) course to violinists, it takes some prompting before the class begins describing the movement they see. Words like "communicating" or "self-expression" are used before someone mentions a movement word.

Many of us violinists simply never saw ourselves as people who move for a living, and therefore we pay very little attention to the quality of our movement. The irony is that dancers and athletes expect to retire in their thirties or forties, whereas musicians expect to go on playing into their golden years!

Maybe we think that a violinist only really needs to be aware of how he *sounds* rather than having any concern for how his body *feels*. Perhaps we have even bought into the self-image of one who must suffer for his art and consider it necessary or even somewhat glamorous to feel pain for the purposes of musical expression. No matter why we have arrived at this level of disregard for how we use our bodies when we play, it is exactly this disregard that causes so much pain and anguish among violinists who suddenly find themselves unable to play because of injury.

Pain

Statistics tell us that over forty percent of all professional musicians play in *pain*. Four out of ten orchestral players go to work every day and either suffer through it or medicate themselves just to get through rehearsal. This high an occurrence of physical distress would be considered unacceptable in most other professions.

Injury

Then there are the musicians who are in the *injured* category—those who finally have to stop playing because of the chronic pain they experience on a daily basis. These folks are harder to account for statistically since many of them have been forced to choose other careers. Violinists suffer from a long list of injuries ranging from neck and back strain or a mild case of tendonitis to raging pins and needles and numbness in the arms and hands.

All the horrible symptoms that prevent violinists from playing are categorized under very broad diagnostic terms like carpal tunnel and thoracic outlet syndromes. However, such terms only identify the primary consequence of the condition, which is that the median nerve is compressed at its thoracic outlet. This description fails to address the origin of the violinist's problem, which is moving in ways that compresses the nerve. Such broad terms obscure the fact that her condition has come about not because she plays the violin, but because of *how* she plays the violin.

Limitation

There is another group of violinists who have not perhaps experienced chronic pain and injury but suffer with a different kind of trauma: feeling *limited* in ability no matter how long they dedicate themselves to their craft. The anguish these players feel is deepened by the misapprehension that they are helpless to change this, since they do not know why they have encountered these limitations when others have not. The frustration, disappointment, and self-doubt these players experience is just as crippling to a professional career as a physical injury and just as likely to lead to loss of that career when disillusionment finally overwhelms any remaining sense of joy that playing brings.

Even players who are not injured, in pain, or who don't feel particularly limited on the instrument can improve their playing by learning to move more freely. One of the biggest motivations that violinists have for doing the hard work of re-mapping their bodies and changing their movement patterns is the difference in sound that they produce when they find balance in their structure. Once a player has experienced playing with her bones in right relationship to each other and her muscles only doing necessary work, there is no forgetting how liberating it feels and how fantastically deep and rich the violin sound becomes. This is true for all musicians, including singers. The natural resonating chambers of the body are profoundly affected by the amount of space they are allowed, specifically by how and where the bones meet and also by the quality of the tissue surrounding the bones. When this tissue is not excessively tightened, more resonance is available.

Pain. Injury. Limitation. These are the three best reasons for violinists to study how the body is designed to move. Understanding your structure and using it in accordance with its design will gradually melt away pain, injuries, and limitations. Good doctors can help you with medical resources and good teachers can provide quality pedagogy, but you are the only one who can change your movement from the inside-out, and good movement is the key to success. You are the only one who can directly access your brain and change the map you hold there which dictates whether you are moving in a healthy or harmful way.

The Field of Somatics

Somatics is a term which translates literally from its Greek roots as "the study of the body," but definitions of the term make it clear that it refers specifically to tissue cells rather than reproductive or bacterial cells. Because it is the tissue cells in our joints which inform the body kinesthetically about its movement, the word somatics has come to be used in a more general manner to refer to any practical study of how the body operates in *movement*.

Somatics is a relatively new field of study in western culture. Despite the obvious importance of athletic activity in ancient Greek society—it was the Greeks, after all, who established the Olympic games—remarkably little was written then about *how* the human body moves. This is particularly remarkable, considering how much written discourse the ancient Greeks produced regarding just about everything else that concerns human existence. They wrote about music, beauty, politics; mathematics, friendship, love, and the philosophy of human conduct; but about human movement they wrote very little.

This all changed just over a hundred years ago when several pioneers in the field of somatics began their explorations. They all had their own reasons for beginning their work, and many claimed that their work was like no other. Certainly each made unique and vital discoveries about the functioning of the body in movement and expressed themselves in distinctive ways. Underlying all of this work, however, is the common thread of intent to discover how we humans can align our movement with our design so that our functioning is optimal.

Prominent pioneers include F.M. Alexander, Moshe Feldenkrais, Rudolph Laban, Irmgard Bartinieff, Joseph Pilates, Alexander Lowen, and Mabel Todd.

Body Mapping is more recent and was developed by William and Barbara Conable, two teachers of Alexander Technique. Body Mapping is supported and enhanced by findings in the fields of anatomy and neuroscience. However, it was discovered and developed specifically while dealing with the movement issues of performing musicians.

Training Movement, the Senses, and Attention

Why do we face such high rates of injury among today's professional musicians? Because the training of movement has been neglected; because these musicians received ear training but no training of their kinesthetic sense; and because their attention was mis-trained. Movement, the senses, and attention must be retrained if musicians are to shake off the shackles of pain, injury, and limitation, and music instruction must forever incorporate movement training if future generations are to be protected against the miseries of the current generation.

Training Movement
Injunctions such as "plant your feet" or "get your shoulder down" need to be replaced with more accurate information about how the body is actually designed so that diligent students do not mis-map themselves as a result of what their well-intentioned teachers tell them.

Training the Senses
In music education the auditory sense is usually trained at the expense of other senses necessary to play and perform well. It is essential for the future health of musicians that we learn to train all relevant senses, including the kinesthetic, visual, and tactile senses.

Training Attention
Contemplate young violin students who have been asked to "concentrate" on their vibrato and have found that the more they concentrate, the stiffer and uglier the vibrato becomes. These poor students are perfect examples of the awful consequences of concentration. Concentration is one of the worst things a student can be asked to do because concentration narrows attention. When attention narrows, so does the body: furrowed eyebrows, needlessly tensed muscles, and mental strain are inevitable products of concentration.

The remedy for concentration is focus. Focus is what the eye does. When a camera focuses, trees and grass are not excluded from the photograph just because they are not the main subject of the photo. In fact, they are essential to the photo in order to place the subject in a context. When a student focuses on vibrato, it is contained within his peripheral context and nothing of his experience will be excluded. We call this inclusive attention. Inclusive attention is a fine condition for a musician because everything needed is in awareness. Shifting from one item of focus to another is very easy for the brain—from vibrato to intonation, for instance. Shifting concentration is quite difficult and slow in comparison to shifting focus.

Next we will look at training movement, the senses, and attention in greater detail, starting with training movement by correcting and refining the body map.

Training Movement by Correcting Errors in the Body Map
When music training is on a secure somatic foundation, we train movement by ensuring that the violinist's body map is generally accurate and also adequate to meet the specific movement requirements of violin playing. To be adequate, the body map needs to be highly refined in the areas of the body directly involved in playing: the arms, including the collarbones and shoulder blades, and the head and neck.

The body map is the internal, neuronal representation we have of ourselves in the brain that dictates how we move. In the field of neuroscience, it is routinely called the body scheme, body image, or internal representation. According to neuroscience we are hardwired from the beginning of life to build and adjust our body maps, and it is these body maps that allow us in childhood to learn how to move as the adults around us move.

The body maps of healthy toddlers are extremely accurate. Two-year olds have not yet had time to abdicate from their natural poise and balance. They have only recently *discovered* their balance in their keen search for a way to be upright and to take their first steps. With relatively underdeveloped muscles, a novice toddler must rely, to a large extent, on the balance of his bones, one against the other, in order to bring himself to standing.

Unfortunately, children quickly alter how they use themselves by modeling the adults in their world, who are frequently quite poor models. It is often easy to pinpoint the source of a child's mis-mappings from observing her parents' postures and mannerisms. In the last decade, neuroscientists have discovered the existence of "mirror neurons" in the brain which fire during movement and while merely observing another person perform a familiar activity. Experts surmise that this firing during observed movement is the reason we humans are able to improve existing skills in any physical activity by simply observing others perform the same task. Clearly, we need to consciously choose who we wish to emulate so that we don't become unwitting victims of our clever mirror neurons!

When the body map is accurate, the movement dictated by the map will look and feel free, poised, easy, and balanced. Conversely, when the body map has inaccuracies in it, movement is stiff, awkward, and injury-producing. There are some jobs which can handle a bit of mis-mapping in certain areas without any serious consequences because the movement required by the job is not demanding or repetitive. And even though violin playing requires being accurately mapped in multiple areas of the body, a violinist will not require as refined a map of the tongue as a singer needs or as refined a map of the ankle as an organist must have.

The body map is comprised of three aspects: *structure*, *function*, and *size*. That is, what our body is like, what it does, and how big it is. We map both the individual parts of the body and the integrated whole. The breakdown into these three aspects becomes very useful during the process of accessing and changing our body map, because the errors causing pain, injury, and limitation can come from any one of these. You may be suffering from an error in structure, function, or size, so you will need to examine all three aspects.

It is important to understand that the term "body map" is not a metaphor. When we begin changing our body maps, there are measurable, observable differences in the way the movement neurons fire in the brain. We speak physiologically and literally when we speak of the body map. Richard Nichols, Professor and Chair of the School of Applied Physiology at Georgia Tech, writes very clearly about the arrangement of the cells of the cortical representation (body map) on the surface of the brain:

In the cerebral cortex, it has been known for a long time that cells in the primary motor and sensory areas are associated with different parts of the body, and that these cells are spatially arranged in such a way as to represent the anatomical correspondence of these parts.[1]

Nichols goes on to explain the importance of an accurate cortical representation to a musician:

The maps in the executive areas of the cortex that represent the anatomy of the body are clearly dependent upon the motor and sensory experiences of the individual. In the case of a highly trained artist such as a musician, it is expected that the cortical areas become reorganized in a way that reflects the motor planning practices of that individual.... Some motor practices can, however, lead to pathological changes in the musculoskeletal system, such as tendonitis or carpal tunnel syndrome. If movement is based on an inaccurate knowledge or perception about the anatomy of the body, then pathologic changes can result. These practices can lead to alterations in cortical representation, which can then become reinforcing of the faulty motor practice. Overtraining of one specific motor pattern can also lead to pathologic changes, such as focal dystonias, in the central nervous system. These conclusions underscore the importance of educating musicians in anatomy and physiology of the motor system so that practices that can lead to pathology in the musculoskeletal system can be avoided.[3]

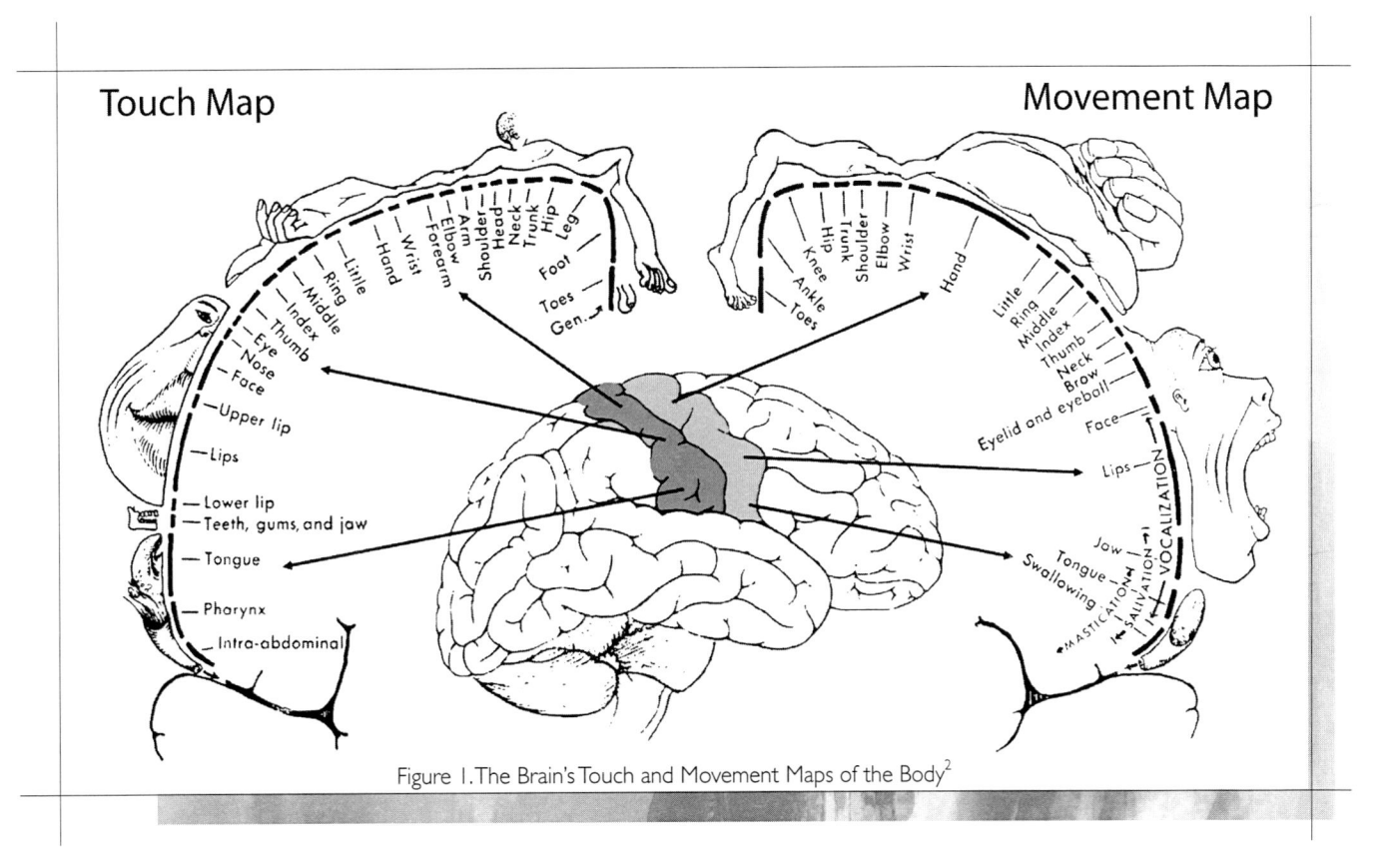

Figure 1. The Brain's Touch and Movement Maps of the Body[2]

Earlier in his article, Nichols addresses the changeability or "plasticity" of the map:

Recent research on rodents, non-human primates and human patients with neurological disorders has also shown that the representation of anatomy on the cortical surface is subject to considerable plasticity. In the cases of injury or overtraining, the cortical representation can change.[4]

It is because the body map is tangible rather than metaphorical that we are able to access it and it is because of its plasticity that we are able to change it.

Body Mapping

Body Mapping is the term that William and Barbara Conable came to call the method of movement reeducation they developed during the 1970s. Coincidentally, they settled on this name with no prior knowledge of the term *body map*, which was already firmly established in the field of neuroscience.

Body Mapping was discovered in the teaching studio of cellist and Alexander Technique teacher William Conable and was then further developed and written about by Barbara Conable, also an Alexander Technique teacher. Before her retirement, Barbara went on to train a group of musicians whose mandate is to continue developing and teaching the work to other musicians. Those musicians are called Andover Educators.

The purpose of Body Mapping is to teach musicians to learn to consciously alter their own faulty body maps. It is a proactive technique, taken on by the individual, of examining her own body map and contrasting it with the true mechanical design of the human body, with the express purpose of learning to move in the most balanced, fluid, and natural way possible. Hundreds of musicians have used Body Mapping to correct how they move in order to heal themselves permanently of injury and pain and to enhance their abilities at their instruments.

Process of Accessing and Changing the Body Map

Before you can change your body map, it is first necessary to access it and discover where your own particular mis-mappings lie. There are many different ways of accessing and changing your map. Studying anatomical images such as those presented here, self-inquiry, and palpation are three of the most powerful tools; but drawing, mirror work, and imitation of beautiful movers are also extremely effective methods.

Being aware of how language or gestures reflect cultural body map errors like "sitting up straight" or "having good posture" can also bring new insights about your map. Frequently a combination of these methods works best. For instance, you can watch a video of one of the great players (choose someone who makes it "look easy") and then watch yourself play in the mirror or on video, taking notice of how your movement differs from his. Or you can draw or describe your spine, then study your anatomy book to compare your conception of a spine with the reality.

As you read through *WEV*, it is important to take the time to consciously access your own internal map by using some of these methods. Gather as much information as you can about how you perceive your structure in the given moment. *WEV* addresses many of the most commonplace mis-mappings that violinists share. However, it is possible and even likely that you will discover some mis-mappings that are unique to you.

A Word about Drawing

Even if you do not have a lot of confidence in your drawing abilities and are just using a few simple lines to depict conceptions of your structure, you are bound to gain some new insights by drawing. Initially, when I began reading Barbara Conable's *How to Learn the Alexander Technique*, I didn't believe that drawing would be of much use to me because I didn't have much confidence in my own drawing abilities. When I finally decided to give it a try after several pages, I made a surprising discovery about my own map. When I began to depict my upper spine with the simple lines I was using, the distinctive bump I drew at the base of my neck vertebrae revealed that I internally perceived this as something quite distinct and isolated from the rest of my spine. I had always known intellectually that it was supposed to be all one unit, but somehow I had very different information in my internal representation—and this was what emerged on paper when I took up the pencil to draw. And, unfortunately for me at that point, it was this misinformed part of my brain that had been dictating how I moved!

Because self-inquiry is such a powerful tool in accessing the body map, there is a sample of this process below. It is in this process that the aforementioned three components of the body map become so useful in accessing and altering our maps. We inquire very specifically about each component: the *structure, function, and size* of each anatomical unit. As you progress through *WEV*, apply these series of questions to each new segment of the body that we explore.

A Sample Self-Inquiry

Because the spine plays such a vital role in helping us to regain our natural balance and poise, it makes sense to begin with exploring the map of the spine in this sample.

On a sheet of paper write the following three questions:
1. What is my spine like (structure of my spine)?
2. What does my spine do (function of my spine)?
3. How big is my spine (size of my spine)?

Now, spend a few minutes trying to answer these questions as thoroughly as you can. Describe what your spine looks like, what it feels like, where it is, what its role in your body is, and how big it is. You may discover that you only have a vague awareness of your spine, or you may find you know more about it than you thought. Whatever you discover, this is the starting point for uncovering your own mis-mappings.

When you feel you have exhausted your own bank of knowledge regarding your spine, read on, examine the illustrations, and compare your answers with the truth about your spine.

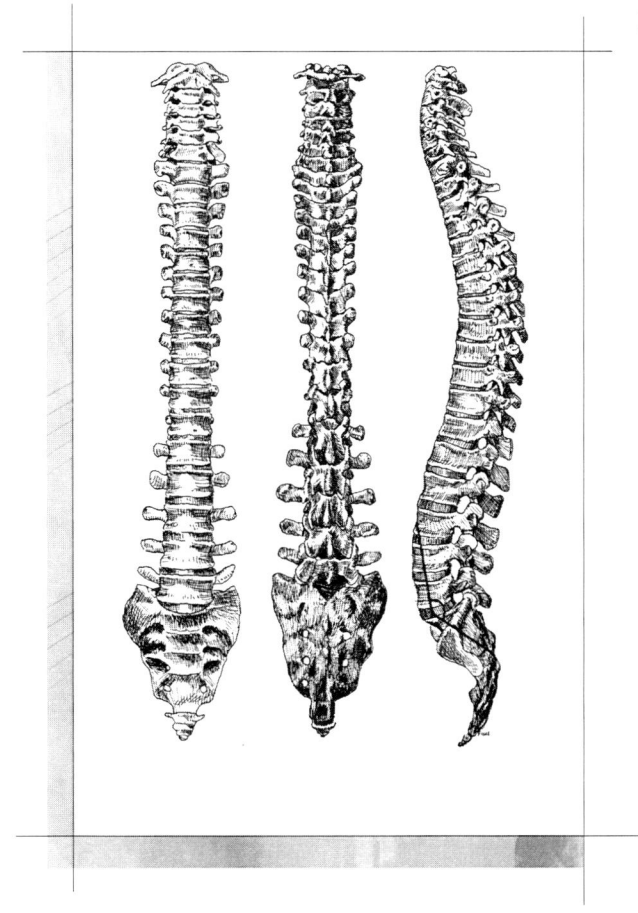

1. What is my spine like?
    a. A spine is segmented into twenty-four separate vertebrae with a joint between each vertebra. Some violinists have their spinal "column" mapped as being one long piece of bone (like a Roman column), which would certainly restrict the free movement through the torso that a violinist needs in order to spiral around and communicate musically with fellow string quartet members.
    b. A spine has four curves. Did you mention the curves in your description, or do you have your spine mapped as straight as a broomstick? Violinists who have been told to sit up straight when they play in orchestra frequently end up mapping a straight spine; this removes some of the natural springiness that the spine can afford a player.
    c. There are two halves to a spine—a front and back half. The front half of each vertebra is rounded and smooth so that the internal organs which nestle against it are not punctured by any bony protrusions. Conversely, the bony back half is designed with protruding processes. The front half of the vertebrae are also stacked vertically one on top of the other, like building blocks—unlike the back half. Did you make a distinction between the front and back halves of the spine in your description, or do you play the violin with only an awareness of the back half of your spine—the part you can palpate with your fingertips?
    d. The front half of the spine has soft disks between each vertebra. Each disk is a tough-skinned sac filled with a gelatinous fluid. Did you include these cushiony disks in your description or do you have bone meeting bone in your map?
    e. The back half of the spine allows space for the spinal cord to run up through it. Did you mention the spinal cord in your description or is it located externally to the spine in your map?
    f. Included in the structure of the spine is the manner in which it meets other structures. Did you mention that the spine forms a joint with the skull at one end and joins with the

pelvic bones at the other, or is your spine a free-floating unit in your body map? Violinists need absolute clarity on the location of the head joint with the spine, since a free, secure support of the instrument depends on it. Players who have not mapped the sacrum of the spine as being securely joined on either side by the two pelvic bones will always be engaging too many muscles in an effort to anchor the spine at its base. Did you mention that the back half of the spine is structured so that each of the twenty-four ribs forms its joint with the spine? Once again, if the security that comes from having our bony form accurately mapped is not experienced, there will be excessive muscle use in the torso.

2. What does my spine do?

   a. An essential function of the spine is to *bear the weight* of the head and upper torso. Which half of the spine do you think is best designed to bear a heavy load: the front half with its soft, regularly-spaced disks cushioning the weight between each neatly stacked vertebra, or the bony back half where the fragile spinal cord is housed? (And yes, this is a leading question!)

   b. Equally important as the weight-bearing function is the *weight-delivering* function of the front half of the spine. A violinist who has not mapped the spine's front half function of delivering the torso's weight unobstructed into the pelvis and then down into the chair will always feel the lower back and abdominal fatigue and spasming that comes from muscularly holding herself up in the chair. Did you mention the weight-bearing/delivering functions in your description of your spine?

   c. As alluded to above, the function of the back half of the spine is to house and protect the all-important spinal cord. The omission of this function of the spine is as serious a mis-mapping as omitting the skull as the main source of protection for the brain! Because the back halves of the vertebrae are not stacked vertically as they are in the front, it is clear that the back-half of the spine is *not intended to bear or deliver any weight!* Much of the back and neck pain and injury that violinists suffer stems from trying to drop weight down through the *back of the spine.* Because it is structurally incapable of bearing weight, the superficial back muscles end up compensating.

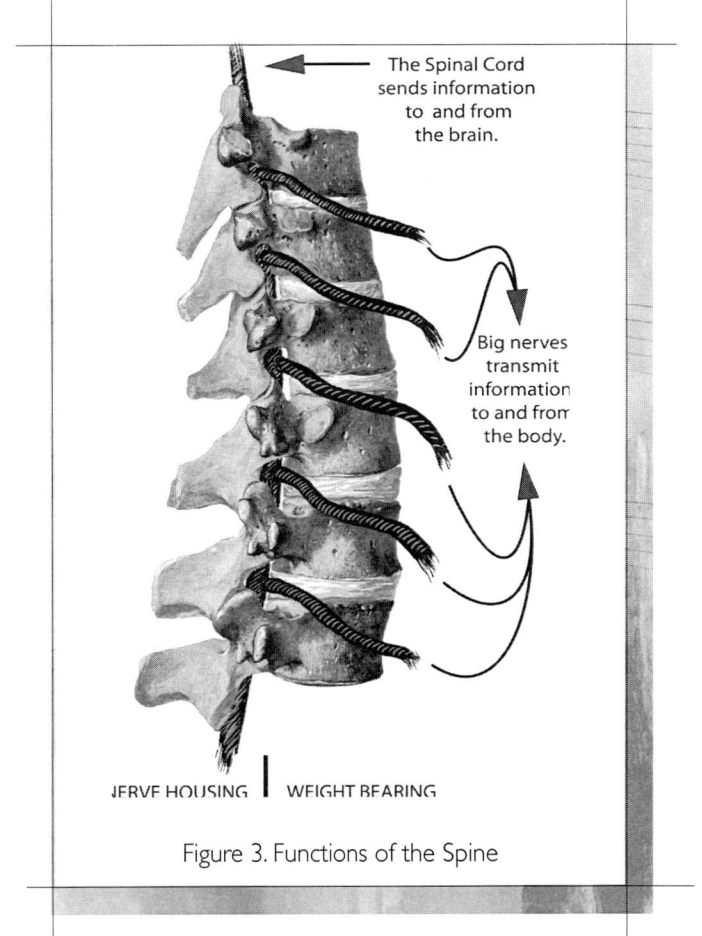

Figure 3. Functions of the Spine

d. Because of the segmented nature of the spine, one of its functions is to be able to twist, turn, spiral, and bend in all of our most musically appropriate ways.

e. Perhaps the most important function of the spine is its ability to gather and lengthen. Most violinists understand that the spine is meant to bend, twist, and spiral, but have not been taught that it is also designed to provide movement in a lengthwise direction. The vertebrae naturally move apart on exhalation and gather together again on inhalation. Attention to breathing (see chapter 5) is the best way for a beginner to rediscover this function of the spine, but with practice, you will discover that by releasing the muscles of your neck and torso out of downward pull you can get a lot more length than just the subtle lengthening that an exhalation provides. This extra length is essential for the freedom of a violinist's arms, and is most often used to provide the extra reach needed on down bows, while on up bows, the spine returns to its gathered state in order to repeat the cycle. When this natural gathering and lengthening of the spine diminishes, violinists lose the sense of freedom and lightness in their arms which makes violin playing feel easy. If you did not mention this movement of the spine along its length, you will need to study the explorations for arm support and breathing described below very carefully until you are sure you are experiencing this function of the spine.

3. How big is my spine?

The short answer to this question is, "BIG!" Because we cannot see or feel with our fingers ninety-five per cent of the circumference of our spine, many of us mis-map it as being only a very small structure than runs up the back. When holding an anatomical model of an adult spine, it is impossible to wrap one hand around the lumbar vertebrae. That's how huge it really is! A violinist needs to know how deep into the core the spine sits so she can begin to let it hold her up stem-like, rather than using so many unnecessary muscles in the lower back and abdomen to stay upright.

Take note of what surprised you in these facts about the spine in the preceding mapping exercise because these are likely the areas where you have mis-mapped yourself and where you will want to consciously begin changing the inner picture of your design. At this point, however, note that a violinist can be beautifully mapped and be completely unconscious of it. Many of the great "naturals" were natural to a large degree simply because their movement never became unnatural! They never lost their natural inheritance of free movement because their body maps remained accurate in all the areas essential to violin playing. Having said that, nearly everyone has something to discover about the inner representation of their body which can be beneficial to their playing.

We have discussed the various methods one can use to access the body map, among them drawing, palpating and self-inquiry. Next we discuss the best ways to go about altering a faulty body map.

Just as you studied the images of a spine in the above sample exploration, you need to surround yourself with images of the various parts of the map that you are working to change. Purchase some additional anatomy books and prop them up around the house so you are absorbing the visual truth all throughout the day. Trace the images until you know the intricate lines of the pelvis or shoulder blade so intimately that you can draw them from memory.

As you study the images, take the time to palpate your own bones so that you are also absorbing the three dimensional reality of your bony structure under your own fingertips. There is an enormous amount to be learned from feeling along your own bones once you know what structural details to look for.

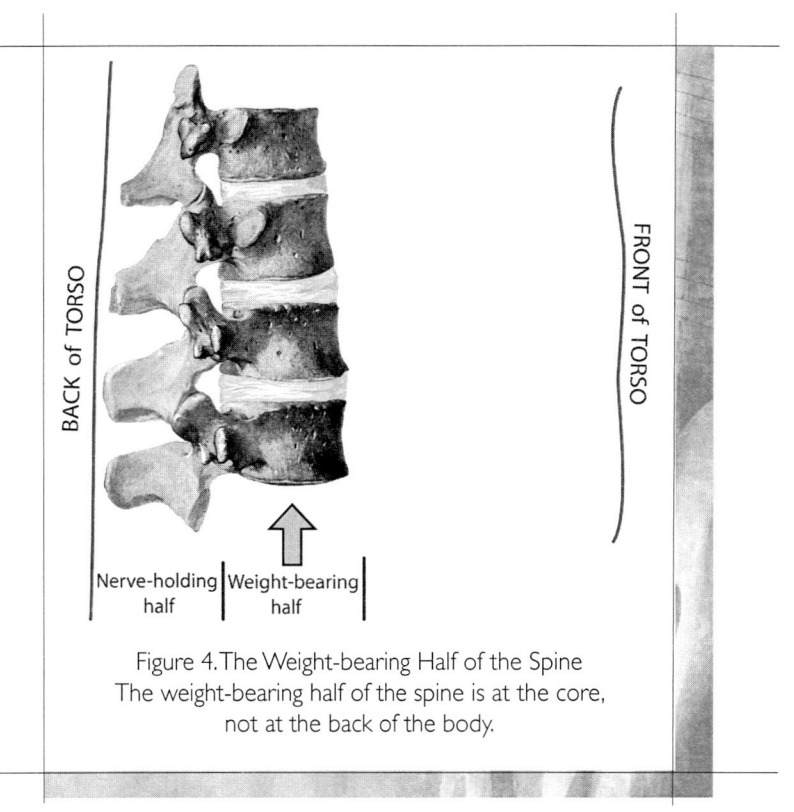

Figure 4. The Weight-bearing Half of the Spine
The weight-bearing half of the spine is at the core, not at the back of the body.

And, finally, as mentioned in the sample exploration of the spine, invest in some good anatomical models. They can be easily purchased online from medical supply companies and are reasonable in price. (Sometimes schools of medicine or chiropractor offices are willing to part with old models when replacing them with newer ones.)

Oftentimes, you will know you have a mis-mapping simply because the image or anatomical model you're examining just doesn't quite jibe for you. You might even feel some disbelief at the truth. When this happens, you know you are on to something. The first time I held a model of the upper arm bone and the shoulder blade, it seemed foreign to me. After many long moments of staring at it, the truth about my structure finally dawned on me and my eyes actually welled up with tears of relief at finally understanding the root of my problems. There had been pain in the muscles surrounding that area for many years and I thought I had exhausted all of my alternatives for ever feeling relief. But my moment of revelation was very sweet when I finally recognized how those two bones were supposed to fit together and that I could learn to use my arms in the way they were designed.

As you become more aware of how you move, you will likely begin watching others around you, particularly your students, to see if they share any of your mis-mappings. It can be very informative to look around you on the street and notice how other people use themselves, both the mis-mapped and the supremely well-mapped. We can learn from everyone. Videos of great violinists and all other great performers, including musicians, dancers, and athletes are very instructional in getting to know what balance in movement looks like. Watch all of the toddlers in your life—they are some of the best teachers available to us.

Once you have discovered where your body map is faulty and have been enlightened regarding your true design, the rest is simply absorbing the necessary changes into your everyday activities. You must practice new ways of movement in the same manner that you practice a new violin technique. Practice everyday, remembering that your body *is* your instrument of movement. The same patience and discipline that you've undoubtedly developed in learning to play the violin is necessary and will be very useful in learning how to use your body in a new, balanced way.

Reading *WEV* through once and understanding its contents, as interesting as it might be, will not change your body map. It is a process of self-exploration and self-observation throughout your daily activities. It requires a genuine interest in how you habitually stand when washing the dishes, how you usually nod your head when conversing with others, and how you react in highly stressful or emotional situations. Changing your body map requires actively taking on the information in this book—to become a scientist performing balance experiments within your own body structure. Every moment of the waking day there are opportunities to experiment with balance:

If I stop leaning my upper torso backward away from the sink, do I feel like I'm closer to balance around my lumbar core? Does this release my arms so I can reach the dishes in the sink more easily?

If I stop vigorously bobbing my head when I'm trying to affirm others in conversation, do I feel my neck muscles become freer, allowing my whole body to free? Does this subsequently allow me to actually better take in what I'm hearing because I'm truly present?

The next time I feel pressure coming from the conductor, can I consciously choose to keep my neck free and my bones balanced before bringing my violin to playing readiness? If I succeed at this, do I notice that I am exuding more strength, competence, and professionalism than at the last rehearsal, when I scurried to meet the conductor's demands, or when I sighed or scowled in distaste at his remarks?

Changing your body map can definitely improve your comfort and skills as a violinist, but there are many other life perks that may come as a result of learning how to move easily and freely according to your body's design.

Training the Senses

Most of us are taught from an early age that we have five senses which inform us about ourselves and the world: visual, auditory, tactile, gustatory (taste), and olfactory (smell). As violinists, we are trained, to varying degrees, in the use of three of these: the auditory, visual, and tactile senses.

Because society names these five senses for us, we are consciously aware of them and learn to use and develop them according to need.

It is interesting that linguist anthropologists have discovered some cultures in which individual colors are not named, but merely grouped into categories such as warm or cool. These findings are fascinating. In these studies, very young children from these cultures were given colored blocks to stack. At age three, the children were able to distinguish between specific colors. Reds were stacked with reds and greens with greens. However, by the time these children were only four or five years old, their ability to tell the difference between specific colors proved to be greatly diminished. They were now stacking blocks only according to warm and cool shades!

The reason for the change? Their culture had not *named* the individual colors, and so they had lost the ability to see each color as being unique. The ability to regain discernment of individual colors was also tested on these children. Within a short period they were capable of recovering the ability to distinguish between green and blue or yellow and orange once the differences were brought back into awareness.

These studies are pertinent to Body Mapping because of a parallel that exists in our culture. We have a sixth sense which is not named in our culture, and correspondingly, most of us have lost our ability to use it effectively. This is not the sixth sense frequently linked to the paranormal; it is our sense of *movement,* or in fancier language, our sense of *kinesthesia.* Because our culture does not name or emphasize this sixth sense, most of us only use the sense of kinesthesia in very limited ways.

Kinesthesia is the sense which informs us about our movement. From its Greek roots, the word *kinema* translates directly as "moving" and *esthesia* as "perception."

Kinesthesia Exercise

To experience how your own sense of kinesthesia informs you, try this:
1. Hold your hand in the air so that you cannot see it and wiggle and wave your hand and fingers without any of them touching one another.
2. Notice that you are not using any of the other five senses and yet are still receiving information about your movement.
    a. You can identify how fast your fingers are moving.
    b. You can tell whether they are moving side to side or forward and backward.
    c. You can sense if the movement is easy and fluid or stiff and unnecessarily tense.
    d. You can tell if you're using the wrist or just the fingers.
    e. You can feel where the finger bones are in relation to one another, even though they are not touching each other.

3. Now, imagine that your pinkie grew five inches in length. You can actually feel what that would be like—what the added weight would feel like on that side of your hand. This is your kinesthetic imagination at work.

Just as we can close our eyes and see images in our heads or hear entire melodies without making a sound, we can have a kinesthetic experience in our imagination.

Any information we receive about ourselves kinesthetically is delivered to the brain by kinesthetic sense receptors found in the muscles and connective tissue. These sense receptors are especially plentiful in and around the main joints of the body.

Training Our Sense of Kinesthesia

It may sound like an impossible chore to train a sense we were not even aware we possessed. However, training our sense of kinesthesia is a process very similar to how a violinist learns to play in tune, and we know that it is possible to learn how to do that. You may remember a time when consistently playing in tune also seemed an impossible task!

So, what is this process? To learn to play with good intonation, we must first hear the note we are playing. Many of us have had the experience of recording a piece in the practice room and being pretty happy with the intonation until we hear the recording! This is a classic example of not really hearing in the moment what we are playing, and is, of course, why recording ourselves is such a good idea. It forces us to listen differently. Lack of awareness of kinesthesia is the same as not hearing an out-of-tune note. Many violinists play for hours at a time without having any awareness that they have been dropping their weight into the lower back region, or pulling down on the collarbone. They only know something is not right when they get home with pain in the lower back or a stiff neck or numbness in the hands. Violinists must learn to pay attention to the information they are constantly fed from kinesthetic sense receptors in the joints. These receptors are there to tell us when we start to go off balance on the body's bony structure, and we can develop the ability to receive this message before major discomfort and pain set in.

Once an out-of-tune violin student has learned to hear the note he is playing, his next chore is to discern whether he has found the centre of the pitch or whether the note is too flat or too sharp. At this stage, a student might wrinkle his nose because he is now hearing that the pitch is not in tune, but does not yet have the skills to determine which way it needs to be moved in order for it to ring true again. Developing the student's skill of discernment takes patient modeling and quizzing on the part of the teacher until the student has developed a certain level of confidence in trusting that his ear knows the difference between a note that is too low and one that is too high.

This is very similar to the second stage of training our sense of kinesthesia. If the violinist knows he is not on balance on his core, or that he is using too many muscles in his neck and shoulder region, his next skill to develop is to be able to discern in which direction he needs to correct the imbalance. He will need to patiently quiz himself as he practices: "Am I sending my weight down behind the core of my body or in front of it? Are my arms pulling down to the floor or hunching around my ears? Am I locking my knees back or am I locking them muscularly in a bent position?"

Staying with our "good intonation" analogy, the final step is, of course, the necessary adjustment of the finger until it locates the ringing centre of the pitch. Just how far to go without surpassing the pitch center is a skill that is gradually learned after much practice. The same concept applies to honing a sense of kinesthesia. When a violinist accustomed to leaning back off of his core balance discovers where balance is, he will need to practice going there many times a day with and without the violin so that eventually he can find it quickly and easily. At first, he might feel that he is actually leaning forward in space rather than simply being on balance on his bones. This is because he is more forward than his habitual place, and his inaccurate body map is still trying to tell him that his habit is better than balance! Gradually, however, by using the images given here to remap his true body design, by using mirrors, videotaping himself, and getting reliable feedback from a movement re-education teacher (Andover Educators and/or Alexander Technique teachers), a violinist can learn to find balance on his core.

If we have lost our ability to fully use our kinesthetic sense and to be able to consciously question our own kinesthesia for information, we have entered a dangerous territory where we begin to lose the accuracy of our body maps. When the body map begins going askew, so does functioning. When unconscious habit begins to guide how we move rather than moving according to an accurate body map, the bones lose their right relationship with one another, muscles and tendons become strained and distorted, and nerves receive unnecessary and harmful pressure. This is the beginning of what all violinists dread: pain and injury.

A heightened, conscious kinesthetic sense *can* be learned, and is the only solution for guiding the body permanently out of pain and limitation. Teaching the importance of the kinesthetic sense to students prevents the younger generation of violinists from ever developing pain and limitation in the first place.

Training Attention

Attention needs to be trained. It is usually overlooked altogether as something that needs to be taught. Attention needs to be coached in lessons and rehearsals as much as intonation or rhythm. Most of us completed our music studies without ever receiving any conscious training regarding our own quality of attention. If we were rambunctious little children, we may have been reprimanded by teachers: "Johnnie, please *concentrate!*" That was probably the extent of comments on the state of our attention, and that request is often more for the benefit of the teacher than it is for the student! In fact, asking a student to concentrate is more harmful than not mentioning attention at all, because it is actively *mis-training* a student's attention rather than simply leaving the quality of the student's attention to chance.

As performing violinists, we need to cultivate an *inclusive attention*. When we are on stage, we want to have contact with the cellist for the next entry, be kinesthetically sensing the support of our spine, and also be aware of the candy-wrapper lady in the audience! It's all important, because it's all stimuli that we will respond to whether we like it or not! We may as well acknowledge it and choose our response to it.

Really good sight-readers instinctively know something about inclusive attention. The old adage to read ahead hints at what we are talking about. A sight-reader who is so concentrated on the note she is playing now, and perhaps only the next one, is going to suffer because she hasn't included the whole line of music in her awareness at once. If she can see there's a shift to fifth position four measures ahead of where she is presently playing, there is ample time to decide on the best fingering and no last-minute sense of panic. However, if awareness is so narrow that the violinist is only concerned with staring at notes one bar at a time, she will always have a sense that she is about to "fall off the sight-reading train."

In performance, if we try to shut out the fact that there is an audience listening and just "concentrate" on what we are doing, we put way too much pressure on ourselves by making ourselves too important in the whole picture. The audience is extremely important simply because they are there in the room with us, sharing an experience. They are part of a whole assembly of human beings connected by the common desire to share in the creation of something beautiful and *our* experience cannot be whole without them. It is unfair to an audience to close them out of our awareness, but it is also unfair to ourselves. When we narrow our attention, there is also a physiological parallel which happens: the body begins to narrow, which means too many muscles are working unnecessarily. This causes the breath to become more shallow, our vision to go blurry, and, altogether, these things can make us feel as though we are going to faint. Not an ideal condition to be in for a public performance! (Attention is a bit like frozen orange juice: in its concentrated form, it is too strong to be of any use!)

Letting go of concentration in performance is a difficult idea for some people to accept. However, choosing not to concentrate does not mean allowing your awareness to wander unchecked around the concert hall, to the detriment of your performance. The beam of light from a flashlight is a good analogy for qualities of attention.

Imagine you are in a dark alleyway at night, lit only by the flashlight you are holding. When you hear another person in the alley with you, you are not going to want to concentrate your precious light on just one part of this person, because you want as much information as quickly as possible in a glance. If you concentrate your beam on just the person's hand, for instance, and it is moving toward you, you won't know if it means you harm or is being proffered for a friendly handshake. You need the context that an inclusive beam of light can give you. If you have enough distance from the person, you can still have the beam focused on his hand while being able to view his entire figure lit up by concentric circles of light. You can then easily, fluidly shift the focus of light to his face without losing sight of what his hand is doing *because all of him is always included somewhere in your field of vision*. In this way, you are able to see his facial expressions and stance, read the situation, and know immediately what would constitute an appropriate response.

Likewise, when playing in a string quartet, you never want to have all of your attention concentrated on just one thing. If you concentrate too much on your second violin solo, you may not notice the unplanned accelerando that the cellist has begun and could be thrown right off the rails. An inclusive attention allows this kind of unexpected occurrence to immediately swim into focus so you can respond to it in the best way possible.

Using a concentrated light beam in a rapid, sequential illumination of an alleyway stranger (hand-face-hand-elbow-face) is analogous to a kind of concentrated attention called "scanning." A violinist who scans in the practice room concentrates on vibrato, then yanks *all* of her attention away to intently concentrate on playing octaves in tune, then snatches all of her attention back for an upcoming spiccato section will feel exhausted at the end of her practice session. However, a violinist who has trained an inclusive attention never loses context for whatever she is focusing on at any given moment. Everything that requires her attention during a practice or performance will be gently illuminated at all times, so that no effort is required to move focus to where it is needed.

The term used to describe the entire illuminated area of attention at any given moment is *gestalt*. The gestalt is the contents of one's consciousness at any given time and how those contents are organized. As violinists, we want to train our gestalt to encompass everything around and within us so that our focus can fluidly roam, attending to whatever requires it, but never turning into exclusive concentration.

We protect ourselves with an inclusive attention because the chances of being startled by anything are diminished when we stay awake to the endless possibilities of incoming stimuli.

Training an Inclusive Awareness

The best way to begin training an inclusive awareness is to spend time every day on the floor in what is called *constructive rest*.

Constructive Rest Exercise
1. Lie on the floor with your knees up and your feet flat on the floor. Rest your arms at your side or put your hands on your belly.
2. Begin by noticing what information you are receiving from your tactile sense. Can you feel the texture of clothes on skin? of the rug under you?
3. Add to your awareness any sounds that you may have previously shut out: trucks on the road, the hum of a furnace or fan, birds outside.
4. Keep adding into your awareness new stimuli that your senses bring you.

5. While allowing all of this information to be present in a widening field of attention, shift the focus of your awareness onto the muscles of your neck.
6. Can you still hear the birds outside as you note which muscles (if any) of your neck are tight?
7. Are the muscles at the nape of your neck pulling your head back?
8. Can you feel any holding at the front of your neck underneath the jawbone?
9. This brings kinesthetic information into your gestalt.
10. Continue in the same manner, fluidly easing the focus of your attention to any part of your body that you begin to notice is held or fixed, all the while maintaining awareness of the whole body as one in context of the surrounding sensual stimuli of the moment.
11. If there is pain present, either physical or emotional (nerves, stage fright about an upcoming performance, anger), notice that it can no longer overwhelm you, once you have put it into the larger context of available experience.
12. Recognize the other emotions you are feeling, such as:
    a. Compassion for yourself (for the good work you do in spite of the limitations you might be enduring at the moment).
    b. Compassion for others (for the challenges that your pianist or cellist might be facing in their lives).
    c. Gratitude.
    d. Love (for others in your life, for your instrument, for the music you are presently working on).
13. Place the pain you feel within this context. This shrinks its importance down to its correct proportion.

Working with inclusive awareness during constructive rest teaches you how to use it in a quiet setting. You will gradually learn how to apply it to violin playing in both practice and on stage.

Inclusive Awareness While Playing the Violin
1. Choose a passage of music you view as challenging. Perhaps there is a large shift you are worried about missing, or a long passage of continuous sixteenth notes.
2. Play it as objectively as possible (videotaping is helpful).
3. Notice what happens in your body as you approach the difficult passage.
    a. Do you feel muscles tightening? If so, where?
    b. What is happening in the facial muscles?
    c. Around your eyes?
    d. Around your mouth?
    e. Notice what your eyes are looking at. Are you staring?

4. Next, prepare to play the passage again. This time, as your eyes reach the measure just before the passage starts, begin to use your peripheral vision to take in what objects or colors you notice behind or perhaps slightly to the side of the music stand.
5. Keep those objects in the fringe borders of your awareness until you have completed the passage.
6. Note the differences as compared to the first time.
    a. Was your world wider?
    b. Was your face wider (instead of marked with a frown)?
    c. Were your eyes freed from staring?
7. Repeat the exercise again, but now notice several new items by moving your eyes around the room and outside the window.
8. Challenge yourself to add one piece of information that your tactile and auditory senses are sending you.

When you take your inclusive awareness skills into a rehearsal or performance situation with others, you need to allow the most important item of the moment to swim into the focus of your gestalt and allow others to be either close to the focus, a little further out, on the periphery, or far out on the periphery. In this way, whatever most needs your attention at the moment (the rushing violist, your own intonation) can easily swim into the center of your focus until something else becomes more important. It is all present for you already; just allow it to move around within your field of attention at the appropriate time.[5]

Chapter 2
Balancing around the Core of the Body

"And the middle of two extremes is always where balance is found!"

Two of the most common questions violinists ask are: "How should I sit?" and "How should I stand?" The short answer for both questions is "Balanced around your core." This chapter explores how to do this. We start by defining *balance* and *core*.

Balance

Dictionary.com defines balance as "a state of equilibrium or equipoise; equal distribution of weight."

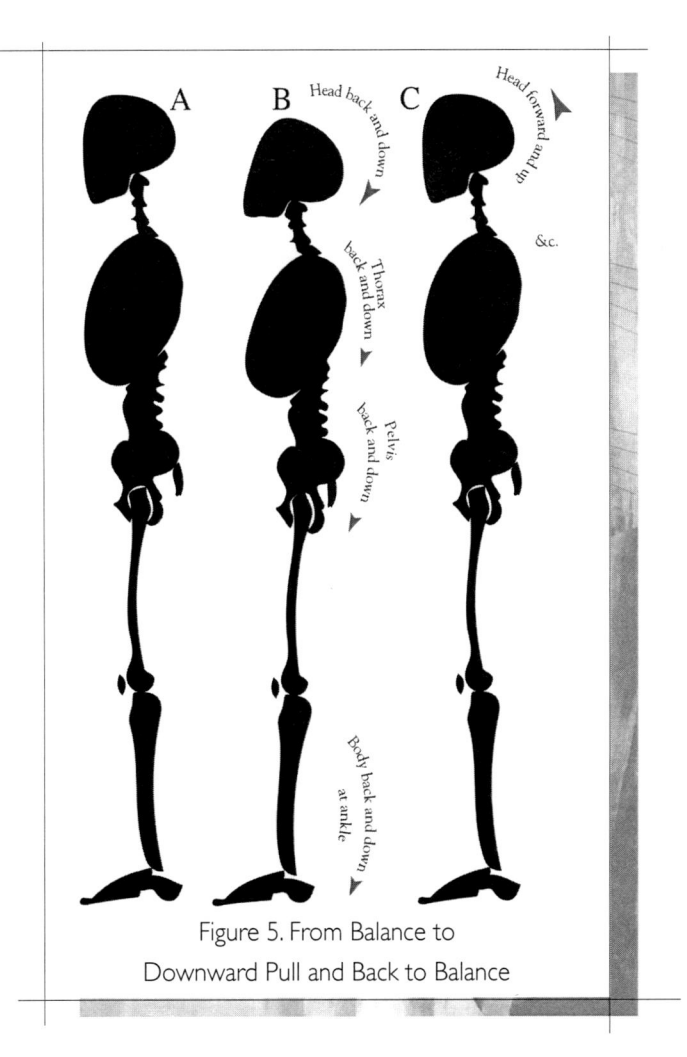

Figure 5. From Balance to Downward Pull and Back to Balance

It is very helpful when defining a term to contrast it with what it is *not*. The following image illustrates very clearly what balance on the bony structure is and what it is not.

Figure 5a shows a silhouette of a human skeleton that is balanced beautifully, like a stack of building blocks.

Figure 5b shows how the bones are pulled off of perfect balance when unnecessary or inappropriate muscular effort is used to hold the body upright. This illustrates perfectly the *downward pull* pattern first identified by F.M. Alexander.[6]

For example, the pattern of downward pull always begins in the tightening of the neck muscles. When the head's balance on the spine has become mis-mapped, neck muscles always tighten in compensation. The tighter the neck muscles get, the farther the head is rotated in a back and downward direction away from its perch on top of the spine. The head is heavy—it weighs on average between ten and fifteen pounds—and the farther it is rotated back and down away from its point of balance, the more the neck muscles must work to hold it up. The more chronic neck tension becomes, the more the location of the head's joint with the spine becomes mis-mapped because all that unnecessary neck tension overrides the sensations coming from the location of the joint itself.

A person in chronic downward pull will often have the joint of his head with the spine mapped as being at the back and sometimes as low as the bottom of the jaw rather than high and central, between the ears. These mis-mappings cause the head to remain rotated back and down, and this continued back-and-down pull of the head reinforces the mis-mappings: a vicious cycle. And this, unfortunately, is just the beginning. Once the head is pulled off balance, a whole series of muscular compensations ensue through the rest of the body. Figure 5b illustrates clearly how, in a domino effect, the rest of the bones of the body are pulled back and down out of balanced relationship with one another, leading to mis-mappings at every major joint of the body.[7]

The specific mis-mappings can vary greatly from one individual to the next. However, figure 5b illustrates the most common pattern of compensations seen in violinists:

1. When the back of the head moves back and down, the chin juts forward and up.
2. This drags the neck vertebrae forward through space, causing the head to be held muscularly well forward of the vertical mid-line of the body.
3. The body instinctively tries to counterbalance the imbalanced head by pushing the sternum up and pulling the shoulder blades together at the back.
4. This however, puts a great deal of strain on the small muscles of the lower back, causing the pelvis to jut forward through space in an effort to relieve some of this pressure.
5. The knees then instinctively lock back in order to prevent the body from toppling over backwards.
6. In turn, this puts undue pressure on the ankle joints.
7. Free movement at all of the major joints of the body is now restricted because the joints are being held in positions by the body's *moving muscles*.

8. When a person uses moving muscles to stay upright instead of relying on the body's *support muscles,* which automatically engage when the bones are on balance, the moving muscles are called for "double duty"—the duty of holding up the body as well as the duty of trying to move it.

This double duty is the cause of much of the muscle and tendon agony that violinists experience. For instance, if a violinist's head is not balanced on top of the spine, then the neck muscles needed to move the head freely while playing (this freedom of the head is clearly evident in great players like David Oistrakh) are contracted even before raising the instrument to play. In turn, because the shoulder blades and collarbones are pulled back, the natural violin shelf that a balanced collarbone provides is not as available to the player. This leads to more unnecessary muscle work in the neck, jaw, and upper back muscles to make the violin feel secure.

Arm movement itself is restricted because the shoulder blades are pinned back and down. With each additional muscular compensation in the pattern comes new mis-mappings at the major joints of the body. In order to return to the balance shown in figure 5c, a remapping of all of these joints may be necessary, but the first step is always to remap the relationship of the head to the spine. When the head's joint with the spine is accurately mapped, there is a rotational release of the head forward and up which allows for the possibility of re-establishing a balance for the bony structure at all the other places of balance. This leads to a release of all the unnecessarily held muscles through the rest of the body.

When a violinist remaps the head/neck relationship to find balance and begins to free the neck muscles, it is the beginning of rediscovering the whole body balance shown in figure 5c. When the head is allowed to regain its natural, balanced perch from its pulled-back position, it encourages the release of the holding at other places of balance through the body because of what neurophysiologists are now calling *automatic postural patterns* (APPs). Neck muscles release, the head rotates forward on its fulcrum in a return to balance (what Alexander called "allowing the head to go forward and up"), and this allows release for all of the other muscles holding through the rest of the body that have been compensating for the lack of head balance.

When a violinist rediscovers balance throughout the whole body, she is always delighted with the new ease she feels and the much bigger, freer tone which emerges from her instrument as a result.

There is a repeated emphasis throughout *WEV* on the importance of finding a free neck, since success in remapping the rest of the body is dependent on successfully freeing the neck.

Experimenting with "Back and Down"

Imagine you are in your practice studio, playing with your back to the door. Someone walks in unnoticed by you, and—*boom!*—slams the door after entering! Did you feel your neck muscles grip and your head being jerked back and down? This response to an unexpected, perceived threat is common among all mammals and is called the *startle pattern*.

Frank Pierce Jones, an American Alexander Technique teacher, wrote about the startle pattern in his book, *Body Awareness in Action*:

> *Another "total reflex" that involves the relation between head and trunk is the "Startle Pattern," the stereotyped postural response to a sudden noise. Recorded photographically, it provides a vivid example of how "good" posture can change to "bad" in a very brief time.*[8]

Jones measured the reflexive responses of subjects who were startled by loud, unexpected noises. The "stereotyped postural response" that he mentions involves the same tightening of neck muscles and pulling down of the head on top of the spine that F.M. Alexander discovered. The startle pattern has been found in other mammals to be the trigger that spurs them into flight from danger. When the danger has passed and the antelope or zebra is once again safely grazing, no evidence of the startle pattern remains. Alexander's great discovery was that humans frequently display, to differing degrees, a chronic, ongoing startle pattern, whether or not there actually is an imminent threat.

The Good Posture and Relaxation Diseases

Many of the violinists I work with are curious to know why so many of us have become mis-mapped and have lost our natural, balanced poise in the first place. After all, if you watch any healthy toddler walking and running, you will never witness a head pulled back and down or a sternum pushed up and out. It is not our natural state. We have already touched on how it may all begin with the startle pattern becoming a chronic habit, but there are other possible causes. We know for certain that young children learn by mimicking; it is not uncommon to see shared postural habits between siblings of a family, and then to meet their parents and recognize that same posturing in the senior family member. Some believe that it is our western lifestyle, right down to the furniture we sit in, that is partly to blame for our mis-mappings. In non-western cultures around the world where sitting on the floor or squatting to sell wares at the market is still common, there seems to be less of a departure from the ideal structural balance that we *all* had as toddlers before we were required to sit in chairs and desks.

It is a fact that, in our culture, the kinesthetic sense is not recognized nor taught to our children and students, and this certainly plays an enormous role in the loss of our natural, structural balance. However, more than just the omission of the word "kinesthesia" in our language, it is the pervasion of myths and inaccurate terminology regarding posture which strongly reinforces the habits of downward pull. I'm referring to the commonly heard admonitions to "sit up with good posture," or conversely to "relax." Throughout the remainder of *WEV*, these cultural myths are labeled as the *good posture* and *relaxation diseases*.

In this context, the word "dis-ease" is used in a very literal sense. A person who has found balance on her bony structure will feel more *at ease*. Breathing becomes *easier*, muscles release, and there is an accompanying sense of calm. Because muscles are not being asked to do the double duty of working to hold up the body and then being expected to be free enough to move it, movement becomes easier and more fluid.

The Good Posture Disease

The first cultural disease is the *good posture disease*. Many of us were so indoctrinated as young school children about what good posture means that, to this day, as soon as the word posture is mentioned, there is an automatic response. Everyone in the room tries to sit up straight; chests are pushed out, causing an exaggerated curve in the spine; necks are flattened; shoulders are pulled back; chins are tucked and breathing is restricted. This is what happens to our children with every admonishment to "sit up with good posture." And just when it seems that these children, being told to "sit up" in backwards-sloping desks at school all day couldn't lose any more of their natural inclination to be on balance, they are handed a violin for the first time.

Now, in addition to being told to stand or sit up straight to play, little Johnnie is told to "get your violin up." Because Johnnie is a good little soldier with his shoulders pulled back, he has no freedom or springiness left in his collarbones. The only way he can get his violin up without this freedom is by pushing his sternum up and out even more. This rotates the whole thorax back and down again and initiates all the hip-joint bracing and knee-locking compensations that figure 5b demonstrates. This is how our good posture disease begins. And then, of course, our body map absorbs this imbalanced disease as the correct way to stand, sit, and play the violin. And remember, the existing body map dictates how we continue to move until we decide to consciously change the map.

Webster's dictionary defines posture in its first sense as "the way a person holds himself." Other words such as *position* and *pose* share the same root as *posture*. Both of these words, by definition, denote some kind of holding still as in "see how the buildings are positioned on the hill," or "the model posed for the art class." As violinists, we most definitely want nothing to do with *holding*. We must be free to move. *Posture* is a holding word, not a moving word.

Webster's second definition of posture is even more telling: "to pretend to be something one isn't." When we *posture*, we are definitely not being who we really are, because we are working directly against our body's natural design. When we stand with "good posture," we are muscularly yanking our body's weight delivery to behind our *core line,* and yet the core line is where we would begin to find our natural balance if we stopped trying to "stand up straight"!

The Relaxation Disease

The *relaxation disease* is less prevalent among violinists than the *good posture disease,* partly because violin teachers rarely say, "Johnnie, you're standing up too straight—you must slouch more when you play the violin!" And yet, frequently to counteract all of the muscle strain Johnnie feels during his violin lesson from his sustained "good posture," he will immediately slump once he packs up his violin and walks out of the studio. Even though violin teachers never recommend slouching to play, they will quite frequently say "Oh my, you're very stiff—you need to learn to *relax!*"

The response they hope to invoke in their students is a sense of emotional ease. Quite often this is said when a teacher is aware that the student is feeling nervous or self-conscious. However, the term is so nebulous that it can be quite infuriating to be given this piece of advice. The student might think: "What exactly is she telling me to relax? Does she want me to relax my left pinkie or does she just generally think I'm uptight? She can't mean to relax all of my muscles, or I'd end up collapsing on the floor."

When I heard the advice to "just relax" as a twelve-year-old student, I often felt resentful. I would gladly have relaxed appropriately to escape the daily discomfort of spasming muscles if I had only known how. But I did not know how, and being told to relax was simply not enough. A teacher will be much more successful if she can explain how the arms are supported by the body, and that the arm muscles are able to move more freely when the structural balance of the bones has been found.

At its best, advice to "just relax" is confusing and frustrating to a student. At its worst, it encourages the relaxation disease. This version of downward pull shares the contracted neck muscles and back-and-down rotation of the head with the *posture disease,* but compensations through the rest of the body manifest somewhat differently. The classic sloucher exhibits the usual patterns of the relaxation disease: a forward-jutting neck and a rounded, slumped spine. The pelvis sometimes tilts in the opposite direction from its position in the good posture disease, and this results in tremendous

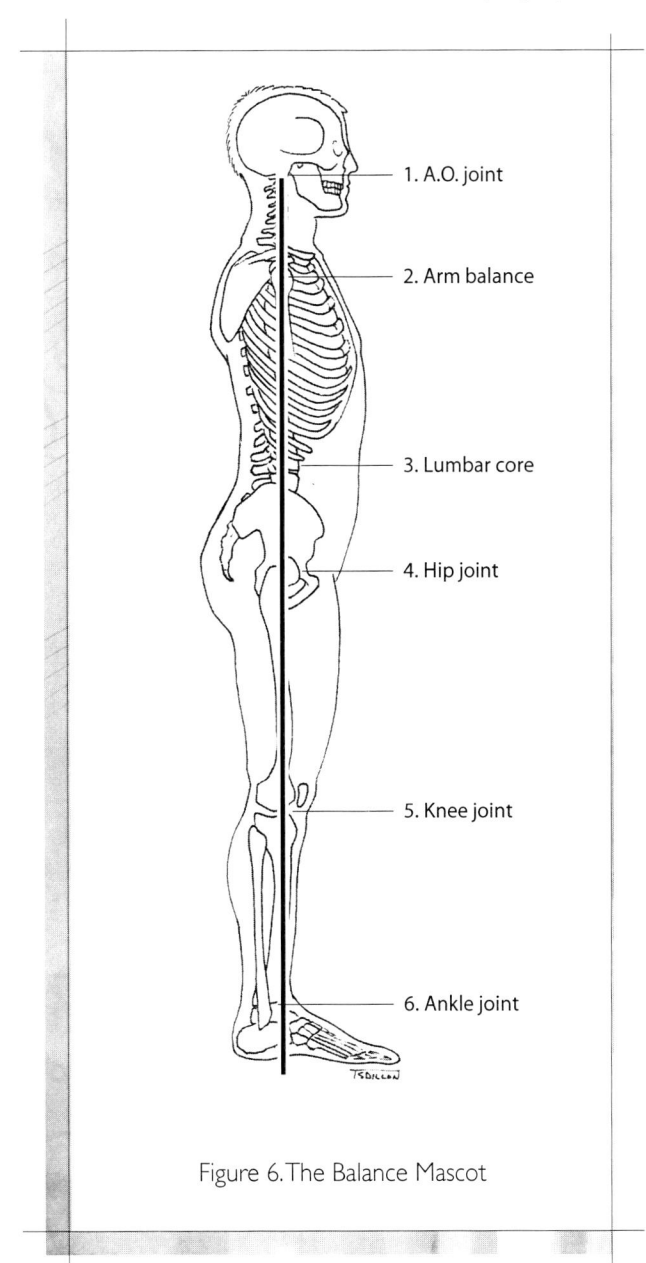

Figure 6. The Balance Mascot

1. A.O. joint
2. Arm balance
3. Lumbar core
4. Hip joint
5. Knee joint
6. Ankle joint

Posture, in all of its pulled "up and back" appearance, is one example of how a tight neck affects the rest of the body. The slumped appearance of relaxation is another. Balance is found when the weight delivery is allowed to happen along the core of the body.

and sometimes very painful and damaging pressure on the tailbone. In standing, the hip joints and knees will still lock, again producing downward pull through the entire body. Ironically, "relaxed," slumped people, like their "posture" counterparts, are tensing additional muscles to prevent themselves from falling over!

Our body maps and those of our students will begin to regain the possibility of structural balance once we have eradicated the good posture and relaxation diseases both from our maps and our vocabulary.

So, having rejected posture and relaxation as options, we are left with what is right in the middle. And the middle of two extremes is always is where *balance* is found! However, before we can go looking for balance in the body, it is necessary to understand what our core is.

Core

Our answer in response to how to stand and sit when playing the violin is: "On balance around your core." Having explored the meaning of balance, we'll now take a look at what our core is. Webster's dictionary defines *core* as: "the inner part of certain fruits containing the seeds; the innermost part of anything."

We are organized around our core in a way similar to how an apple is organized. Our core runs directly down through the body's center, from the top of the spine to the arches of the feet, and through the torso it is comprised of the weight-bearing portion of the skeletal structure. Most of us never give much thought to what lies at the very center of our bodies because we cannot see or touch our insides. Some of us were lucky enough to be taught some basic anatomy in school, but do not remember much of it because we were not shown how to apply this information to our own movement. We learned we had two bones in the lower leg. But if we had also been taught that we should feel our weight traveling down the *front* bone when we stand, the information would have been a lot more relevant. We would have considered this kind of information useful, and probably would have remembered it because we could have had some fun experimenting with it!

At this point it is worth reviewing some of the spine-mapping discoveries we made in chapter 1, since the weight-bearing half of the spine *is* our core throughout the length of the neck and torso. The problem is that many of us have mis-mapped our spines as being in our *backs*. Because our tactile sense

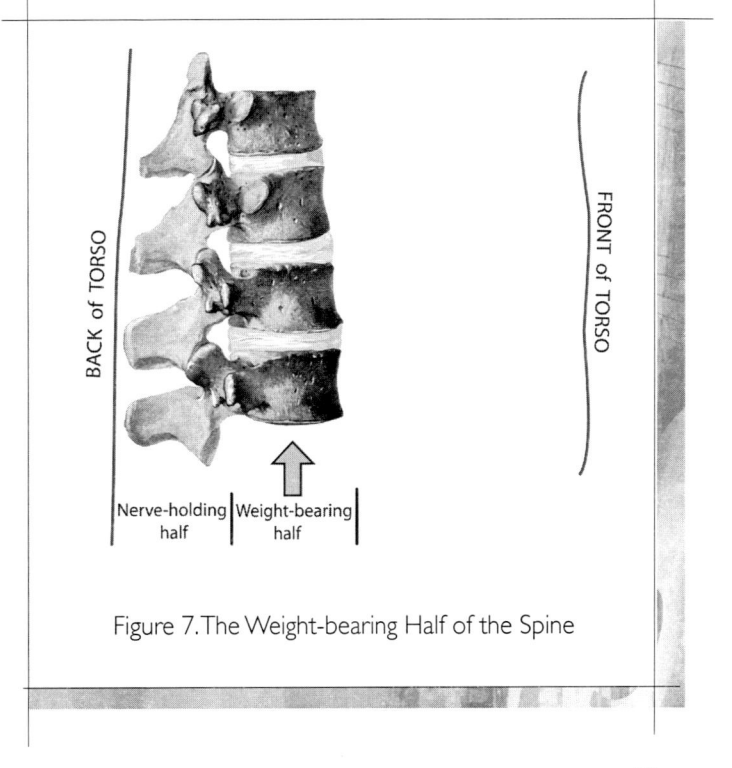

Figure 7. The Weight-bearing Half of the Spine

is so much better developed than our kinesthetic sense, and because we are able to feel only the surface portion of the spine through the flesh in the back, we have been misled into perceiving the spine as synonymous with the back. We have lost the ability to sense where the core, weight-bearing portion of the spine resides, which is down through the center.

So, to review: a spine has two halves—a front half and a back half.

The back half of the vertebrae is made up of protective, bony processes. Run a hand over someone's back and you will feel the tips of the processes that point to the rear only. What you feel is *still* just the tip of the iceberg of the back half of the spine; even the processes that point to the sides (still part of the back half) are buried so deeply that you cannot feel them with your fingertips. The back half is protective and bony because it is designed to house and protect the all-important spinal cord.

The front half of the spine, located right at the core, is shaped very differently. The individual vertebrae which make up this half of the spine are solid, smooth, and rounded, rather like semi-circular stacking blocks. Separating each of these stacked vertebrae in the front are the soft, gel-filled, pillowy disks. The purpose of these disks is to cushion one vertebra from the next as the upper body's weight is borne and delivered through the front half of the spine. The disks do *not* continue into the back half of the spine, because this would interrupt the continuity of the spinal cord from the brain to the rest of the body.

Violinists infected by the good posture disease who spend hours a day playing, all the while sending weight down the back half of the spine, are at risk of slipping a disk. A disk can slip out from its neat stacking between two vertebrae and bulge out on one side when the back halves of the vertebrae are squeezed too closely together by receiving the majority of the body weight from above. A slipped disk is extremely painful because, when it bulges out, it touches and crowds the nerve bundles which stem off from the spinal cord.

Figure 8. The Front and Back Halves of the Spine

When someone stands on balance, as shown in figure 9, a line can be drawn through the middle of the body, bisecting it vertically. This line represents the body's core. One can see how the core line runs through the *front* half of the spine and all major joints of the body.

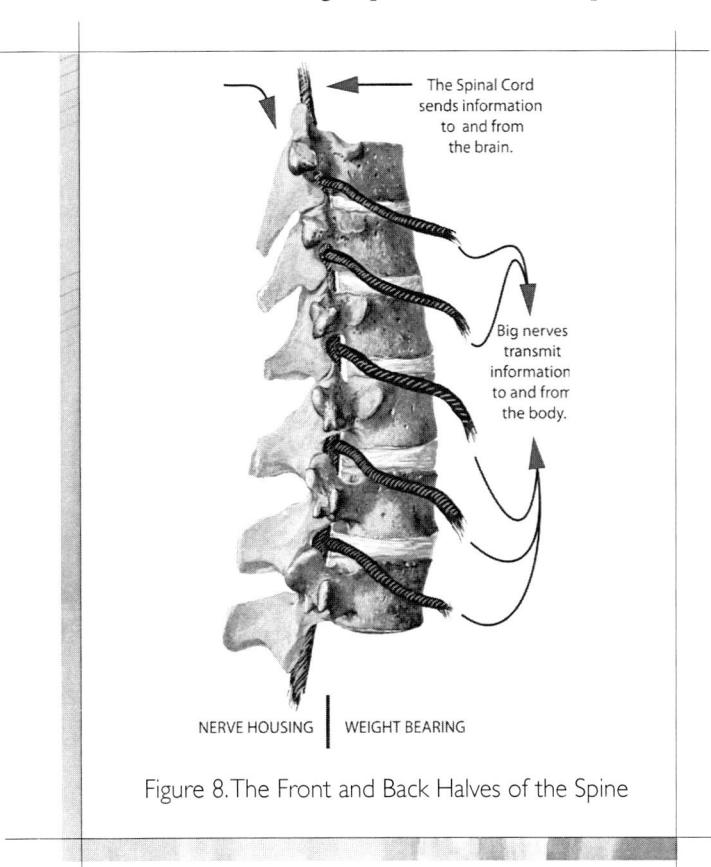

Since we will return to this image frequently, it is labeled as our Balance Mascot. Violinists who organize their movement from a place of balance around the core move effortlessly and freely. Those who do not can be seen massaging their necks and backs because their muscles are working overtime to compensate for the lack of stacked-up balance on the bones along their core.

The numbers that lie along the core line of the Balance Mascot are called the *places of balance*. All places of balance except for number three occur at major joints of the body. Remember that the major joints are rich with sense receptors that feed our kinesthetic awareness. This means that these are the easiest places in the body to start developing our kinesthetic sense. Chapter 3 is dedicated to a detailed exploration of each of the six places of balance.

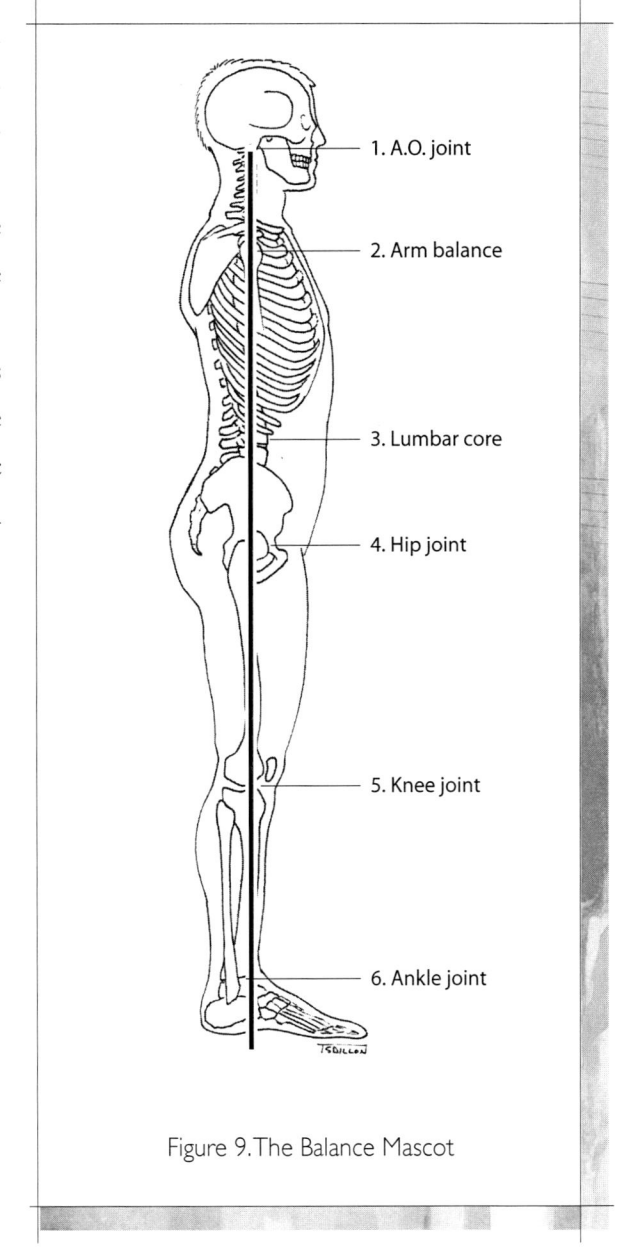

1. A.O. joint
2. Arm balance
3. Lumbar core
4. Hip joint
5. Knee joint
6. Ankle joint

Figure 9. The Balance Mascot

Chapter 3
Places of Balance

"How do I know when my neck is free?"

Place of Balance 1: The A.O. Joint

A violinist who has not found the balance of the head on the top of the spine will never experience a sense of security in supporting the instrument or freedom through the neck and arms when playing. Since we violinists (unlike pianists or cellists) use the head as one of the five points of contact in supporting our instrument, it is essential for us to understand how a head can freely balance on a spine and the mis-mappings which prevent this easy balance.

The atlanto-occipital joint (A.O. joint), like many of our joints, is named for the two bones that meet to form it and thereby provide movement. The atlas is the topmost vertebra of the spine. The occiput is the base of the skull where the head is designed to sit in balance on top of the atlas.

The average human head weighs ten to fifteen pounds. A very large man's head could weigh up to twenty pounds. This is greater than the weight of a bowling ball or the mallet of a sledge hammer. In chapter 1 we learned how the front half of the spine is equipped with soft, cushiony disks between each vertebra. When the heavy head is balanced at the A.O. joint, there is a perfectly designed system of cushions directly below it to bear its weight. When a head

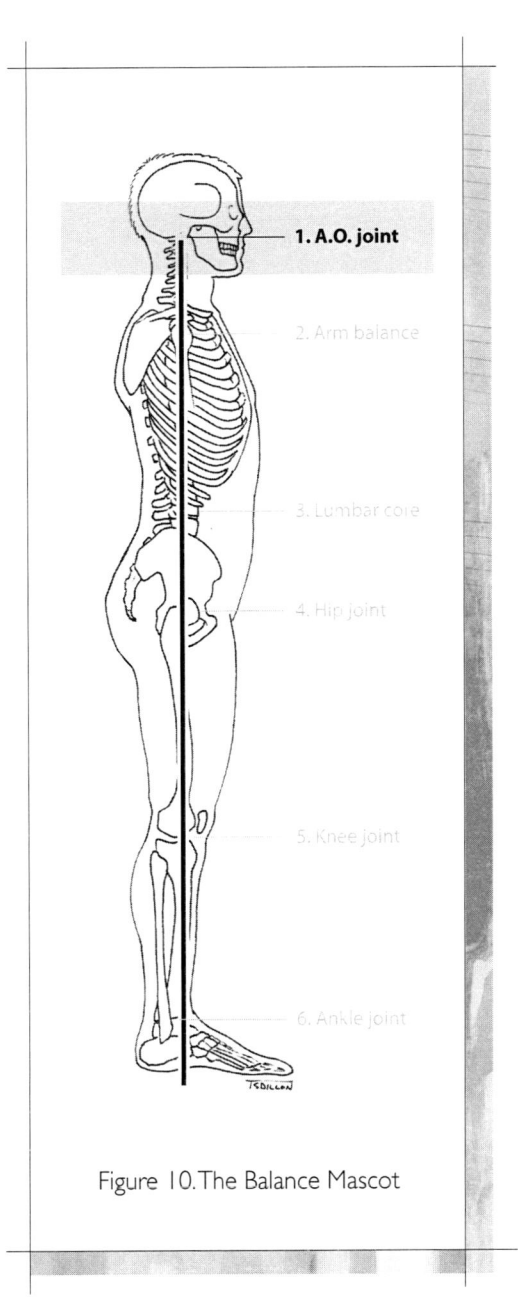

Figure 10. The Balance Mascot

is not perched on the front half of the spine, problems ensue because neck muscles have to compensate for the lack of balance.

Here is a view of the atlas:

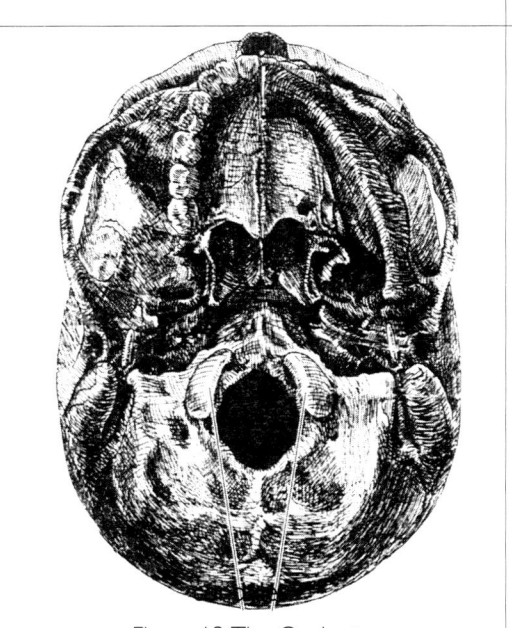

Figure 12. The Atlas as Viewed from Above.

Figure 13. The Occiput
The occiput is the bottom surface of the skull.

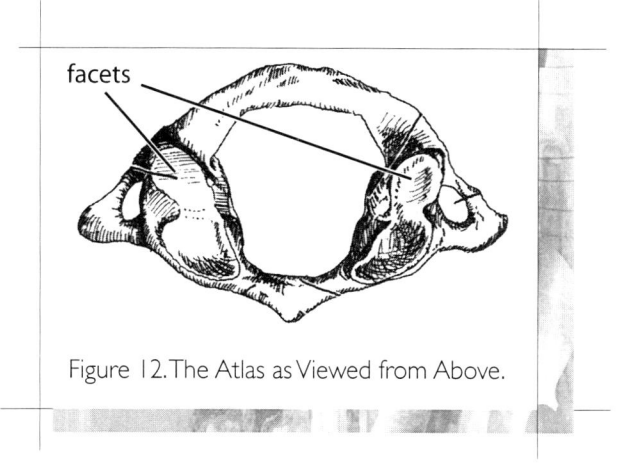

The facets are two shallow hollows located in the atlas, which is the topmost vertebra. The two protruding condyles are found on the base of the skull and fit right into the facets. This design is what allows the skull to nod without losing its balanced perch on the spine, and is why this is sometimes called the "nodding joint."

The balance point for the skull on the spine is exactly midway front-to-back and also side-to-side. It is halfway between the upper front teeth and the back of the skull, and also halfway between the ears.

The two most common mis-mappings that lead violinists into problems in this area are inter-related:

1. Mapping the A.O. joint too far back of the central core.
2. Mapping the A.O. joint too low.

Mapping the A.O. Joint too Far Back of the Central Core

The violinist who has mapped the spine as belonging in the back rather than at the core will always point to the back of the neck when asked to locate the top of the spine. The belief that the head rests on this back half of the spine causes the classic Alexander "back and down" rotation of the head. This rotation is an unconscious effort to fulfill the mis-mapping that the skull joins the spine at the back. Violinists who are mapped too far back always feel an insecurity in holding the instrument.

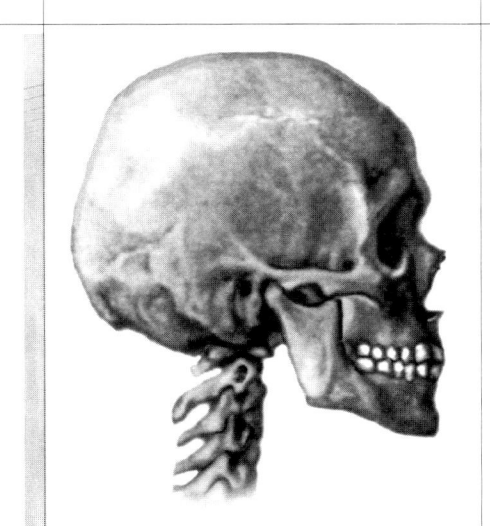

Figure 14.
The head is designed to balance on the spine.

The sensation of insecurity derives from the fact that a head rotated back and down lifts the jaw, preventing it from providing a sufficient overhang directly above the chin-rest for the violin to feel easily and securely tucked underneath. Because the instrument feels as if it is going to slip out from under the jaw, violinists with the A.O. joint mapped too far back of the central core will often compensate by using more neck and upper torso muscles to clamp down on the violin. (See chapter 8 for more details on the numerous ways unnecessary neck tension manifests itself in violinists.)

A violinist with this mis-mapping commonly assumes that she feels an insecurity in supporting the violin because her neck is too long. She mistakenly thinks she needs to build up more height by using a higher shoulder rest, chinrest, or both. This is a result of the head being chronically tilted back and down which lifts the chin and jawbone, often by as much as an inch or two from where balance is found. This, in conjunction with a collarbone being hauled down too low (see chapter 4), gives the impression that at the front, at least, the neck is quite long. Clearly, some adult violinists are very tall with large vertebrae and there are much smaller children with a more petite skeletal structure, all of whom play on full-sized violins. There will be as many different set-ups as there are players, so I am not suggesting that all violinists using very high set-ups are mis-mapped at the A.O. joint. However, most violinists delight in finding a bit more freedom and security in their support of the violin by correcting their A.O. joint mapping to rediscover the central perch of the head over the core.

Playing the violin with a head perched on the front half of the spine rather than being rotated back and down provides a wonderfully secure sensation of being above or on top of the instrument rather than always feeling as if it is something slipping away that needs to be further chased with the jaw. In addition, freeing neck and upper torso muscles that were previously occupied with head-holding and violin-clamping allows for more freedom of movement in the head and arms, contributing greatly to both physical comfort and artistry!

Figure 15a. Head rotated back and down.

Figure 15b. Head balanced on the front half of the spine and lightly nodded onto the violin.

Mapping the A.O. Joint too Low

The second mis-mapping of the head/neck relationship is mapping the A.O. joint as being too low. Frequently, as violinists gaze in the mirror to fasten the top button of a blouse or adjust a necktie before a performance, they repeatedly mis-map the location of the top of the neck as being where the bottom of the jaw meets the neck, because this is what they see from the front view. Just a glance at figure 15 reveals that where collars and ties end is not where necks end. There are at least three-to-four more vertebrae above the top of the collar before the neck meets the head at the A.O. joint.

As mentioned earlier, mapping the A.O. joint too low is related to mapping it as being too far back. A head rotated back and down due to the first mis-mapping sends too much weight down the back half of the spine. The weight of the head coming down the back compresses the back half of the spine, causing an overarching in the cervical vertebrae; this in turn causes the jaw and upper neck vertebrae to jut forward of the core balance line. A person with this chronic mis-mapping can only nod her head by using several of the upper cervical vertebrae. Her actual A.O. joint, way up between her ears, is almost completely immobilized. Because her movement originates from a lower point, she is mis-mapped into thinking that her head joins her neck several vertebrae lower than at the A.O. joint, which in reality is at the very top of her spine.

Once again, a violinist who perceives the top of her neck as being lower than the A.O. joint uses unnecessary neck muscles in her efforts to hold the violin. She takes her head to the violin by sticking the head and neck out to meet the violin, thereby unnecessarily using three or four neck vertebrae to move the head. When a violinist discovers the balance of her head at the A.O. joint, she brings the violin *to her,* where it nestles comfortably and securely in the deep crook that the collarbone and underside of the jaw create when in right relationship to each other.

There are other reasons that violinists mis-mapped the head/neck area. Abstractions from teachers can frequently mislead a student into a mis-mapping. For example, violin teachers who use the common image of "dropping the weight of the head onto the violin like onto a pillow" can be grossly misinterpreted by a student and can lead to a loss of head balance on the spine. Dropping your head onto a pillow generally means releasing all of its weight into the pillow in order to go to sleep. In violin playing, however, we do not want to drop all ten pounds of the head onto the instrument. The proportion of the head's weight actually required to stabilize a one-pound violin is tiny! A student who attempts to drop the full weight of his head onto his violin is no longer able to maintain the balance of the head on top of the spine; rather, he aims for the chinrest as the place to rest the weight of the head instead of maintaining the head's balance on top of the A.O. joint.

When describing how the head approaches the instrument, the term *nodding* is much better than speaking of "dropping the head." If the teacher has already clearly demonstrated to the student where the head balances on the spine and how the bottom of the skull nods in the facets of the atlas, the next logical step is to demonstrate how to allow the head to lightly nod onto the chinrest from the A.O. joint. (One very effective teaching model that can be used to demonstrate how high up the nodding, or A.O. joint, is, is the bobble-head doll, which children in particular love to emulate. A bobble-head can only nod its head from the joint way up between its ears, simply due to the fact that it has no moveable vertebrae.)

This nodding of the head onto the chinrest allows a wonderful, freeing lengthening through the vertebrae of the spine rather than the compression that is caused by a rotated and dropped head. This particular lengthening of the spine is exactly the "up" part of "forward and up" that Alexander Technique students experience after a teacher has guided them out of the back-and-down rotation of the head. Neurophysiologists today recognize the validity of Alexander's forward-and-up release of the head and its ensuing lengthening effect on the spine, and have named this sequence of release (among others they have since found in the body) an *automatic postural pattern* (APP). So, not only do we violinists gain freedom of the head and neck muscles by learning to nod instead of dropping our heads onto the chinrest, we also gain more length and freedom through the spine, and consequently through the arms.

The important point here is that a head lightly nodded into the chinrest is still balanced on the spine and is free to move anywhere, all the while providing one of the five sources of support for the instrument. Watch footage of any of the great violinists from the last century (most of whom played with no shoulder rest), and it is immediately obvious how free their heads are on their spines. Their heads rarely stay in one spot on the chinrest without some sort of movement for more than a few moments. Frequently one can see them lifting their heads right off the chinrest, or swiveling it from front to side. The only way that this kind of head freedom is possible is by taking full advantage of the four other points of contact with the instrument that help to keep it secure. These other places of support are the collarbone shelf, the side of the neck, the left hand, and the friction of the bow hair on the string. If all five points of contact are being used in supporting the instrument, the head has very little to do except balance on its own structure and provide some intermittent, stabilizing contact with the chinrest.

When teaching, it is essential to discuss and demonstrate all five points of contact. There are many violin teachers who advocate holding the violin only between the "shoulder" and head, or worse, between the shoulder and chin. In doing this they squander the opportunity to teach the

---

Figure 16. The Five Points of Contact
1. Jawbone
2. Collarbone shelf
3. Side of the neck
4. Left hand
5. Friction of bow hair on string

far greater freedom available when support from all five points of contact is achieved, including the equilibrium provided by the counterbalance of the left hand from underneath and bow contact from above. These teachers encourage their students to wave their left hands around while the violin is essentially clamped rather than balanced and mistakenly think that by teaching a student to hold the violin securely with the head or chin, the left arm and hand will be freed.

In fact, *because* of the immobility of the upper arm structure and the head and neck in this exercise, exactly the opposite happens. Once again, this forces the head to sit on the violin instead of on the spine, which pulls the head forward of the neck, rotating the whole sphere downwards at the back of the skull and putting a great deal of pressure on the spinal cord half of the spine. In addition to this horror, because the head no longer has the support of the bony structure directly underneath it, additional neck muscles rush in to do the work of keeping the heavy head from toppling the body right over. As we have already discussed, neck tension is the beginning of tension throughout the rest of the body.

Thought Experiment

To fully comprehend how much work it is for muscles to hold a head up that is not balanced on the bones underneath it, try this.

1. Imagine that you are holding a ten-pound bowling ball in an upright position, balanced on your fingertips which are inserted in the finger holes of the ball.
2. You can feel the ball's weight, but since this is delivered straight down through your vertical forearm bones, you are able to balance it with a minimal amount of muscular work.
3. Now, using your kinesthetic sense, imagine slowly moving your forearm from a vertical plane to a forty-five degree angle. This gives you a sense of how much extra work is required from your arm muscles to keep the bowling ball from falling.
4. This is what your poor neck muscles are constantly doing if your head is not balanced on your spine!

Methods for Locating the A.O. Joint (see figure 14)

Before it is possible to find balance at place of balance 1, it is necessary to be kinesthetically clear on where the A.O. joint actually is.

> *When neck tension is present, muscles in the arms are restricted in their ability to move freely and pressure on the nerve-housing half of the spine in the neck can cause numbness and tingling through the arms. This is because arm and hand nerves originate in the neck.*

Method 1: Fingers in Your Ears

1. Point both index fingers into the holes of your ears.

2. If your fingertips continued through the soft tissue between them, before they met they would run right into the upper condyles—those convex rocking bones on the base of the skull.
3. Now, like a bobble-head doll, nod your skull very gently and see if you can allow the movement to happen only at this joint, rather than using the top two or three vertebrae to nod your head as so many do in everyday conversation.

Method 2: Tongue Back and Up
1. Point the tip of your tongue as far back into the roof of your mouth as possible, up into the soft palate.
2. The soft palate is directly in front of the A.O. joint.

Method 3: Pivot on the Thumb
1. To fully absorb that your A.O. joint is exactly midway between the front and back of your skull rather than at the *back* of the base of your skull, as is commonly mis-mapped, put your thumb in your ear and your index finger right under your nose.
2. With your thumb still in your ear, pivot your index finger over the top of your head until it reaches the opposite point from your nose on the back of your head.
3. You will experience the distance from under your nose to your ear as being equal to the distance from the ear to the back of the skull.

Method 4: A Line at the Bottom of the Skull
1. Sometimes the easiest way to develop an awareness of the A.O. joint and the head's balance on it is to mentally draw a line along the bottom of the skull beginning with the upper row of teeth or gums to the base of the skull at the back of the head.
2. If this line, like a teeter-totter, is not horizontal, then you know that your head is not balancing on its fulcrum.
3. To help increase your awareness of this line, you can use your tactile sense by running your tongue or a finger between the upper gums and the cheeks and behind the top back molars.

If it seems strange to you that the bottom of the skull is as high as your upper row of teeth, then it is possible that you have mapped your jaw as the bottom of your skull and have probably been lining the chin up with the bottom of the skull at the back. This will cause the head to rotate back and down. It is important to remember that the jaw is only an appendage to the skull as the arms are to the torso.

As you develop a sense of the skull balancing on the top of the spine you will start to experience more release in your neck muscles.

Mapping the Neck Muscles

As stated earlier, when neck muscles are tense, the head is pulled off its beautiful balance on top of the spine, and that causes tension through the whole body. This creates a vicious cycle that can be resolved into a virtuous circle in which we find the head balanced on the top of the spine, thereby freeing the neck; and in turn, freeing the neck secures the balance of the head on top of the spine.

It is important to map the muscles of your neck very carefully to learn how to free them. The freer the neck muscles, the easier it is to experience the balance of the skull on top of the spine, since pressure on nerves reduces and distorts sensation.

Figure 17 gives a cross-section of the neck.

Everything in dark grey not already labeled is neck muscle. Notice that, coming in from the back of the neck, there are five layers of muscles before the side processes of the spine are reached. The body proper of the spine, the core, is in front of these processes. That's a long way through muscle before reaching the weight-bearing part of the spine.

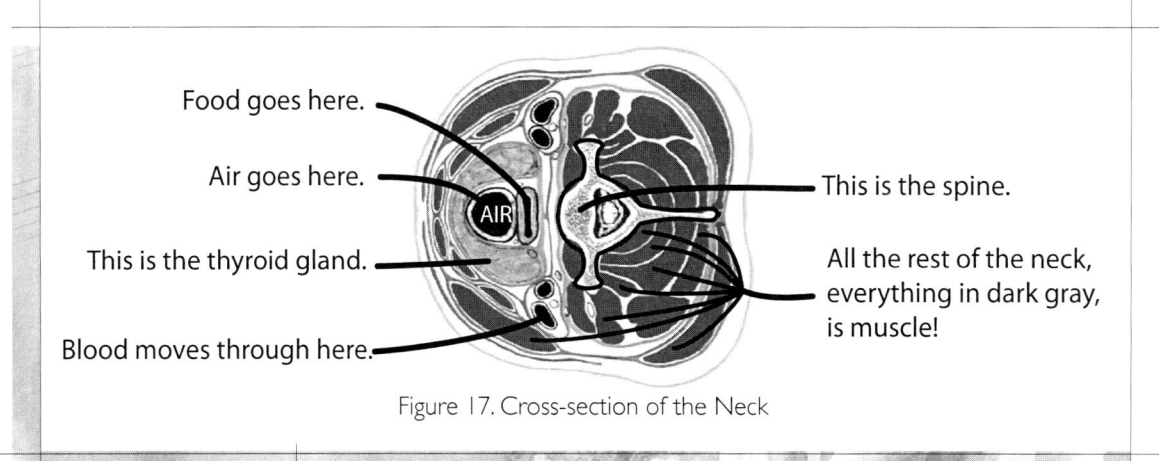

- Food goes here.
- Air goes here.
- This is the thyroid gland.
- Blood moves through here.
- This is the spine.
- All the rest of the neck, everything in dark gray, is muscle!

Figure 17. Cross-section of the Neck

Figure 18. Neck Muscles Viewed from the Side

Notice that muscles cover the entire neck and not just the neck's back or nape. Not just the throat area; not just the sides. Muscles, running vertically, cover the entire cylinder that is the neck.

It is the job of these muscles to move the skull. They can do this because they attach at one end all along the skull's base.

Take note that some neck muscles run underneath the collarbone—the "violin shelf."

Figure 19 shows the difference between free and tense neck muscles. The very first direction that F.M. Alexander gave to himself and his students in order to find good use and freedom was, "Let the neck be free in order for the head to go forward and up." If you learn to free the neck, the head will be released to its natural forward-and-up poise on top of the spine. If you kinesthetically find balance for your head on the spine, the neck muscles will begin to free. It goes both ways!

Notice how tense neck muscles draw the head back and down onto the posterior half of the spine. When neck muscles are contracted, the weight of the head is delivered to the back portion of the spine, where the spinal cord and nerves are housed. This is a lot of pressure to put on nerves.

Look now at the free neck. Notice that the skull is easily balanced on top of the spine and that its weight travels down through the front part of the spine, where the discs provide cushiony support between each vertebra.

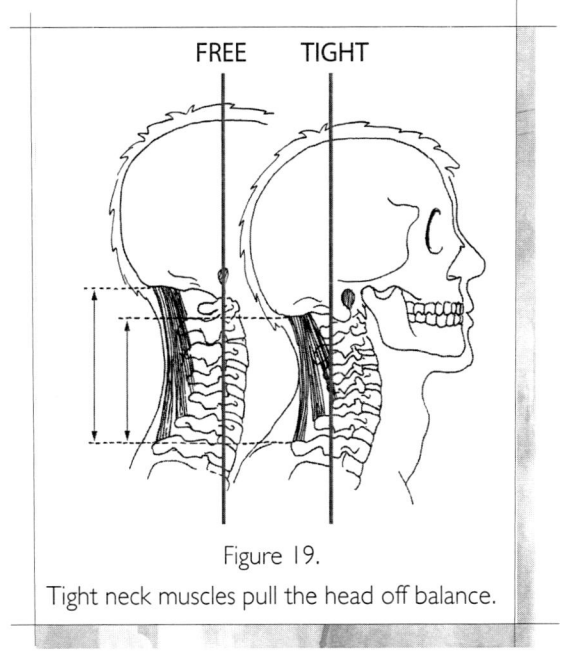

Figure 19.
Tight neck muscles pull the head off balance.

Finding a Free Neck

Sometimes beginner Body Mapping and Alexander Technique students feel very confused about this vitally important first direction. "How do I know when my neck is free?" they ask. One good way to know is by experiencing what it feels like to not use any neck muscles at all while someone you trust gently supports and moves your head for you.

I wish to be very clear that the following exercise is not intended in any way to imitate or replace what an AT teacher is trained to do with her hands. Alexander Technique teachers are carefully trained for a minimum of three years before they are allowed to use their hands on students, and when they do, they are both receiving information about their students and simultaneously guiding the student into release. This exercise is suggested *only* as an aid in mapping the weight of the head and as a safe way to experience freer neck muscles.

1. Lie on the floor with the soles of your feet on the ground and knees bent.
2. Rest your hands on your ribs or on the floor beside you.
3. Your trusted friend should gently slide both hands under your head, cradling it.
4. Your job is to release all of the weight of your bowling-ball head into her hands.
5. As your head is supported, imagine all five layers of muscle in the back of your neck falling away from the bone and toward the floor, much as a Chinese Shar-Pei's loose skin falls toward the floor when on its back.
6. Make sure that you have accurately mapped the location of the bony processes and the bony core of the spine.
7. This image will be of no help to you if you still have the core of the spine mapped as being too close to the surface of the skin: the core, even the side processes, are deep, deep, deep. Remember, it is only the tips of the back processes that protrude out enough to be palpated with the fingertips.

8. When both you and your friend feel that she has received the full weight of your head, she slowly, gently turns and nods your head for you—just an inch or so in each direction—so that you can experience the freedom of movement at the A.O. joint, while at the same time experiencing a free neck.

Having the head supported in this manner so that the neck muscles can release is exactly what happens when someone stands with the head balanced at the A.O. joint, with the one difference: in an upright position, the head's support is the *spine* rather than another's hands. Sometimes it helps students when they move to standing to recall the sensation of hands supporting the head from behind to find more release in the neck and upper torso muscles.

In the search for any new kinesthetic experience, it is extremely important to contrast the new with the habitual. Before rising from the floor, you can take this experiment one step further into movement.

Maintaining Free Neck Muscles in Movement

1. Without trying to change anything from your usual manner of use or any help from your friend, simply observe your habitual neck tension as you extend one of your legs from its bent position until it is flat on the floor.
2. Notice if you are contracting the muscles of your neck in order to move your leg.
3. Return your leg to the bent position.
4. Next, bring your friend back into the picture to cradle your head and repeat the procedure.
5. This time keep your attention on yielding all of the weight of your head to your friend's hands as you move your leg.
6. Are your neck muscles freer than the first time?
7. Keep in mind that, because of the body's interconnectedness, your experience today will be enhanced even more when you do this exercise again after having tried some of the arm-freeing experiments in chapter 4 or the breathing explorations in chapter.

Maintaining a Free Neck While Supporting the Violin

The kind of explorations described above will definitely help you discover what it means to have a free neck. However, in order to play the violin and simultaneously foster free neck muscles, accurate mapping of both the vertebrae and the neck muscles must be done. A clear kinesthetic sense of the front halves of the neck vertebrae stacking up in a column sends the message to the body that there is no need for additional neck muscles to try to hold everything upright. Muscles respond automatically to this kind of mapping of the bony structure. If the structure is on balance, muscles through their own special wisdom know exactly what can be released from duty. We just need to assure them that our bones are working in a way that's got the job covered!

Bringing any object toward the face can cause overprotective neck muscles to tighten and initiate the startle pattern. Just try it with a friend who is not expecting it. Even if we expect it, even if we ourselves are bringing an object (like a violin) toward our face, an approaching object can be the cause of neck muscles tightening—in the violin's case, even before it arrives on the collarbone.

Part of this is due to physical habit. If we are accustomed to using neck muscles to "hold" a violin, they will dutifully prepare for the arrival of the instrument by tightening. But this tightening can also be due to emotional responses and memories associated with playing the instrument. The approach of a violin can be loaded with tightening responses if we carry memories of uncomfortable performances in which the violin did not feel secure physically, or if we did not feel comfortably prepared to perform.

To overcome these obstacles, it is necessary to have a clear, accurate map of the head on the front half of the cervical spine; of the head and thorax balance over the lumbar spine; and of the arms around the core. A thorough explanation of steps two and three below follows under Place of Balance 3 and in chapter 4.

1. As you prepare to raise your violin, feel the support for the head provided by your spine.
2. Check to see if your back upper teeth are aligned horizontally with the base of your skull at the back.
3. Make sure that the core of your neck is nicely stacked. This releases some of the unnecessary holding in the neck muscles.
4. Feel how this release facilitates the poised, forward-and-up balance of the head on top of the atlas.
5. Now take a few steps backward. This helps you to find balance for the torso on the lumbar core.
6. Next, raise your violin and bow right to the top of your head, allowing the collarbone and shoulder blades to rise as needed. Remember that some of the neck muscles run directly underneath the collarbone. If the collarbone is pulled too low when we play it will contribute to tighter neck muscles.
7. Next, slowly lower both arms into playing readiness. The violin should make contact with the left collarbone.
8. In your inclusive awareness, maintain the upward stacking of your core and the balance of your head.

9. Allow your poised head to turn very gently so that the jawbone meets the chinrest Assuming some support from the left hand, the meeting of the jawbone and chinrest often provides ample stability for the instrument for much of what we do as violinists, and in no way risks pulling the head forward of its lovely, balanced perch.

10. Finally, experiment with nodding the head forward in its facets. This reinforces that when we want more security, such as in large shifts down to first position, we can avail ourselves of more weight from the head at the same time as we free the spine and arms.

11. Remember, the goal is to be able to nod the head forward from the A.O. joint without dragging any of the neck vertebrae forward away from their stacked balancing act!

If you know that you have a tight neck, it is very important to your success in freeing it to also study the sections in chapter 5 that deal with all of the structures in close proximity to the neck muscles, such as the pharyngeal (throat) muscles, the tongue, and all other muscles that attach to the hyoid bone.

Place of Balance 2: The Whole Arm

Place of balance 2 falls along the core line, in keeping with the other places of balance, and refers to how the whole arm structure balances around the core.

Because chapter 4 is devoted to a detailed look at each of the joints of the arm, it is sufficient in this chapter to focus on how the arm structure as a whole is designed to rest at a balanced neutral.

First, however, let us be clear on what comprises a whole arm.

A whole arm consists of a collarbone, shoulder blade, one upper arm bone and two lower arm bones, a wrist, and a hand. When asked how long their arm is, many violinists gesture from the hand up to the shoulder joint, stopping there. This is always a clear indication the person in question has not included the collarbone and shoulder blade in the map of his arm. The reason so many regard the shoulder joint as the top of the arm is that a distinction is made in English between the arm and shoulder. And yet, everyone has a different notion of what a shoulder actually is.

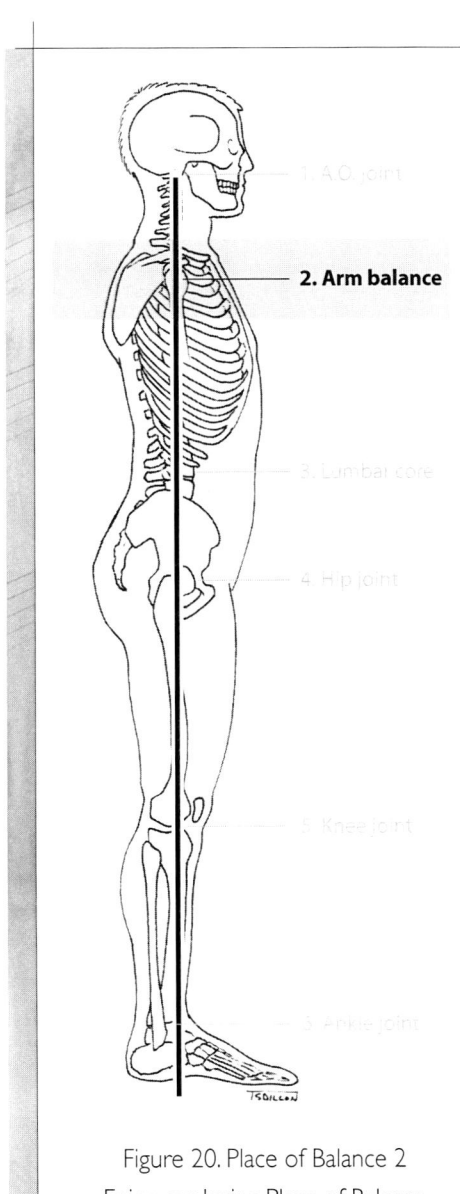

Figure 20. Place of Balance 2
Enjoy exploring Place of Balance 2 and then return it to your integrated whole self.

When I ask students to point to their shoulders, they always point to at least three different places: the shoulder blade, where it forms an overhang above the humerus; the upper humerus; and the trapezius muscles, because these are what are rubbed during a "shoulder massage."

In fact, there is no anatomical unit called a "shoulder," which is why there is so much confusion and mis-mapping in this region of the body. The word "shoulder" is best used not as a noun but as an adjective. There is no one thing that can unequivocally be called a shoulder, but there is certainly a shoulder blade, a shoulder joint and a shoulder region.

A violinist who does not include the collarbone and shoulder blade in the map of his arm limits his facility on the instrument and is also likely to develop tension, pain, and injury in the upper torso region. The quickest way to regain a sense of how the whole arm includes the shoulder blade and collarbone is to go swimming.

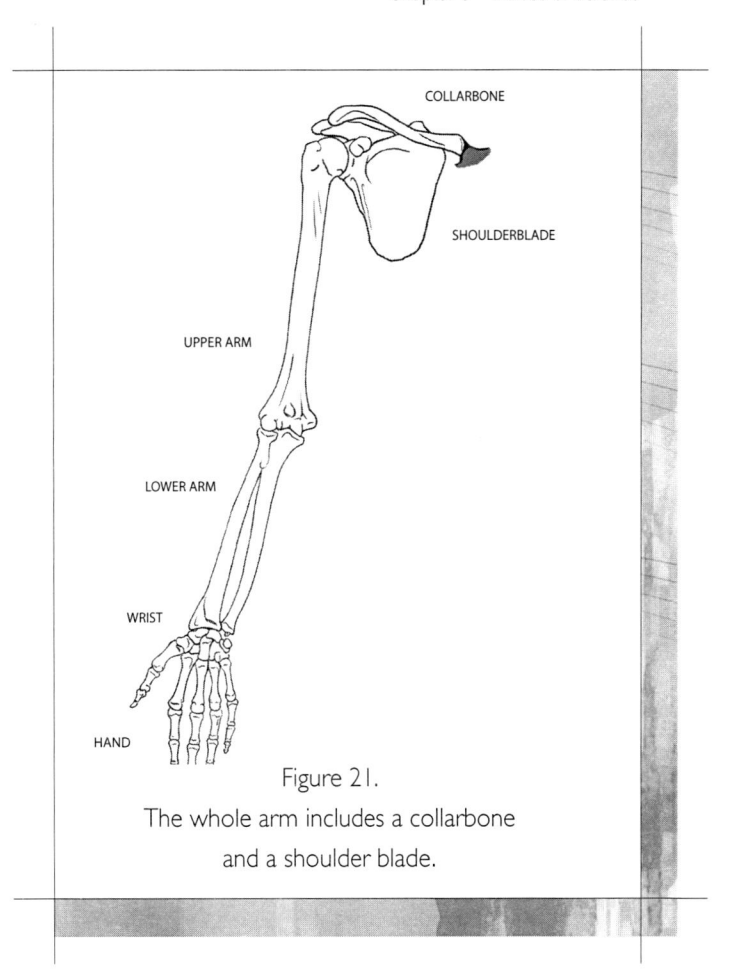

Figure 21.
The whole arm includes a collarbone and a shoulder blade.

Go Swimming

1. Place your left hand on your right collarbone to monitor the amount of movement you allow it.
2. Make a slow, continuous, front-crawl motion with the right arm.
3. Notice how much movement is available to the collarbone.
4. Notice that the collarbone can travel up, forward, and even rotate from its joint with the sternum.
5. While making the same swimming motions with the right arm, move your palpating hand to the right shoulder blade and notice how it has to move up and forward.
6. Next, try to make the front-crawl motion while allowing no movement at all in the collarbone or shoulder blade. *Move only from the shoulder joint and below.*
7. Can you feel how restricted a movement this is? It doesn't work for swimming, and it doesn't work for playing the violin.

Whole Arm Balance over the Torso

Movement is most free and dynamic when there is no muscular effort opposing it—in other words, when it begins from a *neutral place of balance*. Before we can discuss how arms function in the movements necessary for violin playing, we must first understand how they are designed so that at rest they are in a balanced, neutral, both *laterally* (front-to-back) and *vertically* (up-and-down). *Arms in neutral* is the place of no muscular work from which all violin playing movements become more facile.

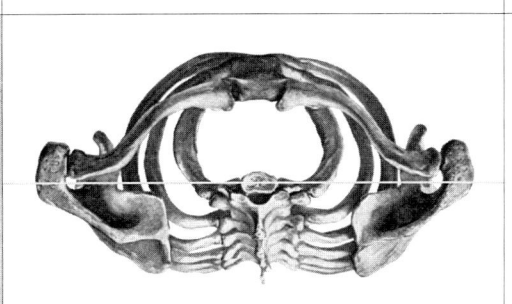

Lateral Neutral for the Arms

Notice in figure 22 how the core is directly aligned with the second arm joint. This is where the humerus hangs at the side when in a balanced lateral neutral.

A violinist suffering from either the good posture or relaxation diseases (or a combination of both), has lost this balanced lateral alignment with the core, and tension and injury will result. For violinists with the posture disease it is particularly important to include the interclavicular ligament in the map of the collarbones. Knowing there is a springy band connecting the two ends of the collarbones helps to counter the habit of pushing the sternum out and pulling the collarbones back and away from one another.

Figure 22.
At neutral the upper arm structure balances around the core.

Lateral Neutral Exercise

This exploration is intended to help you regain a sense of the arms' lateral place of balance. Watch yourself in a mirror as you do this.

1. First put your awareness on the muscles that you feel working as you begin to move.
2. It is important to the success of this exploration to be able to sense the muscular areas working throughout your movement.
3. As with all movement explorations, begin by finding your core places of balance.
4. Release any tension held in your neck of which you are aware.
5. Nod your head from the A.O. joint.
6. Walk backward a few steps. This helps to regain your balance on the four lower places of balance if you have lost it.

Finding Arm Balance from Back of Neutral

1. Bring your arm structure back behind your core line.
2. This is different from "pulling your shoulders back," because that injunction usually encourages thrusting the sternum up and forward, causing the thoracic spine to lose its natural curve.
3. Pay close attention to the muscles that you feel working as you *slowly* release the arms toward your sides *until you do not feel these muscles working anymore.*

4. This is the *place of no work* for your arms.
5. Ask yourself if this place is different from where your arms would normally hang.
6. Note the difference.

Finding Arm Balance from in Front of Neutral
1. Repeat the procedure under *Back of Neutral* above, only now move the arm structure forward through space.
2. Frequently students trying this for the first time will collapse in the neck as if going into a full slump.
3. Again, only move the arm structure around the core.
4. Do not allow the neck vertebrae and head to be dragged forward through space with the arm structure.
5. Keep the head balanced on its A.O. perch.
6. Tune in to which muscles are working, and on returning the arms to the sides.
7. Notice when the muscles reach the *place of no work*.
8. Note how this is different from your arms' habitual place.
9. Is this different from the *place of no work* you found when you went *back* with the arm structure?

As you perform this exploration daily for the coming weeks and months, your kinesthetic awareness will become more and more refined, enabling you to become more able to determine exactly when muscle activity has stopped, thereby indicating where your place of lateral neutral is.

How a Combination of the Good Posture and Relaxation Diseases Prevents Finding Lateral Neutral for the Arms *Note: If you have winging shoulder blades, this section is for you!*

For some violinists, finding the lateral neutral for the arm structure is quite complicated because they have a combination of the good posture and relaxation diseases. This makes mapping the coracoid process a necessary first step in finding lateral neutral.

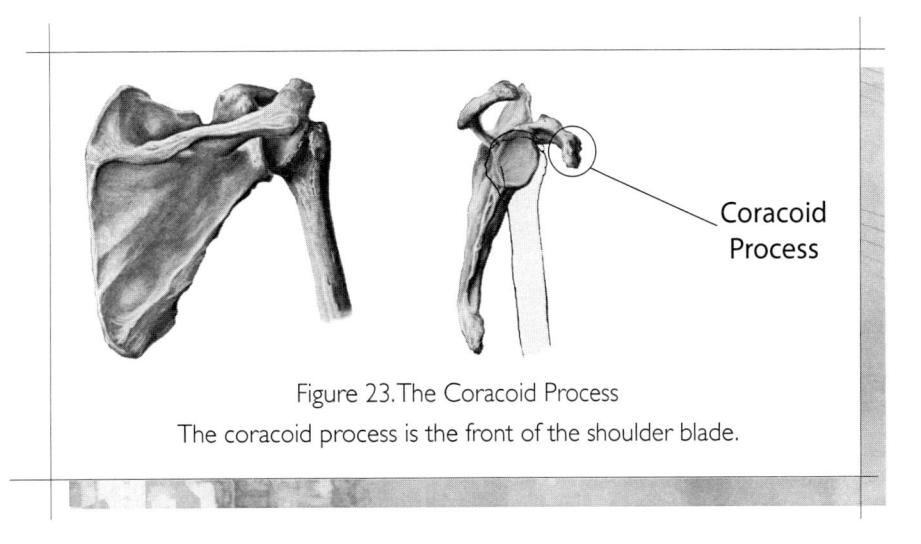

Figure 23. The Coracoid Process
The coracoid process is the front of the shoulder blade.

Mapping the Coracoid Process

When most are asked to point to their shoulder blade, they reach around to the back to find it. For anyone who suffers from tension and pain in the upper torso region, and especially for those who have winging shoulder blades, it is essential to accurately map the *front* portion of the shoulder blade.

Exploring to Locate the Front Bony Protrusion of the Shoulder Blade

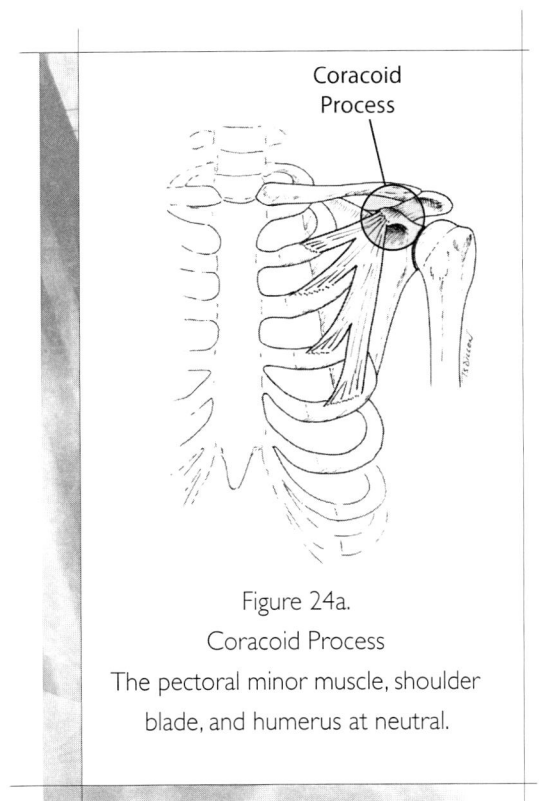

1. Walk your right-hand fingertips along your left collarbone from the sternoclavicular joint outwards.
2. Stop when you reach the upward-curving part of the collarbone.
3. Now walk your fingers about an inch straight down off the collarbone onto the muscle.
4. If you are not a fleshy person, you may be able to immediately locate the bony bump under the muscle. If you are a bit more full-bodied, you may need to wiggle your shoulder blade back and forth in order to find this front bony protrusion. This is your coracoid process.

Figure 24a.
Coracoid Process
The pectoral minor muscle, shoulder blade, and humerus at neutral.

When the arms are at lateral neutral, the coracoid process is on the same plane as the sternum, *not* pulled forward and down from the level of the top of the sternum.

A bit of muscle mapping will help in clarifying how a combination of the good posture and relaxation diseases prevents an easy lateral neutral for the arms. Study figures 24 and 25 with this in mind.

Personal trainers and physiotherapists tell me that they quite regularly see overly tightened pectoral muscles within the general populace, which is what gives that "round-shouldered" look. As violinists who play many hours a day with our arms extended in front of us, the instrument resting on

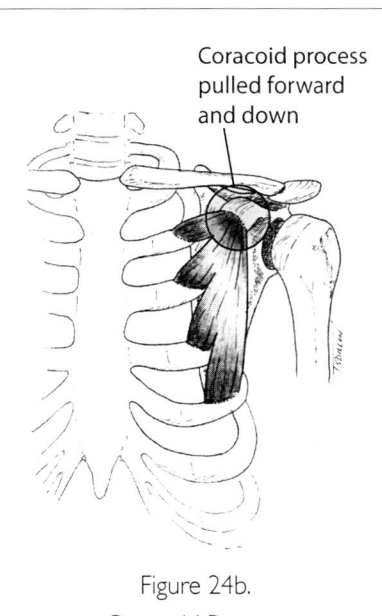

Figure 24b.
Coracoid Process
Pulled Forward and Down

Contraction of the pectoral minor muscle causes "winging" shoulder blades and contributes to a backward rotation of the humerus in its socket.

the upper arm structure (collarbones), we are especially susceptible to mis-mapping the pectoral muscles as too short. However, it is quite common to see a violinist who is chronically tight in the pectoral muscles (the relaxation disease) also chronically tight in the *back muscles,* which attach to the shoulder blades (the good posture disease.) When the back muscles pull back and down on the shoulder blades, the humerus usually goes along for the ride.

Figure 25 shows the muscles which run from the shoulder blade to the humerus; these also usually tighten when the shoulder blade itself is pulled back. The shortening of these muscles causes the humerus to rotate too far backward of neutral in its socket.[9] To accommodate contradictory pulls that the back muscles exert against the pulls of the pectoral minor in front, the shoulder blade often ends up tilting on a sometimes extreme angle. This tilt is known as *winging shoulder blades.*

In order to regain a neutral for the arm structure it is necessary for many violinists to remap the shoulder blades to a neutral tilt. This is aided tremendously by knowing exactly which muscles need to release so that other, underused muscles automatically do their rightful share of the work.

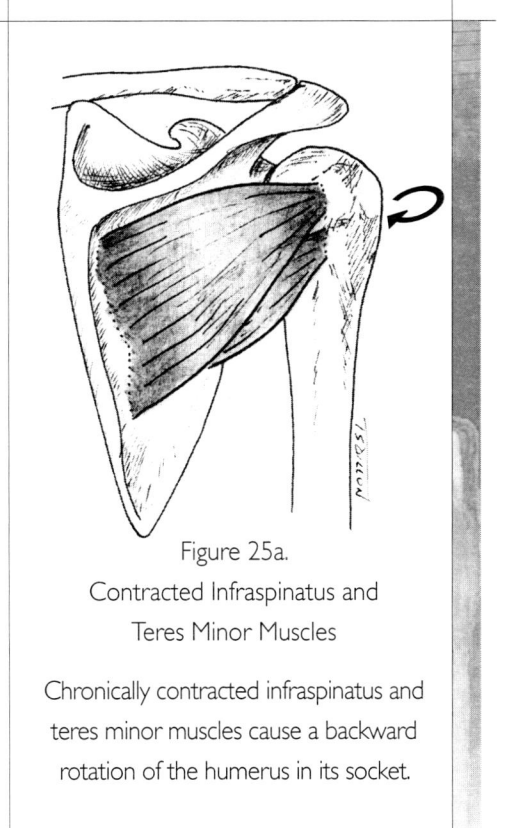

Figure 25a.
Contracted Infraspinatus and Teres Minor Muscles

Chronically contracted infraspinatus and teres minor muscles cause a backward rotation of the humerus in its socket.

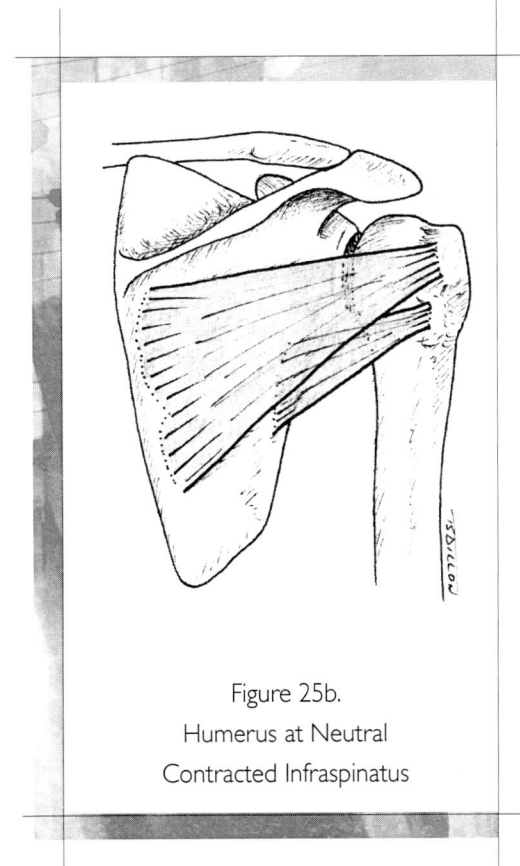

Figure 25b.
Humerus at Neutral
Contracted Infraspinatus

Exploring on the Floor to Find Release in the Front and Back Simultaneously to Regain a Neutral Tilt of the Shoulder Blade

1. With figures 24 and 25 close at hand, lie on the floor with a book under your head and with your knees up.
2. Start by freeing your neck as much as possible.
3. Take a close look at the infraspinatus and the teres minor muscles in the figures.
4. Understand that if you have been holding these muscles as a part of the good posture disease, when you find release for these muscles, you will be looking for an accompanying forward rotation of the humerus back to neutral within its socket.

5. Locate exactly where these two muscles attach to the back of the humerus and focus on softening and releasing these areas.
6. Rather than trying to make the forward rotation of the humerus happen, "think" it into a forward rotational release as you consciously soften the muscle groups that you see in the image.
7. This initiates a release from the good posture disease.
8. After you have found some softening and release here, move on to the image of the pectoral minor muscle.
9. Place the fingers of one hand on the coracoid process of the opposite arm.
10. *While you maintain a free neck and the softening you just found at the back of the humerus (important!)*, allow the muscle that attaches right under your fingers to soften and release.
11. You will probably feel the coracoid process rise to the same level as the top of the sternum and simultaneously feel it gently sinking closer to the floor and out to the sides.
12. Warning: if you feel the shoulder blades jamming in toward the spine, then you have not maintained the muscle release out of the good posture disease.
13. This initiates a release out of the relaxation disease.
14. By maintaining muscle release *simultaneously* on the front and the back you will discover the neutral tilt of the shoulder blade.
15. It is important to work with both front and back muscle releases simultaneously, as one without the other will not teach you what muscular balance around the shoulder blade feels like—it will just be a temporary release on one side of the body only.
16. As always, it is necessary to take these new releases and integrate them into everything you have thus far experienced about balance through the body as a whole.

Vertical Neutral for the Arms

Violinists frequently mis-map the upper arm structure, particularly the collarbone, as resting on the ribs. It is commonly taught that one must secure the violin, which rests on the collarbone, by clamping or dropping the head onto the chinrest. However, this leads to the poor collarbone underneath the violin being squashed down so far

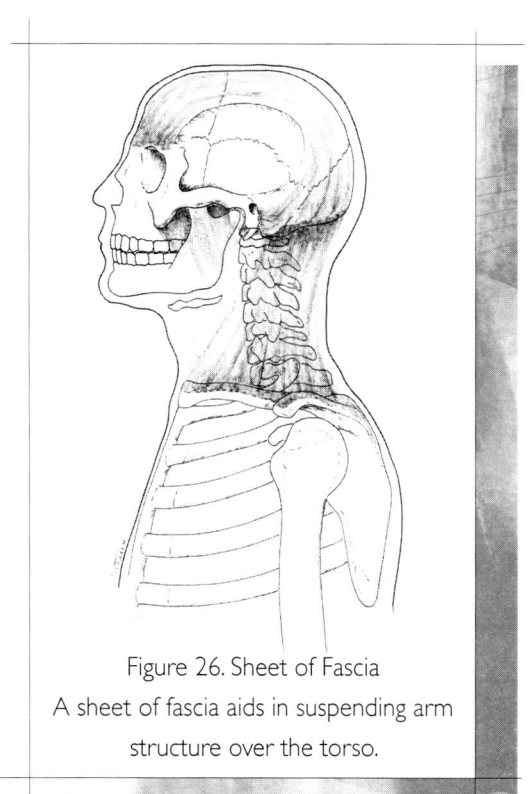

Figure 26. Sheet of Fascia
A sheet of fascia aids in suspending arm structure over the torso.

that it seems that it *must* rest on the ribs. In addition to pedagogy that encourages too much force coming down onto the chinrest, there is also frequent advice from teachers to "keep the shoulders down when you play," which causes the student to drive his upper arm structure further down onto the ribs.

The arm structure, in fact, does not rest on the ribs but is *suspended over them* by a system of elastic soft tissue comprised of ligaments, tendons, muscles, and sheets of fascia. This springy connective tissue attaches along the collarbone and the shoulder blade and inserts throughout the entire upper body to suspend the much denser bone matter of the arms in a similar fashion to that of the springy ultra-light tent poles that suspend the much heavier fabric of a dome tent in order to keep it upright.

Of particular importance in this suspensory system is the expansive sheet of fascia that is part of the scalp from which the collarbones and shoulder blades are suspended. *In other words, the arms are supported, in great part, by being suspended from above—from the very tops of our heads.* Finding this source of support for the arms comes as a huge relief for violinists who have lost it and are wondering why their upper torso muscles are so tight when they play. Any player who has mapped her arms as resting on top of the ribs carries them too low, and the result is a strain on the muscles of her upper back and shoulder region because it is these muscles that are being asked to *hold* the arms onto the torso while simultaneously trying to *move* them. Many of the stamina problems that violinists have in holding the instrument high enough and for long periods stem, not from a problem with the instrument's set-up itself, but from having lost this springy, neutral support for the arms over the torso.

Exploring to Find a Springy, Suspended Neutral

You will need a rubber band for this exploration.
1. Loop the rubber band over your left index finger.
2. With your right index finger, slowly stretch the rubber band down to the place where you first meet a gentle, bouncy resistance.
3. Focus on the buoyant support that your right index finger and hand receive from the rubber band.
4. There is no strain on the band, but because of its stretchy nature, it is still providing some support for your finger.
5. This buoyant place of support is similar to the suspended-from-above neutral position for which we are searching for the whole arm structure.
6. Next, pull down quite hard on the band and feel the strain it withstands.
7. This is akin to what many violinists do to the connective tissue that suspends the collarbones and shoulder blades from above.
8. Keep in mind this image of the springy place of neutral in the rubber band as we continue the search for the springy place of neutral in the arm structure.

Finding Arm Balance from Above Neutral

Now perform the exploration for the lateral neutral for the arms, except that this time, move the collarbone/shoulder-blade unit *up* toward the ears (as opposed to forward and back), then *down* toward the ribs. Everything previously written regarding attention to the work of the muscles applies here as well.

1. Find your core places of balance as before and maintain them as you do this exercise.
2. Slowly move the arm structure up toward your ears, being careful not to compress the neck vertebrae.
3. Frequently, students associate a raising of the shoulder region with a pulling back and down of the head; instead, the head should remain balanced on the spine while the arm structure is brought closer to the ears.
4. As you slowly allow the arms to lower and you look for the place where the muscles stop their work, make sure you do not bypass neutral by allowing a new set of muscles to take over and pull the arms all the way down to what might be your habitual, too-low place of holding.
5. In addition to looking for the place of no work in the muscles, also look for the sensation of gentle springy suspension that the elastic ligaments, tendons, and fascia provide.
6. When doing this exploration in front of a mirror, it is helpful to know that neutral is where the collarbones are *roughly parallel with the floor*—exactly where the arms of every healthy toddler come to rest.
7. This is important information for anyone trying to support a violin on the collarbone. "Collarbones parallel to the floor" translates as a naturally secure perch for the instrument!

Finding Arm Balance from Below Neutral

1. Slowly lower your arm structure down toward your ribs, once again maintaining a sense of balance around your core and paying attention to which muscles are doing the work.
2. As you slowly release these bones back up, look in your mirror and watch to see if what feels like the neutral place of no work is as *high* as the place of neutral you found when coming from above.
3. Attentively repeat the whole exploration two or three times, and watch the mirror to contrast the differences between where you arrive coming from above and coming from below.
4. Keep in mind that your place of suspended neutral will be roughly where the collarbones are parallel with the floor.
5. If you have mis-mapped your arm structure either too low or high, a suspended neutral will initially feel so foreign that you may think it must be "wrong."

6. It may be necessary to repeat this exercise every day for months before the place of suspension is secure in the body map.

There will, of course, be some violinists who will find that they have mapped their "normal" as higher than neutral, and will have to re-map accordingly. These violinists hunch the shoulder region up and in toward the torso on the left side to support the violin and in the bow arm to get to the frog. However, as we will see when we discuss humeroscapular rhythm, this hunching is sometimes just a protective compensation for having lost the *healthy* mobility of the shoulder blade.

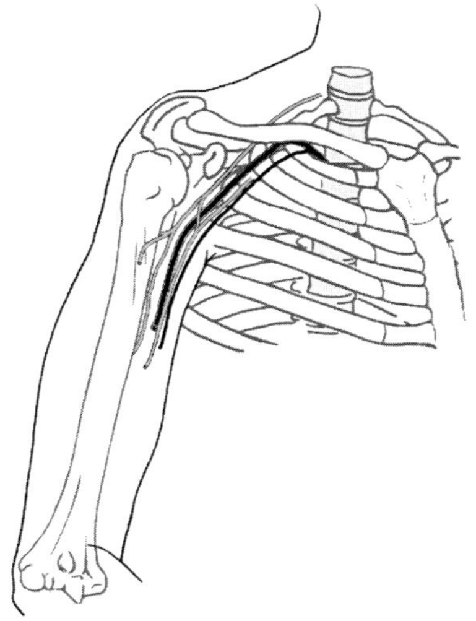

Because the shoulder blade has been chronically denied healthy movement by harmful advice like "keep your shoulders down," some players instinctively hunch at the last instant to protect themselves from strain. And then they are instructed once again to keep their shoulders down! However, because this hunching is a protective instinct, violinists who do this are actually in much less danger of injury than their counterparts who earnestly hold their shoulders down, mapping their arm structure too low.

When the collarbone is continually held too low it impinges vital nerves and blood vessels that run underneath and down the arm into the hand, compressing them and resulting in numbness in the fingers and chronically cold hands. When this happens to the median nerve in particular the condition is known as *thoracic outlet syndrome* (TOS). A violinist suffering from TOS experiences immense relief when she discovers that releasing the arm structure back up to a place of suspended neutral causes her symptoms to disappear and her sound to simultaneously open up—sometimes to a remarkable degree! When we stop squashing the collarbone we have also stopped squashing the instrument, which, of course, means more vibration and therefore more sound.

Figure 27.
Nerves and blood vessels run under the collarbone to the hand.

The other important mapping issue that affects balance of the arm structure over the ribs is the shape of the ribs themselves. If the ribs have been mapped according to the good posture or the relaxation diseases, their shape will be distorted. Particularly important to the balance of the arm unit over the torso is the shape of the uppermost ribs. If the upper ribs are mis-mapped as the same length as the ones below them (causing them to lose their natural beehive shape), or as horizontal rather than higher in the back than in the front, it is impossible for the arms to find balance, since the shape of the structure underlying the arms is distorted and imbalanced. For a more detailed discussion of the shape of the ribs, see chapter 5.

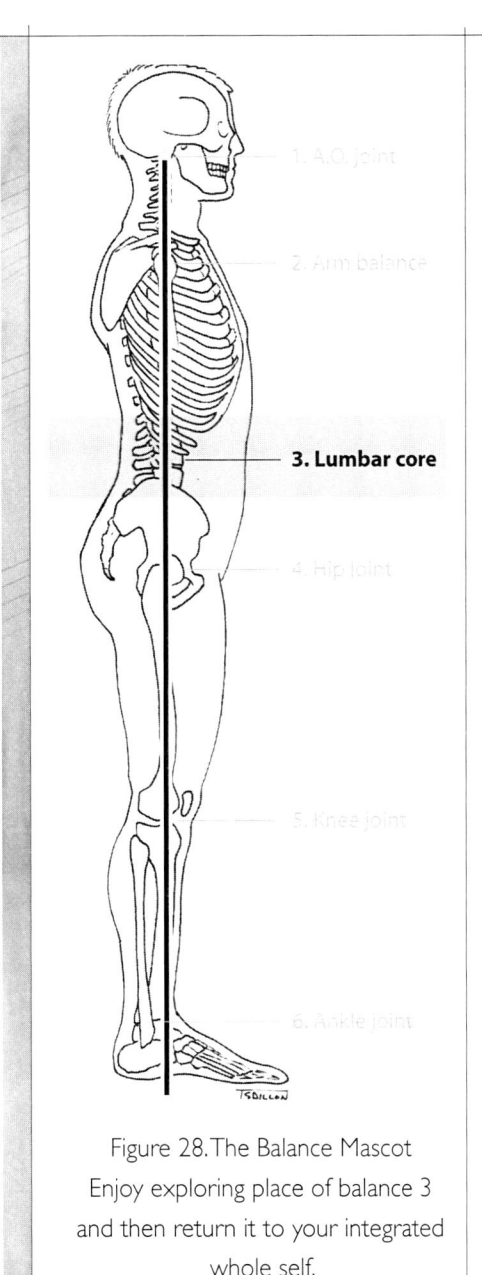

Place of Balance 3: Lumbar Core

In chapter 2, we briefly discussed how the good posture disease results in a downward pull that causes an overarching in the lower back. Violinists are particularly prone to the good posture disease for two reasons:

1. Playing the violin requires raising the arms in front. A person not balanced on the weight-bearing front half of the spine tends to arch his lower back even more when raising his arms in front for *any* activity, be it playing the violin or combing hair.

2. Violin teachers frequently, repeatedly give abstract directions to their young students, such as "get your violin up." Teachers know that when the scroll points toward the floor, the best tone is not produced because the player's bow constantly slides toward the fingerboard, preventing connected contact between hair and string. When the violin is parallel to the floor, the bow moves across a level plane, and so does not fight the force of gravity. When the violin scroll is slightly higher than parallel to the floor, the force of gravity becomes an advantage in keeping the bow closer to the bridge, where the richest tone is produced. However, without any specific information about *how* to raise the instrument higher while staying balanced, students nearly always try to hike the scroll up higher by pushing the sternum up and out, and leaning the whole upper torso back of place of balance 3—*the lumbar core.*

Figure 28. The Balance Mascot
Enjoy exploring place of balance 3 and then return it to your integrated whole self.

Finding Balance on the Front Half of the Lumbar Spine

1. To locate the weight-bearing half of the lumbar spine, place the index finger of each hand at your sides on top of the iliac crest of your pelvis. The iliac crest is colloquially referred to as the hip, as in the instruction "put your hands on your hips.

2. If your fingers could extend straight through the soft tissues of your torso, each one would directly run into the front half of your lumbar spine. This is how central your core actually is.

3. Recognizing that the intestines nestle around this part of the spine rather than just being in front of it often helps students to centralize the spine instead of mapping it as existing only in the back.

4. The very largest and strongest part of our spine is this bottom part, just as the strongest part of a building, the foundation, is located at the bottom.

The easiest way to kinesthetically experience balance on the lumbar spine is to walk backward. Nearly everyone finds balance on the lumbar core when walking backward because we all seem to instinctively know it's a poor idea to lean the upper torso backward when moving in a backward direction! Since we don't look in the direction of travel when we walk backwards, we automatically rely more on our kinesthetic sense to tell us about our balance. We spend very little time walking backward relative to how much of our lives we spend walking forward. For this reason, we have had fewer opportunities to mis-map our backward movement compared to the many ways we mis-map our forward movement.

Rediscovering Balance around the Lumbar Core

I use this exploration regularly to aid violinists in rediscovering balance around the lumbar core. It is a combination of two different explorations, one suggested by Pedro de Alcantara, the other by Barbara Conable.

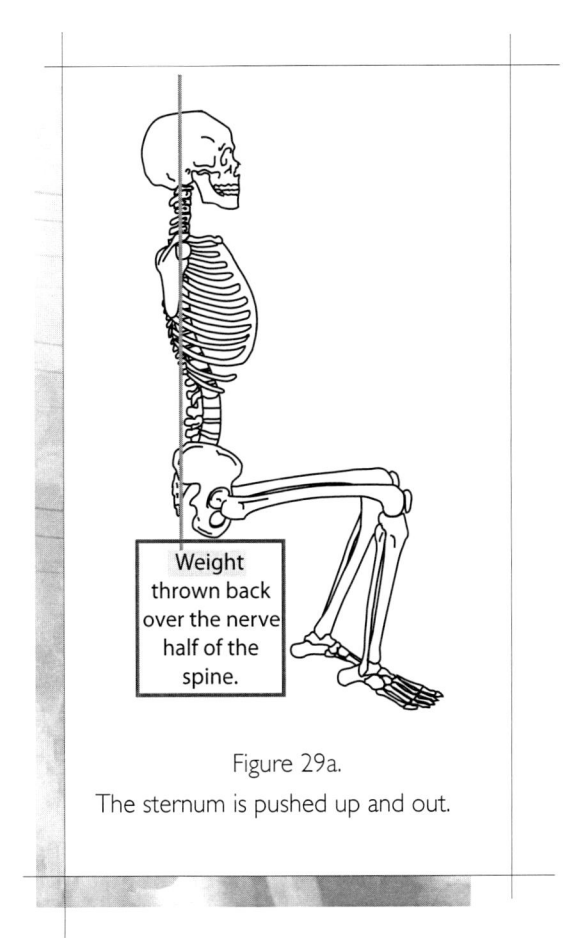

Figure 29a.
The sternum is pushed up and out.

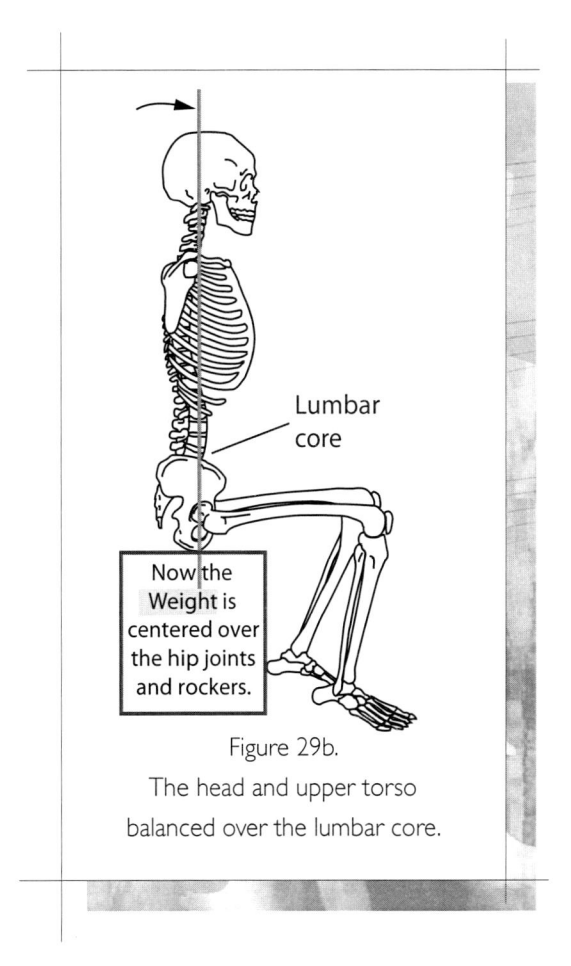

Weight thrown back over the nerve half of the spine.

Figure 29b.
The head and upper torso balanced over the lumbar core.

Now the Weight is centered over the hip joints and rockers.

Part I

1. You will need open wall space, a yardstick or ruler, and your violin. (Watching yourself in a large mirror or on video can be helpful.)
2. Walk forward several paces in your habitual way.

3. While staying attentive to muscular activity in your torso, particularly in the lumbar area (front, back, and sides), take the same number of strides backward.
4. Continue walking forward and backward until you can begin to identify what is different in your torso balance when you change directions.
5. You may experience an actual shift of the torso in space as you begin walking backward. This shift is the upper torso finding balance over the front half of the lumbar spine. In many violinists this is so extreme that it is obvious to the casual observer.
6. Once you find balance, you may feel you are leaning forward. View your profile in a mirror, however, and you will immediately recognize that you are, indeed, not leaning forward but are quite beautifully upright. This feeling of being too far forward occurs because you are forward of your habitual place, not because you are leaning forward of balance.
7. Do enough backward walking to establish balance around your lumbar core before proceeding.

Part 2

1. Raise your arms straight out in front of you.
2. Walk forward in your habitual manner to the nearest open wall space until the middle fingertip of each hand lightly touches the wall.
3. Mark where you stand by placing your measuring stick on the floor in front of your toes.
4. Return to walking backward until you once again find lumbar core balance.
5. Walk backward to the wall.
6. Turn to face the wall, being careful that you don't fall back into your habitual stance.
7. Align your toes with the ruler.
8. Slowly and attentively raise your arms to the wall, being careful not to lean your upper torso back.
9. At this point you may initially revert to leaning backward without sensing it.
10. If you have succeeded in maintaining balance you will notice that it is not your middle fingertips that meet the wall now, but your first or even second knuckle.
11. You have just discovered an inch or two more arm length and more arm freedom for yourself by maintaining balance instead of leaning backwards when you raise your arms in front of you!
12. You may find no shift of the torso at all when walking backward rather than forward, and will therefore find no difference in where your fingers meet the wall the second time. If so, you have already mapped your lumbar core accurately enough for your torso to be balanced above it. This exercise will be most important for you in aiding your students who are habitually back of balance.

13. Take up your violin.
14. As you raise it without leaning back of core balance, sense how the extra arm length allows you the luxury of being over and around your violin rather than feeling that you have to reach your arms way out in front of you to play.
15. Try playing from your newfound lumbar core balance and enjoy the bigger, deeper sound your longer arms automatically produce!

One of the most common mis-mappings that causes a violinist to lose balance off the lumbar core is the notion of a *waist*. Very early on in life, pre-school rhymes and games require us to put our hands at our "waists" as if this was an anatomical unit like a head or arm. Any violinist with a waist in her map will bend to pick up her violin from its case as if there is a major joint at the navel.

In reality, we have bony spine behind our navels, and must map the spine as a continuous anatomical unit that begins at the A.O. joint and does not end until the tip of the coccyx. The spine is designed to provide some flexibility, but does not respond well to being used as a major bending joint.

All toddlers know how to lower themselves to reach toys on the floor by using the hip, knee and ankle joints. They do not try to bend at a mythical waist as adults do, and therefore the integrity of their spines is not continually compromised. An individual who habitually bends from the waist also usually believes that the waist is the middle of the body. He will always be surprised to discover that when measured from head to foot, the actual midpoint of the body is at the hip joint, where the leg bone and pelvis meet at the leg socket—not at the mythical "waist."

A size mis-mapping about the lumbar spine is responsible for lower back pain that many violinists suffer. In response to the question: "How big around is my spine?" a violinist who is off-balance at the lumbar spine will make a gesture with her thumb and index finger to indicate that in her body map the lumbar spine circumference is only the size of a quarter-dollar. When those who maintain this mis-mapping hold a life-sized model of the spine, they are usually amazed at how massive the lumbar and lower thoracic vertebrae actually are.

They try to wrap one hand around these vertebrae and they discover that the fingers will not meet; it takes both hands to fully

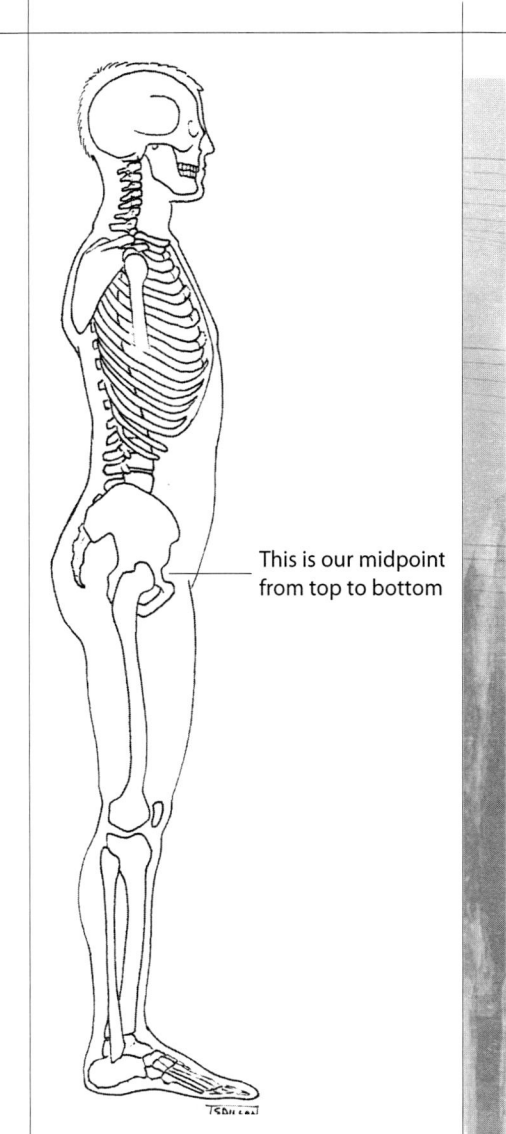

Figure 30. Please Dispose of Your Waist! Photocopy the image of the Balance Mascot (figure 6). Fold the Balance Mascot so that the top of the head bows to align with the bottom of his foot. You will see that the fold runs directly through the middle of the hip joint!

encompass these enormous bones. The size of these vertebrae are usually mis-mapped as too small because we can feel and see only about five per cent of the spine under the flesh in our backs with our tactile and visual senses. This is inextricably linked to mapping the spine as only in the back.

The unfortunate outcome of these mis-mappings is that the moving muscles of the torso, particularly in the lower back, must work much harder to keep the body upright than is necessary to compensate for the loss of support from the enormous front half of the spine. A violinist who suffers from these mis-mappings will always appear to be holding himself up through the torso rather than being easily and buoyantly supported. This is especially conspicuous when he is playing while seated.

When a violinist correctly maps the size of the lumbar vertebrae and begins to kinesthetically sense how they curve right to the body's core to support all of the weight of the head and thorax directly above, lower back pain is alleviated and moving muscles become available to move, resulting in much greater ease in playing.

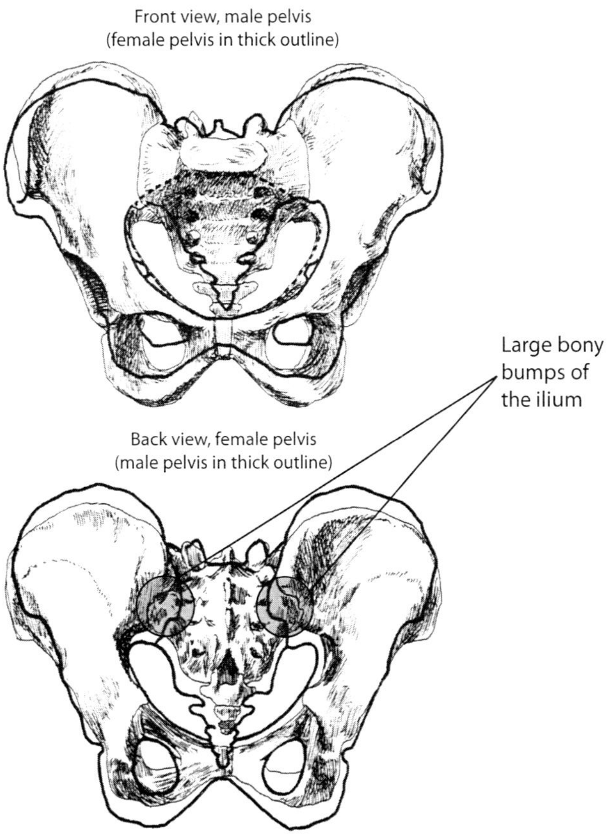

Figure 31. The sacrum is the widest part of the spine.

Sacrum and Coccyx

This fourth curve of the spine, the sacrum, is unique in that it has no articulated joints. In evolutionary terms, what were once individual vertebrae in our ancestors fused over time into solid bone. The sacrum is now the widest and most solid segment of the spine and is vital to the ability to stay buoyantly upright.

The width of the sacrum firmly fitted between the two pelvic bones fosters a sense of security at the spine's base so that the rest of the spine is free to lengthen, spiral, and bend, and allows the superficial torso muscles to stay available as "movers" rather than as "holders."

It is easy to mis-map the sacrum as a vertical plate because that is how it feels when you place a hand over it at the back. Observe, however, that as it makes its way from its centrally situated joint with the bottom lumbar vertebra back to its joint with the pelvic bones, it is close to being horizontal.

Exploring the Sacrum

1. Run your fingers over your lower back on either side of your spine, just above where the gluteal muscles begin.
2. Locate the large, bony bumps that protrude on each side (see figure 31, back view).
3. Just inside these bumps on either side are the sacroiliac joints.
4. As the name implies, these are the joints between the sacrum and the two pelvic bones.
5. The large bumps belong to the edge of the pelvic bones.
6. Put the thumb and index finger of one hand just inside these bumps and experience how wide your sacrum is at the back.
7. Now mentally add on another inch and you have the width of the sacrum on the *inside,* bowl part of the pelvis.
8. Search for this full width kinesthetically. If you have been trying to hold yourself up with the lower back muscles you may notice an automatic release of these muscles as you map the width of your lower spine.
9. You may also notice that the two pubis bones in front are allowed to spring back together if you have been pulling the two pelvic bones together in the back and crowding the sacrum.

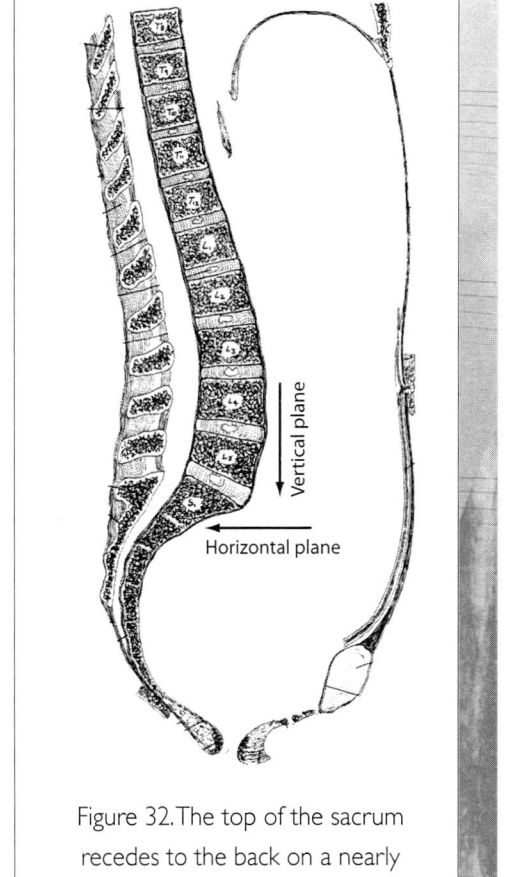

Figure 32. The top of the sacrum recedes to the back on a nearly horizontal plane.

Acknowledging all that space within the pelvic cavity where the sacral bone recedes gives you the exact location of your center of gravity, points out the underbelly of the last lumbar vertebra on top of which everything above balances, and allows all of the internal pelvic organs to unfurl if they have been crowding together because of a mis-mapped lower spine.

Pelvic Arch

Before addressing the fourth place of balance at the top of the femur bones (the greater trochanter), it is necessary to understand how the pelvic arch bridges weight delivery between the Places of Balance 3 and 4.

Figure 33 illustrates how the torso's weight travels through the pelvis to reach the legs when standing or the sit bones when seated.

The design of the pelvic arch is like the arches used in medieval churches and castles as a method of architectural support. In these arches, sloping arcs on each side rise from the ground to meet the keystone which is centered at the top. The equal and opposite forces traveling downward from gravity and upward from the equal resistance the ground provides creates a unifying circuit of force which prevents the keystone from dislodging.

In the human pelvis there is a similarly wonderful and effective arch design at work through the bones as long as overuse of the lower back and gluteal muscles doesn't interfere.

When standing, the weight of the torso is delivered through the lumbar core to the bottom lumbar vertebrae which, together with the wings of the upper sacrum, behave as the keystone of an arch. After the weight arcs sideways through the sacroiliac joint it travels through the sturdiest, thickest part of each pelvic bone to reach its new place of balance: the widest part of our legs (greater trochanter). The final destination of our weight is the place where our feet meet the ground.

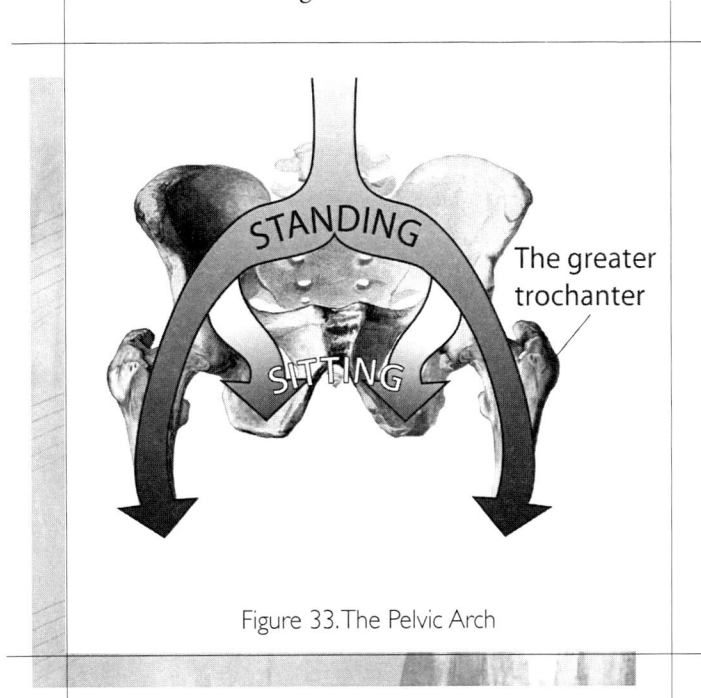

Figure 33. The Pelvic Arch

When sitting, the torso's weight is delivered through the lumbar core to the keystone of the pelvic arch formed by the bottom lumbar vertebrae and wings of the upper sacrum to the place where the sit bones meet the chair.

The sit bones are also known as *rockers,* which is probably a better name for two reasons: First, *rocker* accurately describe the shape of these bones. They are much like the rockers on a rocking chair, and they are not flat for good reason. Imagine the lack of mobility we would suffer if we were designed with a flat base. When sitting on a flat chair, we would lose our marvelous ability to rock the whole torso forward toward a music stand or backward to make dramatic musical gestures. The only difference between a rocking chair's rockers and our pelvic rockers is that our clever design even allows a sideways rocking motion. This makes it possible to lean the entire, unified torso to the right toward the first violinist in a string quartet or to the cellist or violist on the left when the music asks for a special dialogue between two voices.

In addition to this expressive mobility, our rockers, like those on a rocking chair, also provide us with a point of stable rest when we balance the weight of the head and torso directly above the midpoint of the rockers.

A second reason the term *rocker* is more accurate than *sit bones* is that it does not mislead us into thinking that the two bony parts we perch on are separate from the pelvic bones. Not recognizing that the pelvic bones are continuous from the rockers at the bottom to the iliac crests at the top is a serious mis-mapping and can contribute to problems in allowing unhindered weight delivery directly through the pelvic arch.

Violinists who have not mapped the rockers as the bones they actually sit on either send their torso weight through the tailbone or into the legs. A violinist suffering from the relaxation disease sits on the tailbone. Though not common, there have been instances where a musician's tailbone snapped right off due to the chronic pressure sent down behind the sit bones. A violinist suffering from the good posture disease (as is more common), drives his weight into the upper legs where they meet the edge of the chair.

Exploring the Rockers
1. Imitate the good posture and relaxation diseases while seated.
2. Assume an extreme slump.
3. Notice how much pressure you feel coming down into the tailbone.
4. Move into your best good-posture-sitting-up-straight position by arching your back, tucking in your chin, and pulling back your shoulders.

Figure 34. We do not sit on our Legs; we sit on our rockers.

5. Notice how the edge of the chair pushes up into the bottom of your thighs.
6. Pushing the legs into the chair this way to support the upper body limits freedom of movement because it inhibits leg movement for expressive purposes or as an aid in freeing the pelvis and lower back muscles.

Rediscovering the rockers as a place of balance often reveals that the previous lack of freedom in the legs was due to a mis-mapping of the leg bones as being on the same plane as the chair seat.

Figure 35. In sitting, the legs are much higher than the rockers.

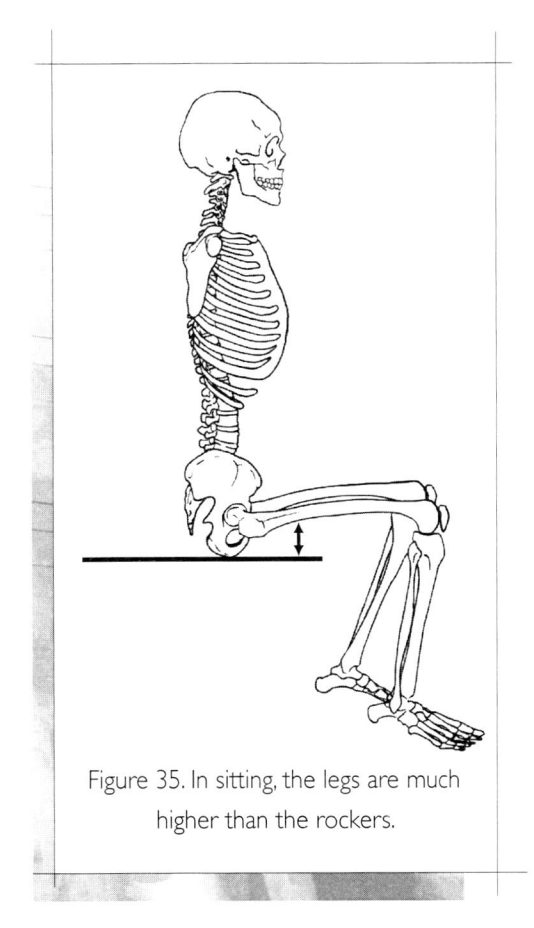

It is true that we have a great deal of muscle and flesh which hangs below the bone and comes into contact with the seat of the chair; however, the bone itself emerges from the hip joint much higher than where the rockers make contact with the chair. This mis-mapping will always produce the feeling that the legs are trapped underneath the body rather than available to dance and gesture to a musical line.

Rigidity in the lower back region sometimes derives from mis-mapping the pelvis as one solid bone rather than two bones that meet either side of the sacrum in the back. Remapping the pelvis as two bones held together with connective tissue frequently helps alleviate this lower back pain and also allows for much more responsive movement through the soft pelvic floor muscle with every breath. (See chapter 5 for a more detailed description of pelvic floor movement.)

Place of Balance 4: Hip Joint

As we discussed above, it is important to remember that this place of balance is anatomical middle of the body, not what we call the waist. The length of the head and torso together equals the length of the leg from the hip joint to the floor.

If you observe, either in yourself or your students, a side-to-side swaying of the pelvis while walking, then take special note of the next mis-mapping. Connected to the myth of the waist is the misconception that the iliac crest (top of the pelvis) is actually the top of the leg. A violinist with a waist in her map walks with a distinctive swaying in the pelvis, *a la* fashion model. If she has mapped her midpoint at the waist she will attempt to swing everything south of the waist when she walks and will have no room in her map for the truth: that the legs dangle and swing from the real mid-line of the body—the hip joint.

Violinists who move from the body's true middle are free to dance around when they play without compromising the spine's integrity. Because the legs are not locked at the hip joint to accommodate the "waist" mis-mapping, all of the leg joints are free to dance, step, and bend while playing. Consequently, their feet are not frozen to the floor.

Unfortunately, violin teachers routinely instruct their students to plant their feet when they play. This is another example of an abstraction in the pedagogy. We humans, in fact, do *not* have roots which run into the ground, so why imagine it? It is simply misleading. Advice to plant the feet often results in the student never feeling free to move his feet to a different place on the floor as he plays. And without constantly refreshing movement from the hip joint in order to move the feet, the leg joints are held and become stiff.

With my own beginnings as a Suzuki violin student, and my continued dedication to teaching Suzuki's method, I am familiar with the Suzuki foot chart. I understand the motivations teachers have in using a foot chart with a very young beginner. It provides clear, visual instruction to the child; she knows exactly where the teacher wishes her to stand; and it is fun for her to place stickers and personal decorations on her foot chart. Suzuki used foot charts himself when he taught; however, it was also not uncommon for him to march group classes around the room in a moving line as they played.

This freedom of movement of the lower half of the body always translates into more freedom in the torso, neck, and arms while playing. If, as a teacher of young children, you feel strongly about beginning a child's instruction with a chart of some description, try using a larger chart that simply outlines an *area*. It will still show the child the general region that you would like her in for the lesson, but allows enough space for the child to move her feet expressively and rhythmically as she plays. I have begun using a chart for young beginners which is decorated like a desert island with a palm tree and sand surrounded by water. The idea is for the child to stay on the island without getting her feet wet. There are no foot positions traced on it, and foot movement is encouraged right from the beginning.

Figure 36. Place of Balance 4
Enjoy exploring Place of Balance 4 and then return it to your integrated whole self.

Finding Your Halfway Point
1. To locate the exact spot where the leg joins with the pelvis, start by finding the greater trochanter.
    a. Place a finger at the creases in your jeans or pants that form at the front pockets when you squat.
    b. Now run that finger right out to the sides and you will be close to the greater trochanter.
    c. It is the widest part of your leg bone and is the bony protuberance you feel at the sides.
    d. You will know you've found the right spot if you feel this bone moving under your fingers as you march on the spot.
2. Walk your fingers up no more than an inch, still at your sides, and you will feel the ball of the hip joint swivel in its socket as you march.
3. This is the exact mid-line of your body. It is also the place where the leg moves in relation to the torso, and conversely, where the torso moves in relation to the leg. For this reason I refer to this as the *bowing joint* when teaching young children how to bow to an audience.

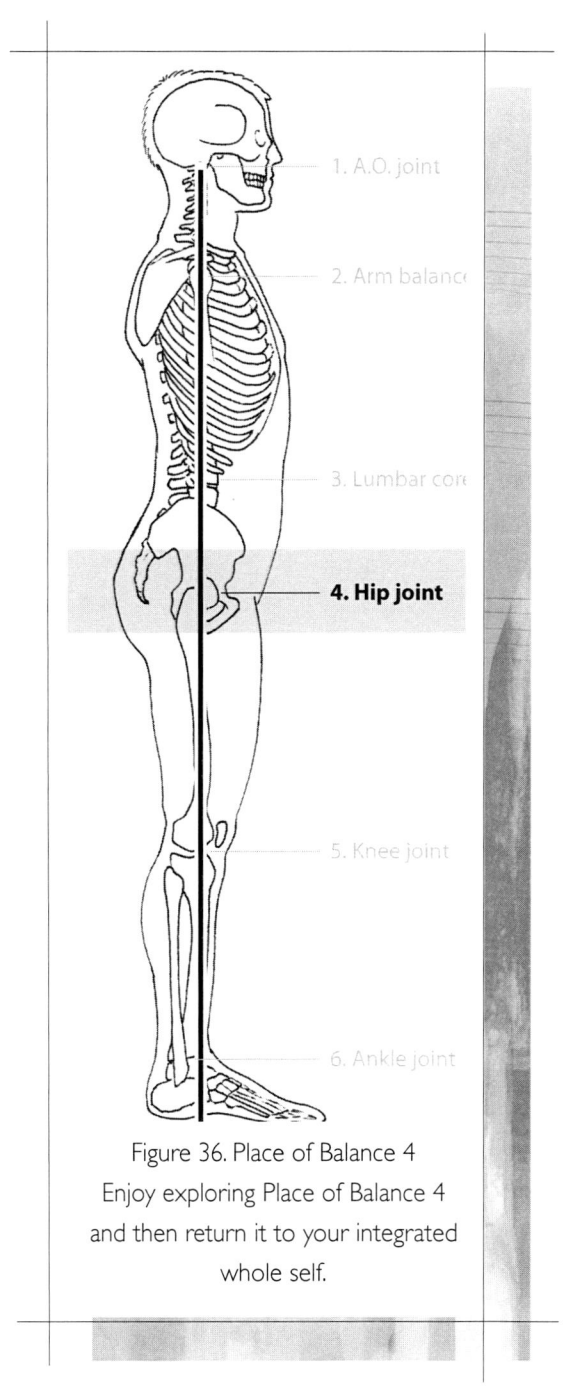

Figure 37. The Hip Joint

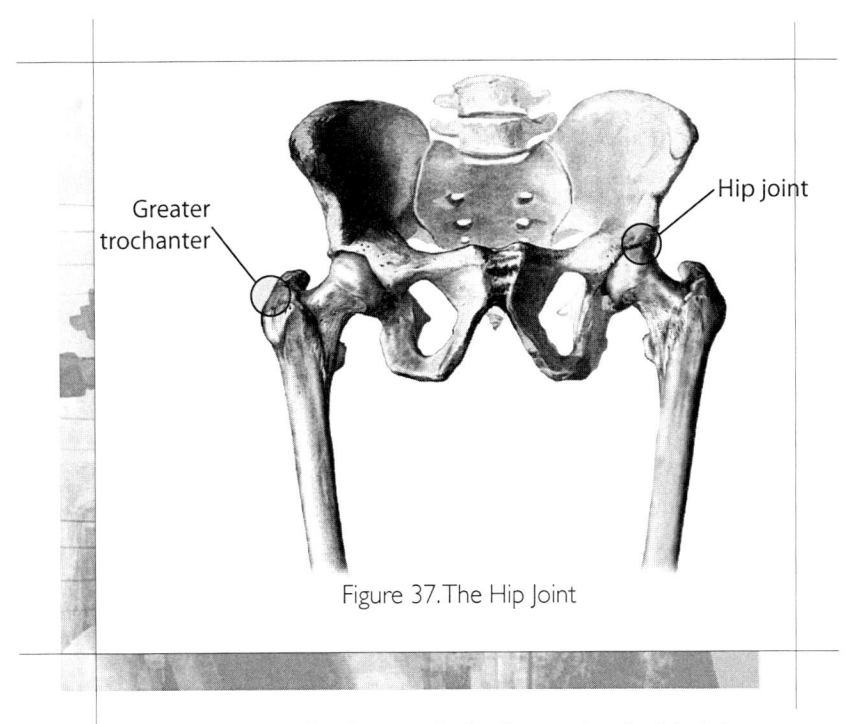

4. Keep your fingers at the hip joint and experiment with bowing from this major joint of the body rather than from an imaginary waist. This maintains the integrity of the spine as you bow. You should feel your fingers being slightly swallowed up by the crease that forms when the socket of the pelvis rolls over top of the ball of the thigh bone.

5. Note that the common practice of teaching young children to bow with the feet touching one another makes free movement from the hip joint nearly impossible. Bowing needs to be done with the feet under the hip joints, not under the pubis bones!

Marching and bowing are not the only movements, of course, that the hip joint affords us. Because of the spherical nature of the ball of the thigh bone, it can move in any direction. Besides being able to swing the thigh bones forward, backward, and sideways, our design also allows us to rotate the thigh bone in its socket.

The range of motion of this bone is appropriately limited in all directions by the boundaries that are created by the depth of the socket into which it nestles. As we will see in chapter 4, the leg socket is much deeper than the arm socket, which explains why we have a greater range of motion in the arms than the legs.

Violinists who suffer from locking at the hip joint nearly always show some evidence of the good posture or relaxation diseases.

Because both diseases entail the upper torso leaning off-balance from its sturdy lumbar core support, the body naturally has to compensate so that it doesn't tip right over. The joint that automatically jumps in with the best intentions to save the day is the hip joint. It pushes forward through space to counteract the imbalance of the upper torso. In fact, the degree to which a player pulls off the lumbar core is in exact proportion to the degree that the hip joint pushes forward off its own plumb line. And the compensations continue down through the knee and ankle joints. When the hip joint pushes forward there is an accompanying squeezing and shortening of the gluteal muscles, so it is well worth taking time to map these muscles in order to learn how to release them.

Figure 38. Find rotation at your hip joint.

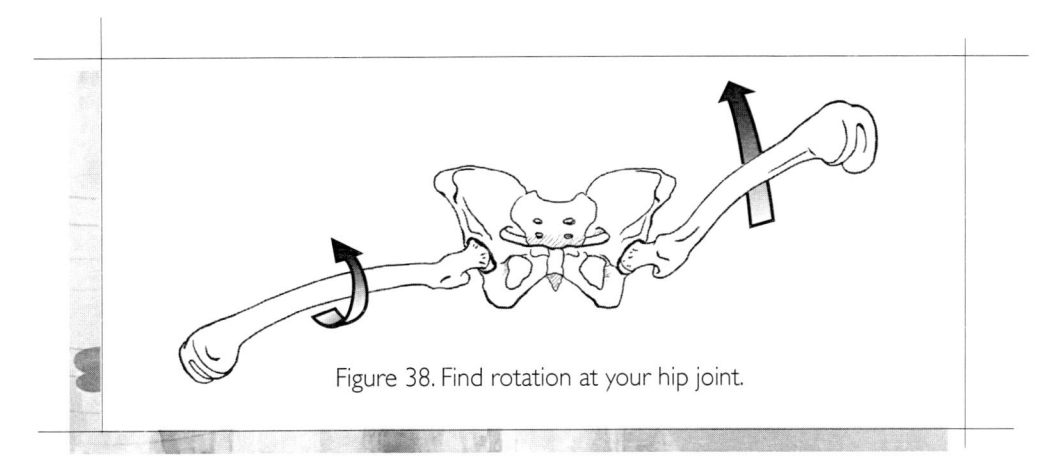

When a violinist plays with the toes pointing excessively away from each other it is often a sign that the gluteal muscles are squeezed together. Once he learns how to release these muscles he will experience what some people call a "dropping of the butt," and the feet will naturally move into a more neutral relationship with one another. This is a result of the spiraling of the musculature that begins at the sacrum and continues, through connective tissue, through the upper leg. When tightened, these muscles pull the toes away from one another; when released, they allow the feet to return to a more natural relationship and the hip joint to return closer to its neutral core line.

Sometimes teachers of small children advocate a toes-pointing-out playing position. Once again, *any held position* of the feet contribute to locking the leg joints, but pointing the toes out can cause an additional tightening of these lower back and gluteal muscles.

Tightening of these muscles causes a pulling-in on the pelvic bones, giving the sensation that the pelvis is much narrower than it actually is. Conceiving the pelvis as narrow leads to mis-mapping the legs as joining the pelvis too close to the front rather than at the sides. This makes the pelvic region feel so cramped that it seems there is no room anywhere but at the front for the legs to emerge.

The idea that our leg bones extend straight out from in front of the rockers, or—even worse—from the pubis is often reinforced by the misleading pin-striping on trousers or the parallel weave of fibers in common jeans. In truth, the upper leg bones originate in the hip socket at the sides, right under the ears and arm sockets, then make a diagonal line inwards to meet with the lower leg bones at the knee joints.

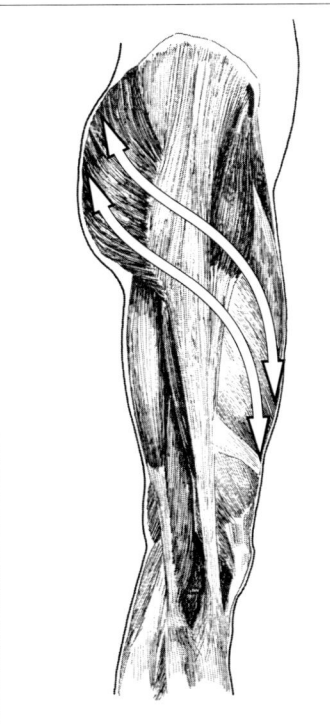

Figure 39. Learn to release these muscles in length and width.

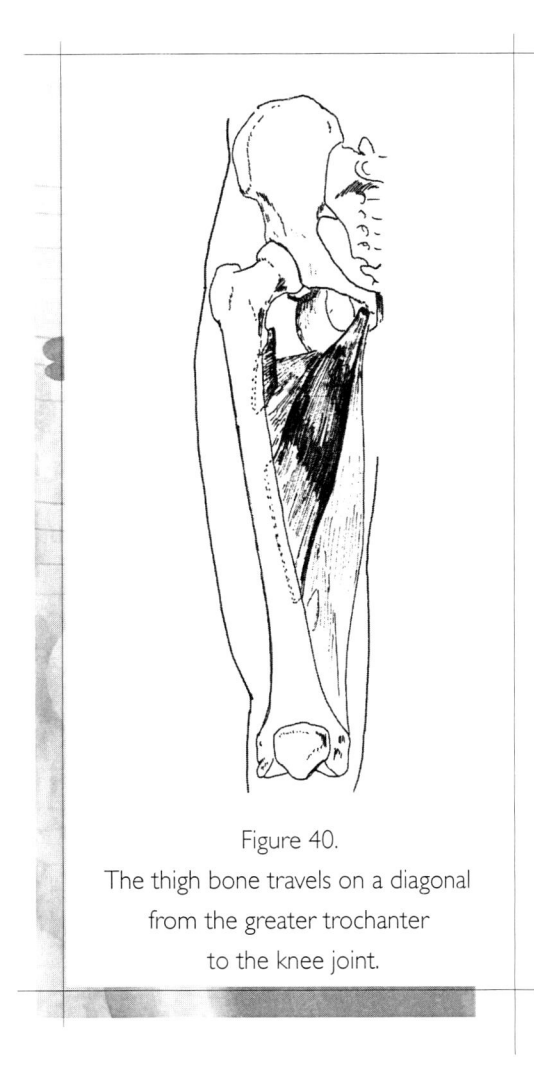

When a violinist fully grasps how wide the pelvis actually is from side to side he experiences a much more secure and stable base on which to sit. In standing, he senses even more width—right from one end of the pelvic arch to the other as the body's weight delivers through each of the greater trochanters, down through the legs, and into the ground.

It is not just the location of the hip joints that is mis-mapped from chronically tightened lower back and gluteal muscles, but also the structure of the hip joint. The more the pelvic bones are pulled in together the less room there seems to be for two leg bones, two pelvic bones, and one sacrum to all comfortably come together in one region. This often leads to mapping the hip joints as being on the inside of the pelvic bowl rather than on the outside of the pelvic bones. Those mis-mapped this way move as if there is nothing stopping the leg bone from poking right through to the inside of the pelvis, and therefore feel that their legs are trapped under them when they sit.

Figure 40.
The thigh bone travels on a diagonal from the greater trochanter to the knee joint.

Finding Balance at the Hip Joint

1. To find balance at the hip joint you need to become familiar with the two extreme positions of the pelvis in relation to the ball of the thigh bone. Balance, of course, is found right between the two extremes.
2. While standing, arch your lower back to an extreme as you would with the good posture disease.
3. Notice how this automatically swings the hip joint way out in front of your mid-line.
4. Fashion models frequently use this jaunty pelvic-thrusting attitude on the catwalk. What happens in your lumbar spine and knees if you try to move with this posture?
5. Do you feel the loss of balance off the lumbar core?
6. Do your knees lock back? The only reason knees ever lock back is to compensate for a hip joint locked forward.
7. Next assume the exaggerated slump of the relaxation disease.
8. Ironically, when a slumping violinist stands to play, it is this same forward-locking of the hip joint that compensates for the extreme C-shape the spine has been forced into.
9. This pattern is commonly witnessed among bass guitar players.
10. To find the other extreme position of the pelvis, use your hands to guide your pelvis into a tilt in the other direction, so that the top of the pelvis moves forward through space, and the lower half, (where the thigh bone meets its socket) moves back through space.

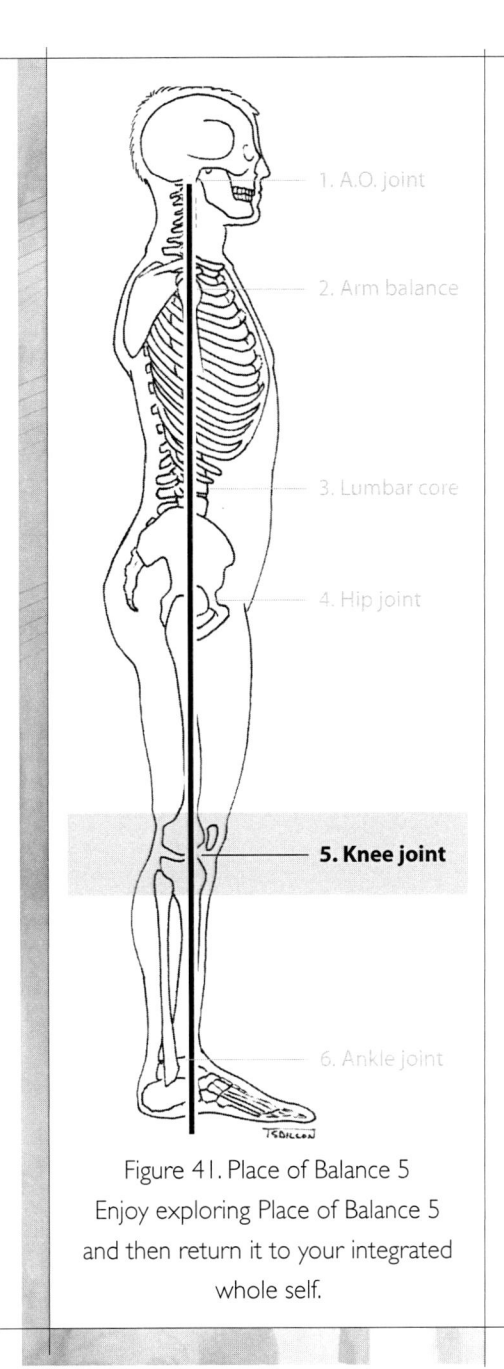

Figure 41. Place of Balance 5
Enjoy exploring Place of Balance 5 and then return it to your integrated whole self.

1. A.O. joint
2. Arm balance
3. Lumbar core
4. Hip joint
5. Knee joint
6. Ankle joint

11. You may sense that your eyes are not looking straight out at the world anymore, because your torso will to some degree be tilting forward and down.
12. A person with this mis-mapping naturally feels a desire to look out straight ahead, and will often crank his upper torso upright by creating an extreme arch through the thoracic and cervical spine.
13. Swing slowly between these two extreme positions until you begin to have a sense of where neutral is for your pelvis.
14. As you search for neutral at place of balance 4, make sure that all of the major joints of your upper body (places of balance 1–3) are already at a balanced neutral position.
15. Otherwise you will continue to compensate in the pelvis for the lack of balance above.

Place of Balance 5: Knee Joint

Unlike other instrumentalists, violinists are very fortunate to be able to perform standing up. However, when hips, knees, and ankles chronically lock, we lose all potential for expressive and freeing movement through the legs and, indeed, the entire body.

In my private studio I place a strong emphasis on finding free leg movement so that stepping into the high point of a phrase or bending at hips, knees, and ankles for a dramatic *pianissimo* moment become expressive movement options.

Violin teachers regularly implore their students to unlock their knees when they stand to play. However, locking the knees is not the source of the problem; it is merely a symptom of back orientation. Knees lock instinctively to protect the disks of the lower spine that are squeezed or pinched when a person loses balance around the lumbar core and compensates by using the muscles of the *back* to hold up the body. It is an extremely poor idea, in fact, to ask a student to unlock her knees if the bony imbalances and compensating muscular work above are not being addressed.

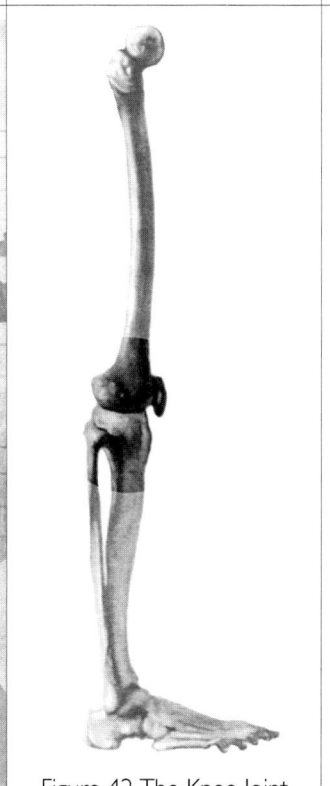

Figure 42. The Knee Joint

Quite often students respond to their teachers' injunctions by keeping the knees slightly bent to avoid being accused of locking them. However, a chronic bending of the knees is simply a different kind of muscular locking, this time in a forward direction. Whether the knees are locked backward or forward, it is the upper leg bone being squarely centered and balanced on top of the large lower leg bone that is lacking and must be remapped.

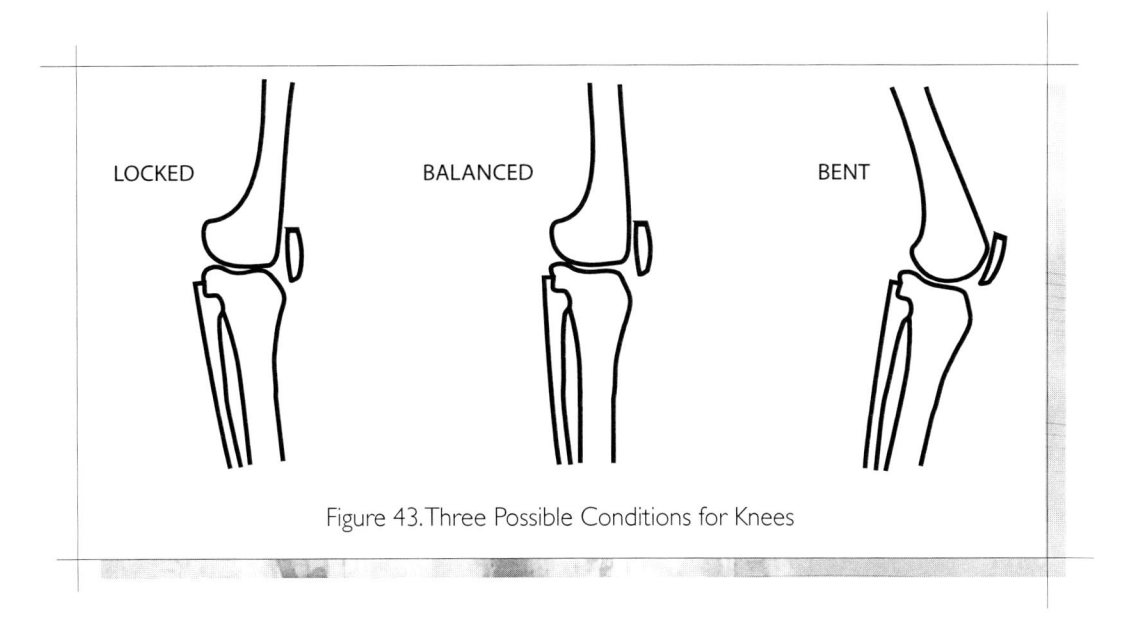

Figure 43. Three Possible Conditions for Knees

If you do most of your playing sitting down, be aware that remapping the knees may be just as important to you as to the violinist who most often stands to play. If you are a knee-locker when standing in line at the grocery store you are very likely a back-oriented player who throws torso weight on the back half of the spine rather than through the core of the spine. Work on standing balance to help find balance while sitting.

Like the hip joint above, there are three possible conditions for knees: they can be locked back, locked forward, or on balance. When knees are on balance, the thigh bone is squarely stacked on top of the large lower leg bone and less muscular effort is required at all places of balance in order to stand.

The most common mis-mapping that causes imbalances at the knee joint is the fantasy that the knee is a *thing*. A knee is a *joint,* and the definition of a joint is "the *space* between two bones where they meet in order to provide movement." Sometimes the *thing* mis-mapped as a knee is a fictional bone lodged between the ends of the femur and tibia.

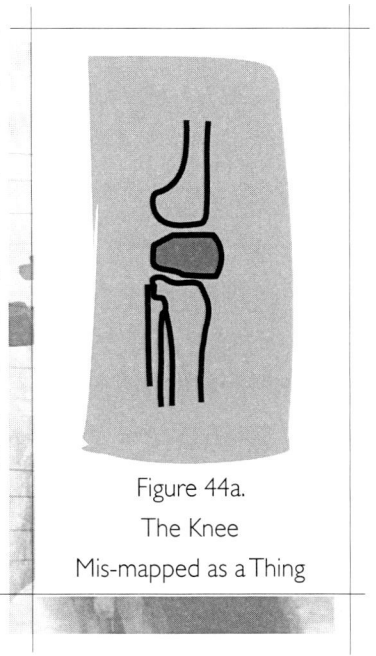

Figure 44a.
The Knee
Mis-mapped as a Thing

Figure 44b.
The Knee
Mis-mapped as a Kneecap

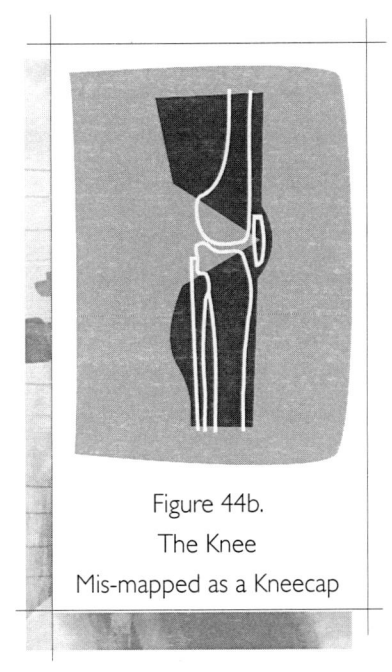

Sometimes the *thing* which people think of as the knee is the kneecap itself. Once again, it is language which contributes to this mis-mapping. We rarely say, "My knee joint hurts." Instead, we point to our kneecaps and say, "My *knee* hurts." In this way, many of us come to believe that the kneecap *is* our knee.

The kneecap, in fact, is a separate little bone that is positioned in large part *above* the knee joint. Only the bottom rim of the kneecap is in front of the joint itself. Thinking the knee *is* the kneecap and trying to deliver weight through it muscularly "locks the knees" and jams the kneecap backward, closer in than it should be to the front of the lower leg bone (tibia). The sensation from this jamming reinforces the notion that this *is* the location of the knee.

This backward jamming also pushes the end of the thigh bone too far back on the tibia, and the weight of everything above travels down the back half of the tibia instead of squarely through its core, frequently leading players to mis-map the *rear* lower leg bone (fibula) as being the weight-bearing one. (See place of balance 6 for more on this.)

Locating the Knee Joint

Mistaking the kneecap for the knee mis-maps the knee as located only at the front. Figure 45 shows that the knee joint has a circular nature, with a front, back and sides.

1. Sit with figure 45 nearby.
2. Palpate around the circumference of your knee joint with your fingertips.
3. Begin at the back and work around to the front.
4. Note that the area a doctor taps with his mallet when testing your reflexes is directly under your kneecap when you are seated and is the place at the front where the two leg bones meet.
5. At the sides you should be able to feel the knobby, bumpy ends of the thigh bone and the tibia that you see in figure 45.

Because of the jamming described above, a chronic knee-locker nearly always maps the bottom surface of the thigh bone as resting *too far back* on the top surface of the tibia. Even when moving the knees out of a locked-back position to bend them, these two bones often continue meeting in an imbalanced relationship to one another (see figure 46b) until remapping is done.

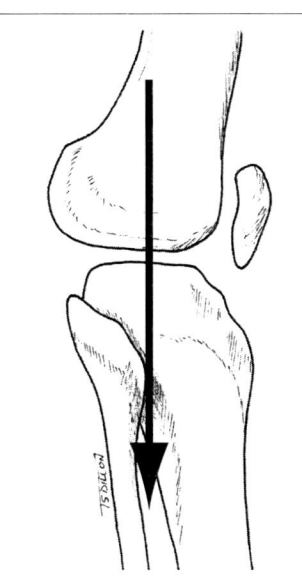

Figure 45. Locked Knees
Locked knees jam the femur too far back on the tibia and cause weight to travel down the *back* of the leg.

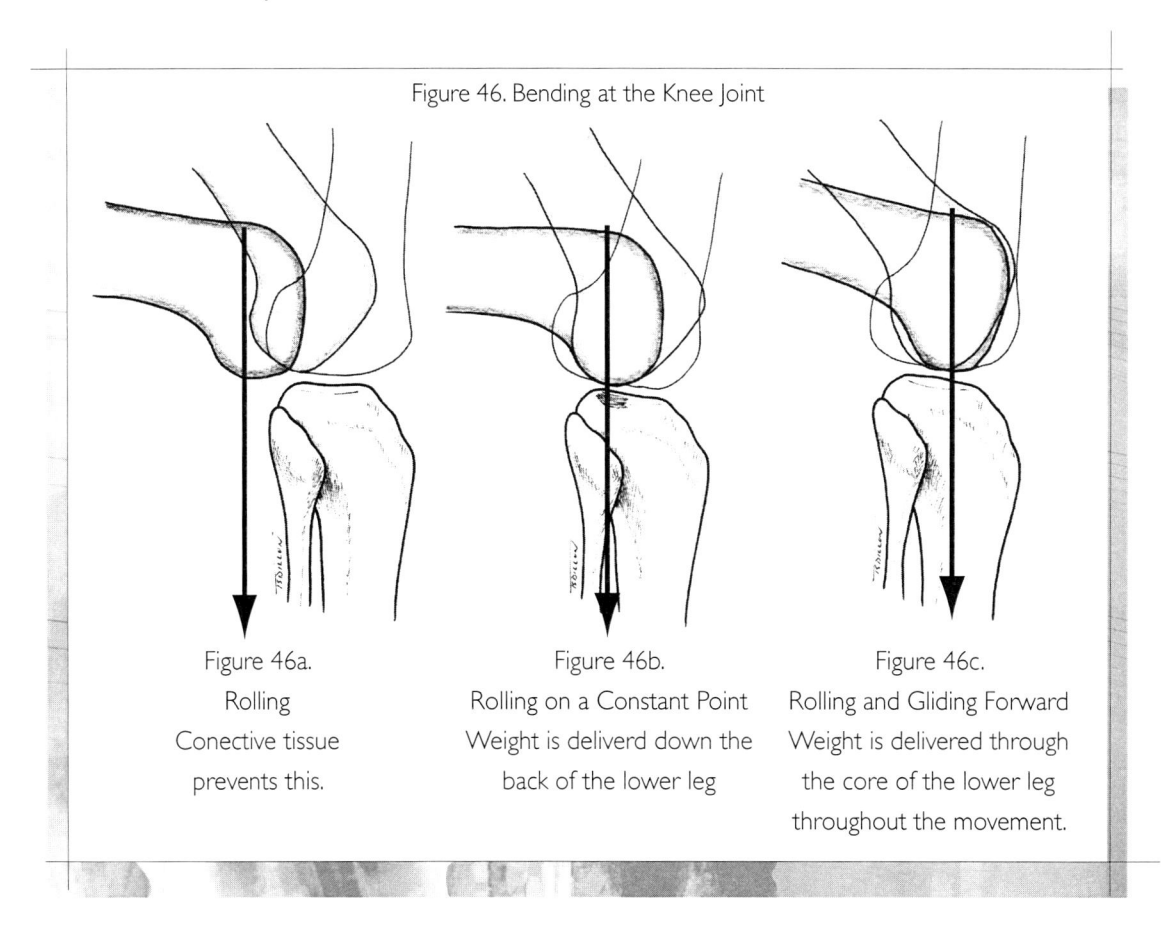

Figure 46. Bending at the Knee Joint

Figure 46a.
Rolling
Conective tissue
prevents this.

Figure 46b.
Rolling on a Constant Point
Weight is deliverd down the
back of the lower leg

Figure 46c.
Rolling and Gliding Forward
Weight is delivered through
the core of the lower leg
throughout the movement.

Three Ways to Bend at the Knee Joint

Speaking for a moment about the functions of the bones only rather than the combined functions of the bones with connective tissue, the thigh bone can move in relation to the tibia bone in three different ways in order to make a bending movement at the knee:

1. Rolling
2. Rolling on a *constant* point of contact with the tibia
3. Rolling and gliding forward

Rolling

If there were no connective tissues at all, the thigh bone could roll right across the top surface of the tibia, like a ball rolling across the floor, eventually rolling right off the back edge of the tibia. Fortunately, this is prevented from happening because the connective tissues *are* there between the two bones.

Rolling on a Constant Point of Contact with the Tibia

The thigh bone *rolls* on *only one contact point* on the top of the tibia rather than rolling right *across* the top surface (as described above). Unfortunately, the connective tissue can allow this to happen when a person does not have the relationship of the two bones mapped accurately. A mis-mapped, jammed-back thigh bone delivers weight through only the back half of the tibia and tends to stay on the back half of the tibia. Rolling only on this one, single, back-of-balance point of contact on the tibia creates wear and tear on the cartilage between the two bones. So far, neither of these options is very healthy for knees!

Rolling and Gliding Forward

The thigh bone rolls and glides forward across *many* points of contact on the top surface of the tibia, allowing the thigh bone to constantly re-establish a new, always centered point of balance on the tibia as it travels through its full range of motion. When the thigh bone is allowed to glide forward as it rolls, the weight of the body above is delivered through the center of the tibia rather than through its back half. When the thigh bones are mapped as rolling *and* gliding, the upper leg feels perfectly balanced on the lower leg no matter where within the range of motion the two bones are because they always meet squarely head-on. The gliding motion which constantly renews the bony balance also allows release of the compensating muscular work around the knees, in the quadriceps, the buttocks and the lower back.

You can never fully experience the weight of your upper body delivering fully into the ground and the easy buoyancy that comes with this balanced weight delivery if the working relationship of the thigh bone and tibia is mis-mapped.

If the neck is already free before going into this balanced kind of knee-bending (and assuming that there is also freedom at the hip joints and ankle joints), there will be a lovely and automatic lengthening through the spine and freeing through the back and arm muscles.

Finding Balance at the Knee Joints While Standing

Balance at the knees depends on balance at the major joints above the knees.

Part 1

1. Check the balance of your head on your spine.
2. Check that your neck muscles are free.
3. Walk backward to help ease your upper torso onto your lumbar core.
4. Search for neutral at your hip joints.
5. Now you are ready to begin kinesthetic experimenting at the knee joints.

Part 2

1. Begin by locking the knees back.
2. Without allowing the lower leg bone to pop out from under the thigh bone, allow the muscles surrounding the kneecap and the whole knee joint to release so that the end of the thigh bone subtly glides forward across the top surface of the tibia to the center, creating a head-on meeting of the two bones.

3. This forward gliding motion brings the two bones into right relationship if they have been chronically locked back.
4. One student described this by saying, "It's as if the lower leg bone stays back, but you don't let the thigh bone stay locked back." You should feel a softening all around the kneecap, particularly right under it, as muscular strain is released from the joint.
5. You should feel more of your weight delivered through your lower leg bone and feet into the ground because you are now directly *above* the lower leg bone, allowing it to support you more efficiently.
6. If you think about freeing your neck, you may feel yourself spontaneously growing taller as your spine is triggered into lengthening.
7. Continue to play with this until the thigh bone finds a poised and centered balance directly on top of the lower leg bone.
8. If you have been a chronic knee-locker for many years, it may take weeks or months to discern where this place of balance is for you.

Finding Balance at the Knees while Bending at the Knees

It is necessary to clarify that what is commonly called a "knee bend" actually requires an equal amount of bending at the hip joints above and the ankle joints below: it is a hip-knee-ankle bend. Work through the following continuation of the exploration above.

1. Once you find the place where the thigh bone and tibia meet head-on, you need to maintain that relationship in order to perform a knee bend.
2. Begin as above with the knees locked back.
3. Without allowing the lower leg bone to pop out from under you, allow the thigh bone to ease or glide forward until you reach a centered head-on meeting of the two bones. Chronic knee-lockers nearly always allow the tibia to pop out from under them as soon as they start to bend their knees because this fulfills the misconception that the thigh bone should meet only the *back half of the tibia.*
4. Move the thigh bone into a bending motion, allowing the lower leg bone to join the knee-bend only when the thigh bone has glided forward as far as it can so that it will maintain solid contact with the ample surface area the top of the tibia provides.
5. The more the thigh bone rolls on top of the tibia (whether in a deep bend or just to bend enough to get your sit bones on a chair), the more it needs to glide forward to be fully and squarely supported by the lower bone.
6. Note that, even in sitting, the thigh bone must be squarely centered over the supporting surface of the tibia so that balance is maintained at all other places of balance, and so that the lower back muscles do not work unnecessarily.
7. When the thigh bone and tibia meet in a centered balance in sitting, you may experience a hollowing sensation at the backs of your knees.

8. This results from finding a more forward point of contact for the head of the femur on the tibia and the muscular release that comes with it.

Finding Musically Expressive Leg Movement

One of the best ways to work with a violinist who is a knee-locker is to get him moving his feet while he plays. He won't like the suggestion at first, because it is very difficult to move the legs when some or all of the joints are locked; however, it will help him to find freedom at this joint to encourage him to use *musically appropriate movement* while playing.

1. Begin by encouraging your student to find three places in a piece where a high note or climactic moment can be physically demonstrated by *stepping into* it.
2. Make sure when the moment is over that the feet return to a neutral place.
3. Next ask your student to demonstrate *pianissimos* in the piece by bending at the knees, hips, and ankles.
4. Challenge him to mark an especially emphatic *fortissimo* musical moment by stamping one foot.
5. After consciously practicing such choreographed moves the student will begin to absorb the myriad possibilities of expressive leg movement, growing into a performer with a natural, spontaneous dance happening in his legs at all times, whether so small that it is unnoticeable to observers or so dramatic that it sends a ripple through the audience!

Regardless of the leg movement you encourage, avoid letting students fall into a seasick swaying from foot to foot that usually indicates legs are locked up at all major joints. There is so much more expressive movement available to us from all six of our leg joints, and the best part is that it frees the rest of the body while enhancing our artistry and further engaging the audience in our performance.

Place of Balance 6: Ankle Joint

Like all leg joints, when the ankle is locked it is to compensate for loss of balance above.
It is impossible to have freedom in the legs if weight is sent down into the wrong part of the foot, gripping with the toes or holding in the ankle or foot in any way.

Figure 48 shows an ankle joint from the outside of the foot. Study carefully how the two bones of the lower leg meet the bones of the foot.

When teaching, I sometimes ask the class to point to the ankle joint. Invariably there are students who immediately point to the bony bumps right above the foot. Some have these bumps mapped as ankle bones; some map them as the upper part of very long foot bones. In both cases the joint is mapped as above the bumps. These students are astonished when they discover that these bumps belong to the lower leg bones and have absolutely nothing to do with the ankle joint. It is the bottom-most surface of the front leg bone, the part that meets and delivers weight into the foot bones, that makes up the ankle joint—not the bumps on the sides.

Sometimes violinists comment that their feet get tired or sore during a practice session. When questioned for more specifics, they often say it is their heels that feel tender or tired. This complaint almost always stems from mis-mapping the smaller rear bone of the lower leg as the weight-bearing bone.

Violinists with the good posture disease who send their body weight down the back of the spine rather than through their mid-line core believe their entire body weight is meant to travel down the back of the leg to reach the foot at the *heel,* since it is directly under the poor, overloaded back. Because there is so much sensation in the heel, it seems that the weight must spread from the heel forward through the rest of the foot.

By design, however, the body's weight should be delivered down the *front* leg bone to be distributed equally to the front and back halves of the foot. This equal distribution of weight takes all the strain off the heels. Occasionally, a violinist with sore heels has only mapped *one* bone in the lower leg. This mis-mapping is nearly always accompanied by the idea that the foot is "L-shaped": that the ankle joint occurs directly above the back of the heel rather than above the middle of the foot's arch.

Notice it is the larger, sturdier bone of the two lower leg bones which is designed to bear the weight from above. Because the larger bone is also the front bone, weight is beautifully delivered into the very top center of the arch of the foot, which then delivers the weight

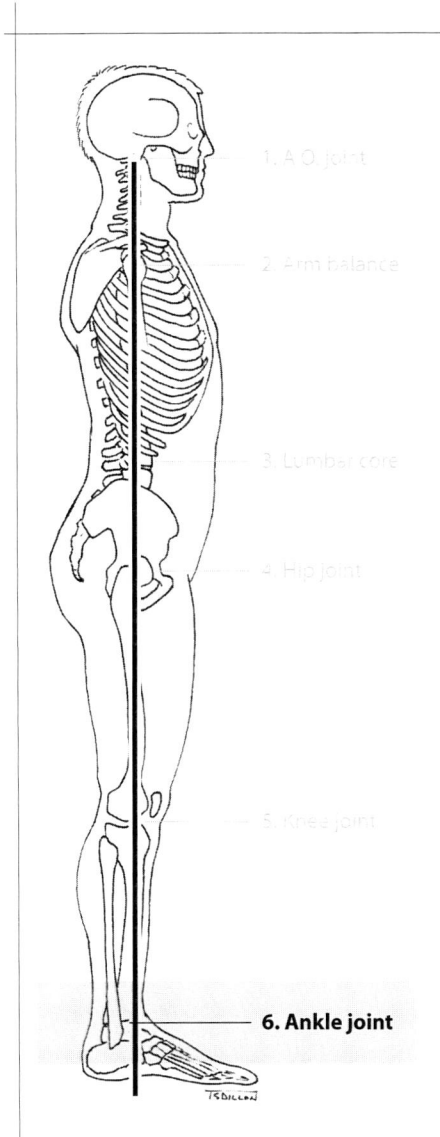

Figure 47. Place of Balance 6
Enjoy exploring Place of Balance 6 and then return it to your integrated whole self.

evenly to the front (ending at the ball of the foot) and to the back (ending at the heel).

A common mis-mapping here is that the arch is found only on the instep of the foot—just the part with which an arch support in a shoe might make contact. There are, in fact, three main arches in the foot.

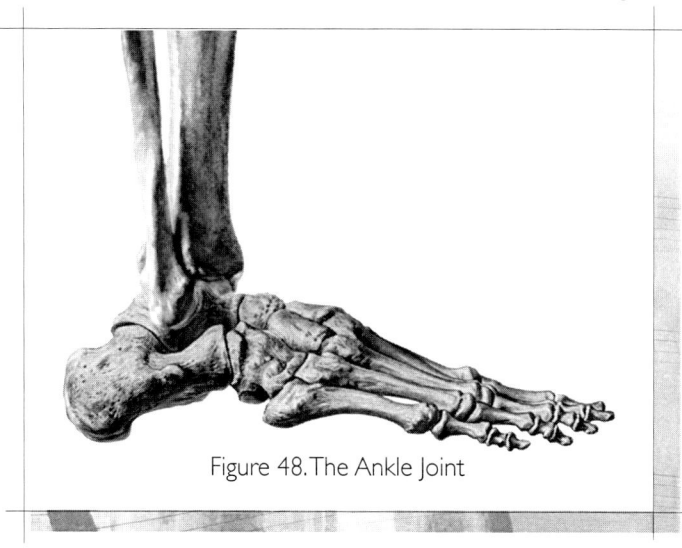

Figure 48. The Ankle Joint

Figure 49. In standing balance, our weight delivers through the front leg bone.

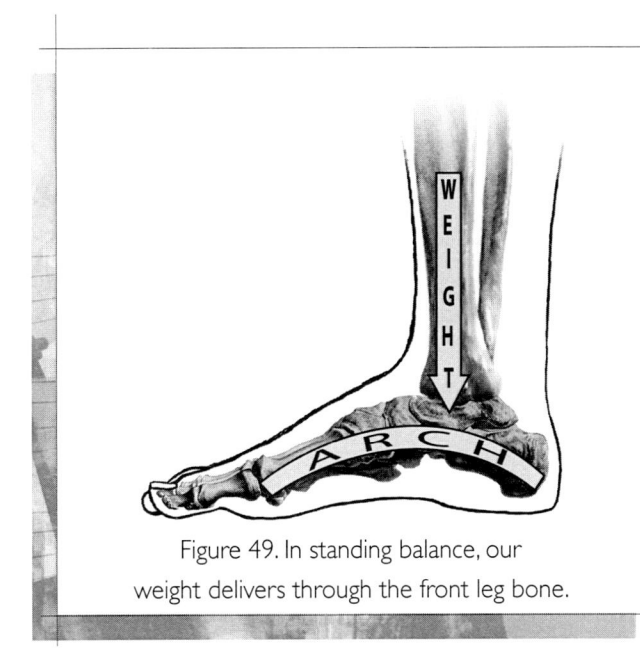

The first (shown in figure 49) is the extremely long arch on the big-toe side of the foot that runs all the way from the ball of the foot to the back of the heel. The second runs in a parallel fashion on the little-toe side of the foot. The third is called the *transverse* arch and runs laterally across the foot from the ball of the big toe to the corresponding place on the little toe side of the foot.

Between the two main lengthwise arches are a multitude of arches. In other words, the whole bottom surface of the foot can be viewed as one long arch from the base of the toes to the back of the heel. Likewise, the entire width of the foot can be viewed as one great transverse arch.

When you allow the body's weight to deliver evenly, front and back, through the lengthwise arches of the foot you experience a lovely, width-wise spreading sensation through the transverse arch. This is caused by the spreading from side to side of the long foot bones as the foot finds its full width.

Palpating the Foot

1. Take off a shoe and seat yourself in such a way that you are able to examine the bottom of your foot.
2. With a finger, trace the three main arches described above.
3. You will find that you are describing the shape of a tripod with your finger.
4. Understanding and kinesthetically experiencing the three points that make up the end points of this tripod is essential to beginning to learn to allow your weight to evenly distribute through the foot when you stand.
5. It is important to be clear that the toes do *not* form a part of the arch of the foot; their function is not to balance, but to propel. If we were creatures never meant to do more than stand balanced on one spot for eternity, we wouldn't need toes—they are only there to allow us the privilege of walking.

Violinists who grip their toes when they stand to play also grip the muscles around the ankle joints. Some students I have worked with found it very helpful to imagine that the lower leg bone is analogous to a wooden stilt. Both are long shafts on which we intend to balance our body weight; both come to fairly flattish ends that meet another surface on which to balance.

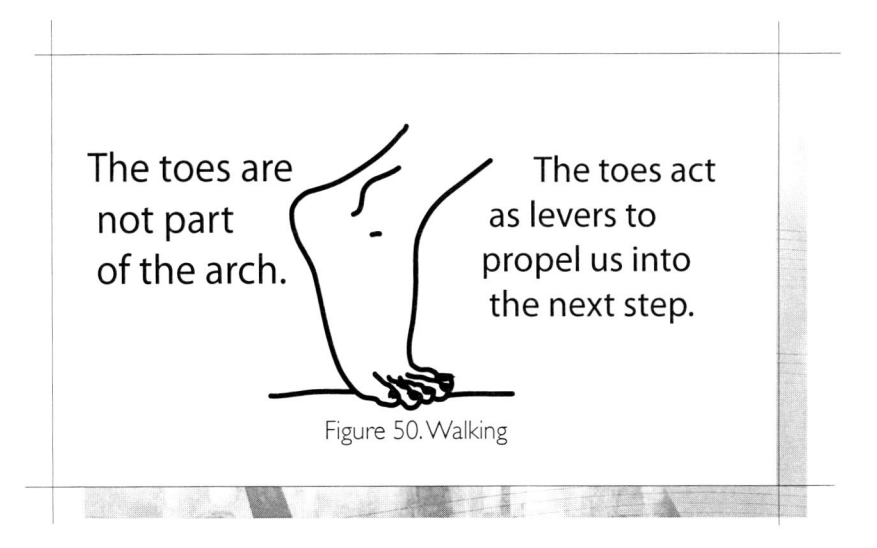

> The toes are not part of the arch.
>
> The toes act as levers to propel us into the next step.
>
> Figure 50. Walking

1. Quickly run a mental balance checklist over the first five places of balance to stack up your body's weight along your core line.
2. Now think about sending your weight down this built-in stilt into the ankle bones.
3. Think about softening the muscles that surround the ankle joint, particularly at the front of the ankle.
4. Search for a balanced and secure perch over the three-pointed tripod of your foot, all the while keeping the toes free enough to wiggle.
5. When you can do this you have found your sixth place of balance in the body, free from toe- or ankle-gripping.

Once you regain the transverse spreading of the foot bones and the propulsion role of the toes in your walk you will also recover a lovely spring in your step. Don't confuse this with an artificial bounce which gives one the appearance of bobbing up and down—it is more subtle than that, and is experienced as a natural outcome of rediscovering the true nature and design of the foot.

Going up on the toes when playing encourages more spreading of the foot bones and triggers a lovely upwards connection through all of the joints of the body, including an extra lengthening of the spine. Neurophysiology has recently confirmed that this is yet one more lengthening reflex in the body similar to the forward-and-up of the head on the spine that F.M. Alexander discovered. Great singers often instinctively rise on their toes when looking for more freedom in their upper range. Likewise, going up on the toes is useful to violinists looking for that extra bit of freedom in the arms that comes from the lengthening spine.

Chapter 4
Arms and Hands

"Many violinists share the belief that the violin is an unnatural instrument to play."

The Whole Arm (Reprise)

Learning about the whole arm is quite possibly the most important information a violinist can take away from this book. So, at the risk of seeming pedantic, here I repeat word-for-word the pages about the whole arm given in chapter 3.

A whole arm consists of a collarbone, shoulder blade, one upper arm bone and two lower arm bones, a wrist, and a hand. When asked how long their arm is, many violinists gesture from the hand up to the shoulder joint, stopping there. This is always a clear indication the person in question has not included the collarbone and shoulder blade in the map of his arm. The reason so many regard the shoulder joint as the top of the arm is that a distinction is made in English between the arm and shoulder. And yet, everyone has a different notion of what a shoulder actually is.

When I ask students to point to their shoulders, they always point to at least three different places: the shoulder blade, where it forms an overhang above the humerus; the upper humerus; and the trapezius muscles, because these are what are rubbed during a "shoulder massage."

In fact, there is no anatomical unit called a "shoulder," which is why there is so much confusion and mis-mapping in this region of the body. The word "shoulder" is best used not as a noun but as an adjective. There is no one thing that can unequivocally be called a shoulder, but there is certainly a shoulder blade, a shoulder joint and a shoulder region.

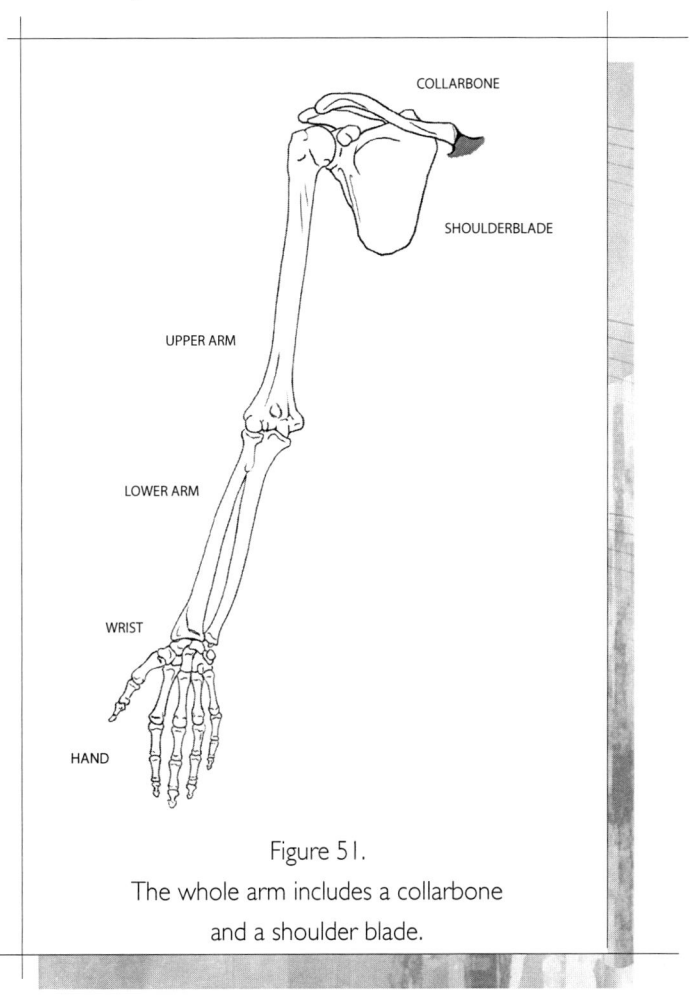

Figure 51.
The whole arm includes a collarbone and a shoulder blade.

Mapping the Four Arm Joints for Violin Playing

Arm Joint 1: Sternoclavicular

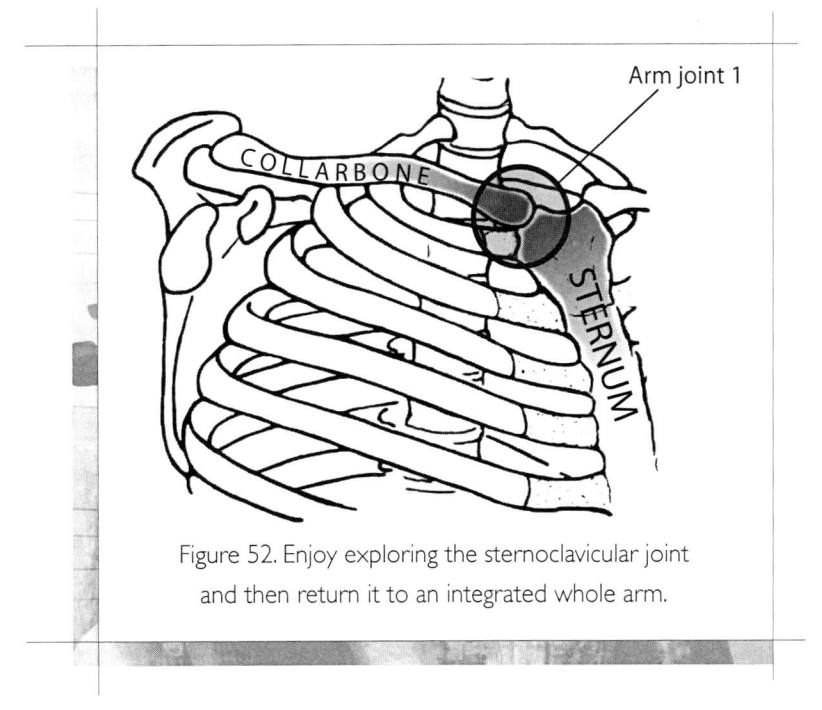

Figure 52. Enjoy exploring the sternoclavicular joint and then return it to an integrated whole arm.

Arm joint 1 is the only joint the arm forms with the torso. If this statement surprises you, then you probably still think of the top of your arm as beginning at the shoulder joint and the shoulder blade as part of the back rather than part of the arm.

The most serious mis-mapping for violinists involving the sternoclavicular joint is not including it in the map of the arm at all; in other words, not mapping it as part of something that participates in movement.

When asked about the job of the collarbone, most violinists mention its role as a shelf for the instrument to rest on, but many are surprised by the notion that the collarbone should move. In fact, players frequently say, "I didn't think it was *supposed* to move from there." But in order for the arms to feel buoyant and supported from above by all that elastic connective tissue, the collarbone must be accurately mapped as the top portion of a long, long arm that swings as a unit from the torso at the sternoclavicular joint.

In order for the shoulder blade to have free and healthy movement, (see Humeroscapular Rhythm under Arm Joint 2: Humeroscapular below), movement of the collarbone in all directions must be accurately mapped, since together, the collarbone and shoulder blade form a unit and move as one.

Put the fingers of one hand on the opposite collarbone and try moving your shoulder blade without moving the collarbone. You will find it is impossible. The only reason a shoulder blade is able to move at all is because it attaches to the collarbone, which in turn forms a joint with the torso from which the whole, integrated arm moves.

Constantly trying to hold down the bow-side collarbone at arm joint 1 while raising the humerus for tasks like string crossings to the D and G strings, or for traveling right to the frog on up bows inhibits shoulder-blade movement as well. Over time, the rotator cuff muscles can become vulnerable to strain and tearing.

It is not uncommon for violinists to mis-map the collarbone as an immobile part of the torso while at the same time falling prey to the good posture disease. This double-whammy of mis-mappings causes the collarbones to be pinned into a position back and away from their joints with the sternum. Although this position makes the proximal bumps of the collarbone very prominent, it makes the part of the collarbone most needed as a place of support for the violin disappear. Losing this place of easy support causes even more muscular holding in an effort to make the instrument feel secure.

Chronically misusing the front of the arm structure in this way inevitably leads to mis-mapping the shoulder blades in a number of different ways.
Play with the collarbones constantly pinned back and the shoulder blades are forced together on the back. This can lead to mis-mapping the shoulder blades as attached to the spine, or in extreme cases, as attached to one another.

Playing while pushing the arm structure *down* as well as pinning it back results in mapping the shoulder blades as not only sitting on the ribs but actually attaching to them because this is how it begins to feel.

If you recognize that you chronically pull your collarbone and shoulder blades back as in the good posture disease, repeat the lateral neutral movement exploration under Place of Balance 2: The Whole Arm in chapter 3. If you know that you are limiting movement in any way from arm joint 1, return to the Go Swimming movement exploration in the same section. If it works to free the shoulder blades, it works simultaneously to free the collarbones!

Some violinists instinctively know there needs to be *some* movement of the collarbone while playing, but may have been told by teachers to keep the shoulders down. In trying to obey both instinct and teacher these players may end up "splitting the difference," the body map taking on an imaginary joint somewhere in the middle of the collarbone. The collarbone may move somewhat, but will feel restricted and awkward because some muscles attempt to hold it down while others try to move it. The solution is to be very clear about where the two ends of the collarbone actually are: one end meets the sternum and the other butts into the side (the acromion) of the shoulder blade. There is no other source of movement between these two ends. The whole, very long collarbone must swing freely from arm joint 1.

Palpating the Length of the Collarbone from One End to the Other

1. Walk the fingers of one hand along the collarbone, beginning at the bump where it meets the sternum, all the way over until you feel the joint it makes with the shoulder blade.
2. Make sure to palpate all three curves of the collarbone (like a very shallowly-curved S) before you stop. You won't be at the shoulder blade until you have felt the collarbone curving out toward the front again.

We do not include the joint where the collarbone meets the shoulder blade as one of the main arm joints because we have no control over its movement—it is involuntary. The *function* of this joint is to accommodate the voluntary movement that happens at the at the other arm joints. However, for purposes of examining upper arm *structure,* it is a very important joint because it marks the end of the long collarbone.

Violinists who have mapped themselves as more narrow-shouldered than they actually are (perhaps for aesthetic reasons), are often delighted to discover how much longer the shelf for the violin really is. Knowing the full length of the collarbone also aids in remapping where the real joints are; it dispels any notion of movement being able to originate from the *middle* of the bone. There are three different directions in which the collarbone can move from arm joint 1: up/down, forward/back, and in rotation. It is possible to be well-mapped in some of the functions of a joint but not to have them all mapped.

For instance, you may be well aware that you can move your bow arm collarbone up to accommodate crossing to the lower strings, and that you can move your violin arm collarbone forward when you need a bit more security for the instrument during a long down-shift in the left hand. However, if you haven't mapped the possibility of rotation at the sternoclavicular joint, you may have difficulty in returning the whole arm to a released and balanced neutral.
Players suffering from the good posture disease often chronically rotate the collarbone in a backward direction, causing the shoulder blades to be dumped farther down the back. The possibility of releasing the collarbone in a frontward rotation is necessary to find an easy balance for the whole arm structure in relation to the sternum.

Exercise for Maintaining a Free Neck While Bringing the Violin to Playing Readiness

The following exercise elaborates on "Maintaining a Free Neck while Supporting the Violin" in chapter 3.

Part 1: Freeing the Collarbone from Arm Joint 1 to Buoyantly Support the Violin

1. Check the six places of balance.
2. Hold the violin in both hands, the left on the violin's shoulder and the right fingers over the tailpiece.
3. Point the elbows to the sides while lifting the violin so that it sits on the top of your head, always maintaining your head balance.
4. Notice that to even get the violin on top of your head, the collarbones have to move up from arm joint 1, and the shoulder blades—at least to some degree—have to follow the humerus.
5. Are you still holding the shoulder blades down in any way? If so, you will feel a strain along the back edge of the armpit as if the two bones are trying to separate. Allow them to release into a healthy humeroscapular rhythm.

6. Most violinists love having their violins on their heads, because, for the first time, it feels like being given permission to involve the whole arm in movement while holding onto the instrument.
7. Maintain this position for several moments, enjoying freedom that you are allowing at arm joint 1.
8. Now, without losing the balance of your head on the spine or turning it to meet the violin, slowly bring your instrument down to playing-readiness, all the while being careful to not bypass the place of springy, suspended neutral for the arms.
9. Once the violin reaches your collarbone, maintain your attention to balance as you turn your head until the jawbone meets the chinrest.
10. If you use a high shoulder pad or chinrest, it is very possible that you will feel that there is now too much bulk between your collarbone and jawbone.
    a. This exercise is a measuring stick for how much padding you actually need in order to be comfortable with the violin because it simultaneously locates your suspended place of neutral for the collarbone while preventing any downward pull or loss of balance of the head from its perch on the spine.
11. Continue adjusting the height of your violin set-up over the next days and weeks as you work with this exploration until you feel that your set-up accommodates *your* design rather than the other way around.
12. Once you are confident you have found the right height in your pad/chinrest arrangement you will begin to enjoy the higher plane on which your violin arrives when you bring it to playing readiness from above. It feels very virtuosic!
13. As you prepare to play, resist any urge to clamp down on the violin and collarbone with your head—the weight of the head should always be on balance on your *spine* as you play rather than dropping it all onto the chinrest.
    a. Clamping with the head or applying excessive weight of the head depresses the collarbone. Do this and you will lose the suspended place of neutral, which is what provides arm joint 1 with its potential to move in any direction.
    b. Instead, enjoy the security provided simply by the sideways turn of the head that brings the jawbone into contact with the chinrest and the slight forward nod of the head on its fulcrum at the A.O. joint. This is enough security for the instrument for most of our violinistic tasks.

Step 2: Allowing Movement at Arm Joint I as You Play

1. Play open strings, moving frequently from E to A, D to G and back across the other way, always ensuring that as you travel to the lowest strings, the shoulder blade follows closely behind the humerus (see Humeroscapular Rhythm under Arm Joint 2: Humeroscapular

below) and that you can feel the collarbone traveling up as it pivots on its joint with the sternum.

2. Keep in mind it is not just the bow-arm collarbone that moves in violin playing.
3. If you are just rediscovering your freedom to move at arm joint 1, experiment with every possible movement from this joint in both arms.
4. On every up-bow, allow the left collarbone to move forward so that the violin moves into the bow.
5. Try improvising a passage above seventh position.
6. As you prepare to move the hand back down to first position, allow the collarbone to move up to temporarily aid in the security of the violin during the downshift.
7. Finally, as required for all healthy movement, when the activity is completed allow the collarbone to return to its suspended place of neutral.

Bringing the violin in from above encourages neutral for the arm in both the lateral and vertical planes; holding the ends of the violin with elbows to the sides encourages lateral neutral and a healthy alignment of the arm bones with one another; and raising the arms above the head helps locate the suspended vertical neutral for the collarbones. Finding this suspended position for the collarbones preempts the tendency to compress them or the violin, which in turn leads to a much greater depth of tone, since compression prevents vibration and vibration *is* sound. And finally, once the arms have been released to neutral, all of that lovely violin playing movement from arm joint 1 is available to them.

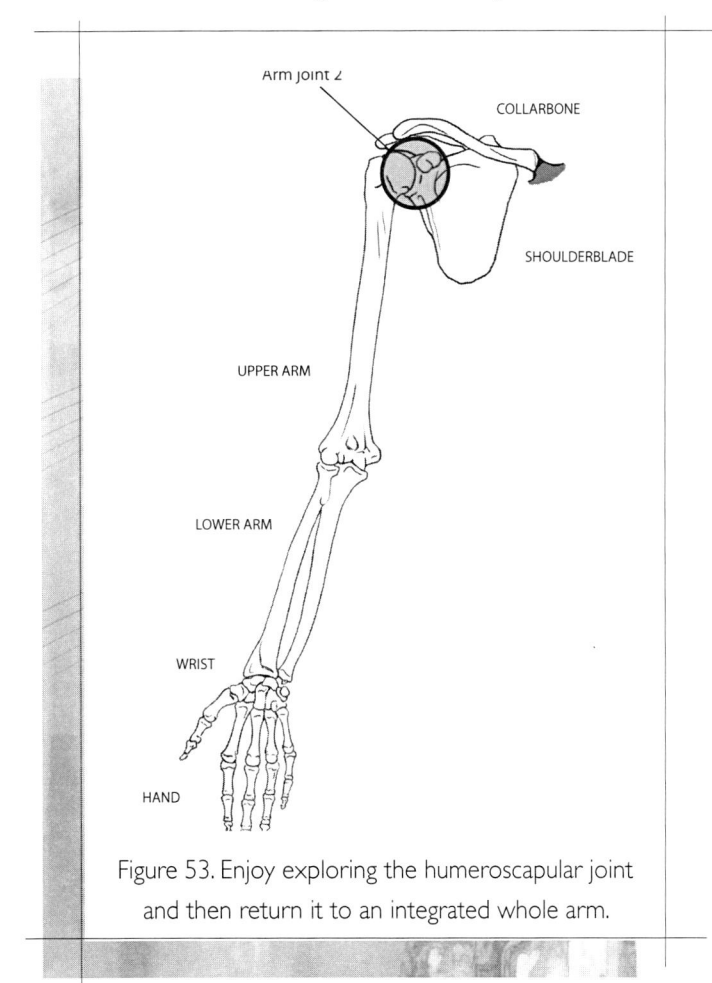

Arm Joint 2: Humeroscapular
Structure of Arm Joint 2

If arm joint 1 is mis-mapped and the collarbone/shoulder blade unit is held back or down, either because of the good posture disease or the "get your shoulders down" advice, arm joint 2 will inevitably be mis-mapped. This is inevitable because the socket for the joint is located *in the side of the shoulder blade.*

If you see in yourself or your students a loss of space in the armpits, winging in the shoulder blades, discomfort in the muscles, or stiffness and popping in the shoulder joint, then the first mapping question to

Figure 53. Enjoy exploring the humeroscapular joint and then return it to an integrated whole arm.

ask is: "What does the humerus meet at the shoulder joint?" A person who has mis-mapped this region is not likely to mention the shoulder blade.

In such a person's map there is no recognition that it is the side of the scapula which provides the socket for the upper arm bone. A structural mis-mapping at this joint frequently leads a violinist to answer the question by saying, "The upper arm bone meets a socket at this joint." However, the socket envisioned is a fantasy socket, completely separate from the structure of the shoulder blades.

In this mis-mapping the shoulder blades are so close together on the back (thus the winging appearance) that it is inconceivable that they could ever extend far enough to the sides to provide a socket for the humerus. Thus there is a mis-mapping at the first arm joint (the shoulder blades too close to the spine) reinforcing one at the second arm joint (a separate socket remote from the scapula), and vice-versa.

In reality, of course, the closer to the spine the scapulae are pulled, the closer into the torso the attached humerus is yanked, thereby giving the visual impression of a closing off of the armpit. This pulling down and in of the arms into the torso prevents an easy movement forward and up when we raise the violin to play because we are asking muscles to work in direct opposition to one another, creating a terrible muscular strain.

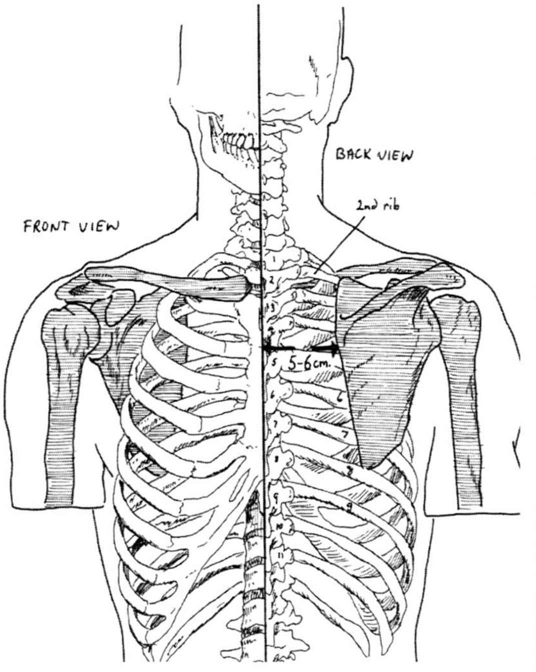

Learn how to release the shoulder blades back to their lateral neutral position so that arm joint 2 is directly under the ears and you will feel an immense relief, both physically

Figure 54. The socket for the ball of the humerus is contained in the side of the shoulder blade.

and emotionally. There is physical relief because the upper torso muscles can stop holding and are free to move the arms, and also because the ribs can move more to allow freer breathing. Emotional relief comes because an accurate map of the shoulder joint frees the arms, revealing why playing the violin may have felt so difficult until now!

Even if a violinist is aware that the socket for the end of the humerus is found in the side of the shoulder blade, she may still have mapped its size incorrectly. To illustrate the arm's ball and socket joint, she might gesture by enclosing her fist in the palm and fingers of her other hand, or by cupping a hand over the rounded part of the shoulder region which in truth is comprised of bits and bobs of several different bones, including the collarbone, shoulder blade, and humerus. Either of these gestures indicates the mistaken belief that the socket is much bigger than it actually is.

Figure 55. The socket is small and shallow relative to the size of the ball of the humerus.

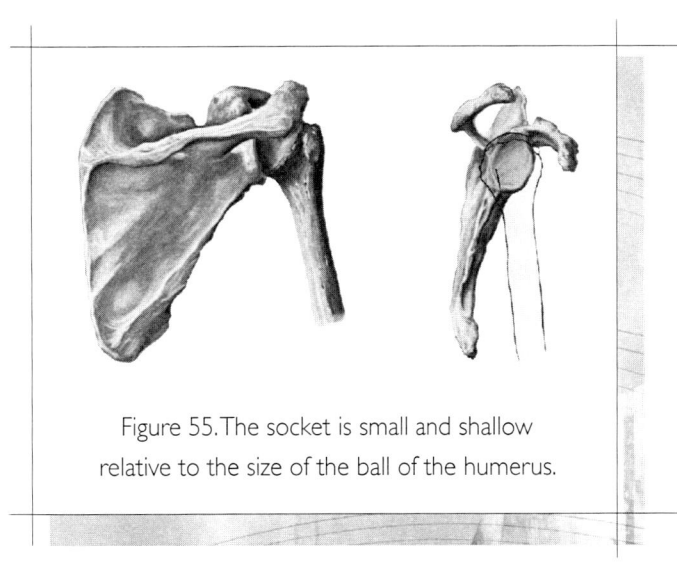

As figure 55 shows, the socket is extremely small—only as big as the pad of the thumb. It is also very shallow—only slightly concave. The very shallow socket in which the large humeral ball moves is precisely why the arm has such extreme ranges of motion at arm joint 2. The ball is not designed to come into contact with the top portion of the shoulder blade that hangs over it; when it does this repeatedly it can put undue pressure on the bursa sac, inflaming it. However, contact will inevitably happen if the overhang is mapped as the top part of the socket.

So, to summarize, the most common mis-mappings at arm joint 2 arise from a mis-mapping at arm joint 1. If the collarbone/shoulder blade unit has not found neutral, the scapula will not follow the rest of the arm easily into movement. This places a great deal of strain on arm joint 2 as the humerus tries to move from the side of the body while the socket for the humerus is dragged away into a "stabilized" position somewhere on the back. The resulting perception is that the humerus and shoulder blade could not possibly meet to form a joint.

This introduces an imaginary joint at the sides of the body, usually involving too many bones, which leads to an oversized socket in the body map. This limits nearly all violin playing tasks, and feels difficult and awkward because everything we do on the instrument requires free movement at arm joint 2—from raising the violin and bow to playing-readiness to drawing the bow across the string.

Solving problems at arm joint 2 is entirely dependent on having healthy movement at arm joint 1, so if you feel restricted in any way in the shoulder joint, revisit all of the movement explorations described earlier that promote easy movement of the collarbone and shoulder blades from a balanced neutral position, and study, study, study figure 55 until there is no doubt in your mind about the shape, location or size of arm joint 2.

Functions of Arm Joint 2

In order to play the violin, there are three basic movements at the humeroscapular joint: up and down, back and forth, and rotation. Once the structure of arm joint 2 is well-mapped and healthy movement is restored, most violinists have no problems mapping the movements of the humerus up and down as well as back and forth. However, it is not uncommon to neglect the function of rotation at arm joint 2. Ignoring rotation at the humeroscapular joint limits both tone and comfort.

In the bow-arm humerus, for example, a loss of forward rotation always results in poor tone production at the tip. If you have a satisfactory sound in the lower half of the bow but cannot sustain it in the upper half, it is probable that you haven't mapped humeral rotation at arm joint 2.

Relocating Humeral Rotation

1. Take a pen in your bow hand.
2. With your usual bow hold, move the pen down and away from yourself, miming a down-bow gesture.
3. Once you reach "the tip" and have pronated as far as you can in the lower arm, keep rotating the tip end of the pen down until it points to the floor.
4. This movement has to come from the forward rotation of the humerus at arm joint 2, and requires the shoulder blade to follow easily along behind it.
5. Next, take your violin and bow. Watch yourself in a mirror as you play full bows, both down and up, looking for evidence of this rotation as you near the tip, and conversely looking for the backward rotational release in the humerus as you begin the up bow.
6. Repeat this without allowing the humeral rotation.
7. Can you hear the weaker tone production at the tip when you disallow the humerus its rotational movement?

Over-rotation in the left humerus is a common mis-mapping among violinists that arises from the frequent injunction to "get your elbow under the violin." This abstraction is often used by teachers in an effort to set up a student's left arm so the pinkie finger (perceived as weak) can reach the strings, especially the lower ones, without straightening or straining. The problem with this advice is that it draws attention to the wrong joint. The only way the *elbow* can be swung under the violin is by the backward rotation of the humerus at *arm joint 2*.

A teacher who instructs a student to "get the elbow under," actually wants to see a *combination* of this humeral rotation, a forward movement of the collarbone, supination at the elbow joint, and the forward movement of the pinkie hand bone (more detail on the latter two movements follows). These four movements together do, indeed, allow the pinkie to reach all of the strings without strain. However, by not acknowledging all four sources of movement and by only speaking of the elbow, this abstraction causes a loss of good quality movement at arm joint 2 and usually ends up distorting the relationship between the humerus and shoulder blade.

Violinists thinking only about the end goal of "getting that elbow under" nearly always drive the collarbone down and into a backward rotation. This withdraws all support the socket in the shoulder blade could provide for the humerus. The humerus then must be contorted into an extreme and completely unsupported rotation in order to complete the movement.

This over-rotation causes the arm to feel "cut off at the pass" in the armpit, thus reinforcing the notion that the arm stops at arm joint 2 and causing loss of the strength and unity derived from an arm mapped as going all the way to the tip of the scapula.

The same disconnection happens in the bow arms of violinists who over-rotate the humerus in a backward or clockwise direction in an effort to "drop the elbow" or "drop the weight of the arm into the string" to produce a bigger tone. In addition to losing the sense of whole-arm connection through the armpit, this pedagogical abstraction causes another serious problem. When arm weight, which is substantial, is "hung" from the bow by rotating the humerus in a backward direction, the collarbone/shoulder blade unit is dragged down out of its balanced, suspended neutral and leads to mis-mapping the unit as resting on top of the ribs.

Additionally, instead of the arm's weight traveling through the bow and into the violin string, most of it is borne downwards through the right side of the torso. This results in loss of rib movement, which in turn leads to restricted breathing. The whole notion of arm weight being *dropped* into the string is misleading and potentially injurious to violinists. It is frequently used by teachers to avoid using words like "press" or "push down on the bow" when they wish to indicate that more effort must be used to keep the string vibrating as the sounding point moves closer to the bridge. Pedro de Alcantara writes:

> *Some players consider the idea of pressure negative, speaking instead of releasing 'arm weight' into the string or suspending weight away from it. Yet the pressure of the bow on the string is like the pressure of breath against lung or of blood against vessel—a lively and vital force acting upon an elastic surface. The string, the bow stick and hair, and the player's arm are all flexible and resilient. Together they create a system of springs that not only withstand pressure but thrive under it.*[9]

Whether or not a teacher includes the word *pressure* in his pedagogical vocabulary, it is necessary to understand that *arm weight* never sets a string vibrating; and it is a vibrating string which produces sound on the violin. It is *friction* that sets a string vibrating; so our challenge as teachers is to find ways to describe how to maintain necessary friction at all sounding points along the string in order to produce a deep tone, rich with overtones.

It is true that it takes more effort to set the string vibrating when playing on the sounding points nearer the bridge because of the string's increased rigidity, but describing this increased effort as "dropped arm weight" is potentially misleading. In watching Heifetz one can clearly see that he has not *dropped* anything in his bow arm. His arm structure is beautifully suspended over his core and he uses his bow arm as a strong chain of interconnected levers which he rotates into the bow to produce the necessary friction for the sounding point he is using.

There are three different joints in the bow arm where this rotation takes place: at the elbow joint (arm joint 3) the lower arm rotates (pronation); at the humeroscapular joint (arm joint 2) the humerus rotates forward in its socket; and at the sternoclavicular joint (arm joint 1) there is sometimes a slight rotation of the collarbone as the scapula follows the humerus (very long-armed violinists do not often need to rotate at arm joint 1).

There is no need to speak of dropping weight if there are no mis-mappings of separation anywhere throughout the arm structure, so that the arm is accurately mapped as connected at *all* of the joints, from the fingertips touching the bow frog to the tip of the scapula, as we see with Heifetz. The desired sound is always available and setting the string vibrating always feels easy, since it is an act of leverage rather than a muscular effort of "pushing down" or the more damaging act of "hanging weight."

Several of the preceding movement explorations stress the importance of allowing the shoulder blade to follow the humerus into movement. Let us now take a detailed look at how these two bones work together for free and easy arm movement.

Humeroscapular Rhythm

Humeroscapular rhythm is the name given to the natural tendency in upper arm movement for the humerus to lead and the scapula to follow. When humeroscapular rhythm is not denied, the shoulder blade follows sequentially behind the humerus in whichever direction it reaches. Humeroscapular rhythm is of much interest to neuroscientists who study movement because it is one of the earliest observable movements in infants developing in the womb. It is clearly evident in young babies in the crib as they reach up to touch a mobile or reach out to grasp a toy. The rule for a healthy humeroscapular rhythm is that the shoulder blade must move soon enough and far enough so that no strain is felt in any of the muscles or connective tissue in the upper torso.

Testing Your Own Humeroscapular Rhythm

1. Slowly raise your arm while paying particular attention to the sensation along the back rim of the armpit.
2. Note the point at which you start to feel the shoulder blade wanting to follow.
    a. This will be shortly after the humerus begins to move and long before it is parallel to the floor.
3. Continue reaching up until your fingers are pointing straight to the ceiling while allowing the shoulder blade as much movement as it needs so that it smoothly follows the humerus.
3. Lower your arm and repeat steps 1–3, but this time, when you feel the urge for help from the shoulder blade, deny it—"hold that shoulder down"—and feel the resulting strain in the muscles of the shoulder blade and upper humerus.
4. Keep going. You will automatically want to hunch up and in toward the torso to try to protect yourself from overstraining.

5. Contrast this feeling of strain (and the resulting contortion) with the easy freedom you experienced in the first reach when you allowed the shoulder blade its rightful humeroscapular rhythm.

Violinists who have not mapped the shoulder blade as part of a whole arm have very likely lost their humeroscapular rhythm. Mapping the shoulder blade as something belonging to the back rather than the arm denies its function to follow the rest of the arm when it is needed. Violinists systematically taught that "shoulders" should not move or that they should "stay down" also lose their humeroscapular rhythm. Believing they will have a freer arm "if I could only stabilize this wobbly shoulder," they push down harder on the shoulder blade.

Whatever the reason for the mis-mapping, any attempt to deny the shoulder blade its sequential movement causes discomfort and injury. Not allowing humeroscapular rhythm in the left arm translates into limited rotation for the upper arm that severely limits ease of movement when travelling up the fingerboard to the highest positions. It also means that the violin gets stuck in one place only, and perhaps even worse, that breathing is constricted, since holding down the shoulder blades prevents the rib movement necessary for free breathing.

Bringing the bow to the string, playing to the tip, and especially crossing to the lower strings while denying a healthy humeroscapular rhythm leads to extreme tension in the upper torso and sometimes even to tearing in the rotator cuff muscles. The rotator cuff muscles are a group of muscles that connect the front and back surfaces of the shoulder blade to the head of the humerus. Their job is to ensure that the shoulder blade stays in right relationship to the humerus—in other words, that it follows the humerus in a healthy humeroscapular rhythm.

Besides harmful pedagogical advice regarding "holding the shoulders down," the other main culprit in destroying people's natural humeroscapular rhythm is the good posture disease. When the shoulder blades are pinned back and the sternum is pushed up in military fashion it becomes impossible to allow the shoulder blades to move anywhere freely, let alone soon enough and far enough.

Rediscovering Humeroscapular Rhythm if It Has Been Lost

Violinists who have mis-mapped themselves out of a healthy humeroscapular rhythm in their playing often still retain it in the front-crawl swimming motion.

1. Place your left hand on your right arm's collarbone to help monitor the amount of movement you are allowing at the sternoclavicular joint.
2. Make a slow, continuous, front-crawl motion with the right arm.
3. Notice how much movement is in the collarbone.
4. Notice that it travels up, forward, and even rotates in its joint with the sternum.
5. Next, make the same swimming motions while reaching back to the shoulder blade with your palpating hand.

6. Notice how it has to move up and forward.
7. Now try to make the front-crawl motion while not allowing movement in the collarbone or shoulder blade.
8. Can you feel how restricted this movement is? It doesn't work for swimming, and it doesn't work for playing the violin.

Humeroscapular Rhythm in Violin Playing
1. Very slowly raise your bow to the string.
2. Notice that the shoulder blade follows the humerus, first in a forward direction, then in an upward direction as the arm is raised.
3. Begin playing.
4. Notice that on every down bow, as the humerus extends out to the front to reach the tip, the shoulder blade wants to fall in line and move behind the humerus.
5. Now, while approaching the frog of the bow on up bows, try for a moment to deny your arm's natural tendency—try to "hold the bow shoulder down."
6. Notice that right before you reach the frog, the "shoulder" wants to hunch up in order to alleviate the strain put on it.
7. Begin a new up bow from the tip.
8. After passing the middle of the bow, be mindful of the place where the shoulder blade wants to join in with the humerus in moving forward and up.
    a. This is the necessary and healthy forward and up movement of the "shoulder" as opposed to the unhealthy hunching to alleviate the strain felt when humeroscapular rhythm is denied.
9. Rest your bow at its midpoint on the string.
10. Without playing, rock the bow from the open E string to the open G string and back again.
11. You should feel the shoulder blade follow behind the humerus during every moment of the upward trajectory to the G-string.
12. Likewise, the shoulder blade follows the humerus back down as the bow returns to the E string.
13. Next, experiment in a similar fashion with the violin arm.
14. Slowly raise the violin.
15. Notice that the humerus travels just a few inches before the shoulder blade wants to follow its frontward and upward direction.
16. Try "holding the shoulder down" as you move the left hand into the higher positions or over to the G string.
17. Contrast this feeling of strain with the ease of movement you feel when you allow the shoulder blade to follow behind the movement of the humerus.

18. In addition to accommodating the left hand in its negotiations of the fingerboard, a healthy humeroscapular rhythm also provides enormous freedom of the violin itself.

If you have been taught that the violin should remain in one place and the bow should do all of the moving, experiment with the extreme ranges of movement possible for the left arm and the violin when you play. You may eventually decide to only use these movements in performance for the occasional dramatic gesture in a musically appropriate place, but it is necessary to regularly practice the full range of motion of the left shoulder blade so that it does not remain mapped as immobile.

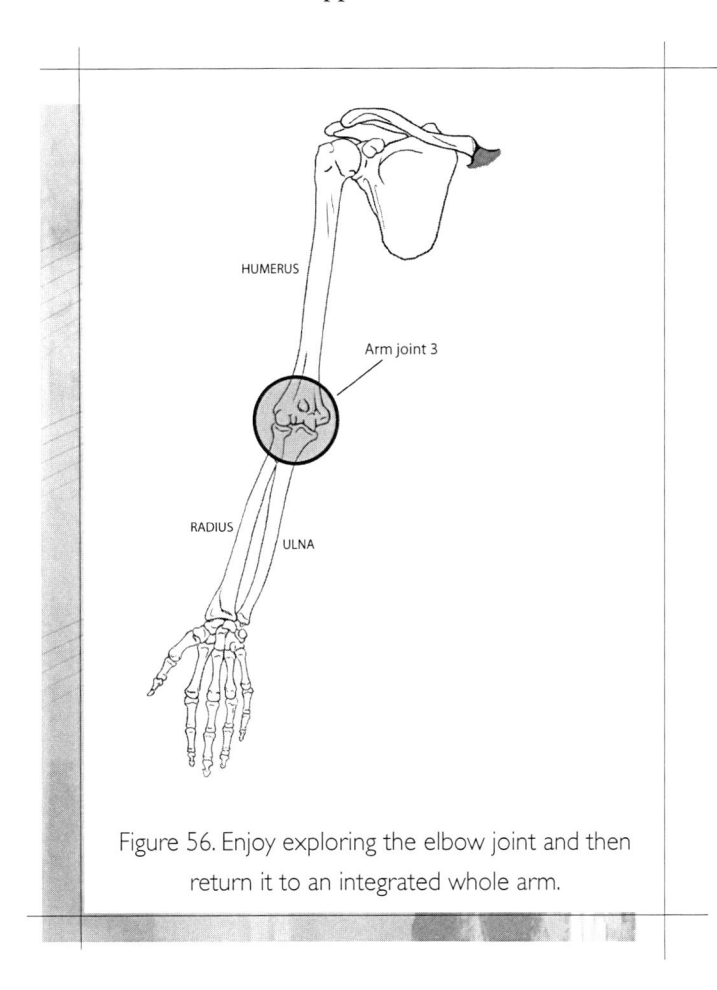

Figure 56. Enjoy exploring the elbow joint and then return it to an integrated whole arm.

Arm Joint 3: Elbow

There are two movements which happen at the elbow joint—bending/unbending and rotation—and there are two lower arm bones—the ulna and the radius. The ulna takes full responsibility for the movement of bending and unbending, and the radius bone looks after the movement of rotation. Before examining the functions of these two bones in detail, however, it is important to understand the structure of the arm joint 3.

Structure of the Ulna and Humerus

Many violinists think of the elbow as one big, old thing rather than as a joint where the ends of three different bones come together. This leads to mis-mapping parts of the ulna as upper arm bone and parts of the humerus as lower arm bone. When I teach, I usually ask students to examine the bony bumps at the elbow to try to identify which belong to the upper arm bone and which belong to the lower arm bones. We usually begin with the bony bump that contacts the table when, with a vertical forearm, we say we are "leaning on our elbows." Normally at least one person surmises that it belongs to the upper arm bone and is surprised to find out in fact that it is the end of the ulna—a lower arm bone.

Next we make the same inquiry about the "funny bone" bump. This is the one that if struck on a hard surface often produces momentary numbness or tingling. Someone nearly always has this bump mapped as belonging to the lower arm. In fact, this bump is the end of the humerus. (I find that the "humerus/funny bone" play on words often helps students remember that the funny bone belongs to the upper arm bone.)

Exploring the Structure of the Ulna and Humerus

1. Palpate the bumps of your left elbow one at a time as you study figure 57 until you become really clear about which bump belongs to which bone.
2. Bend the left arm at the elbow and point the fingers of your left hand to the ceiling.
3. Use your right-hand fingers to trace the indentation between the funny bone bump on the side of the humerus and the elbow bump at the end of the ulna.
    a. What you are palpating is the curve of the backward-C-shaped notch at the end of the ulna into which the humerus inserts.
4. Continue studying figure 57 and palpating your elbow joint until there is no doubt in your mind how the humerus and ulna interconnect.

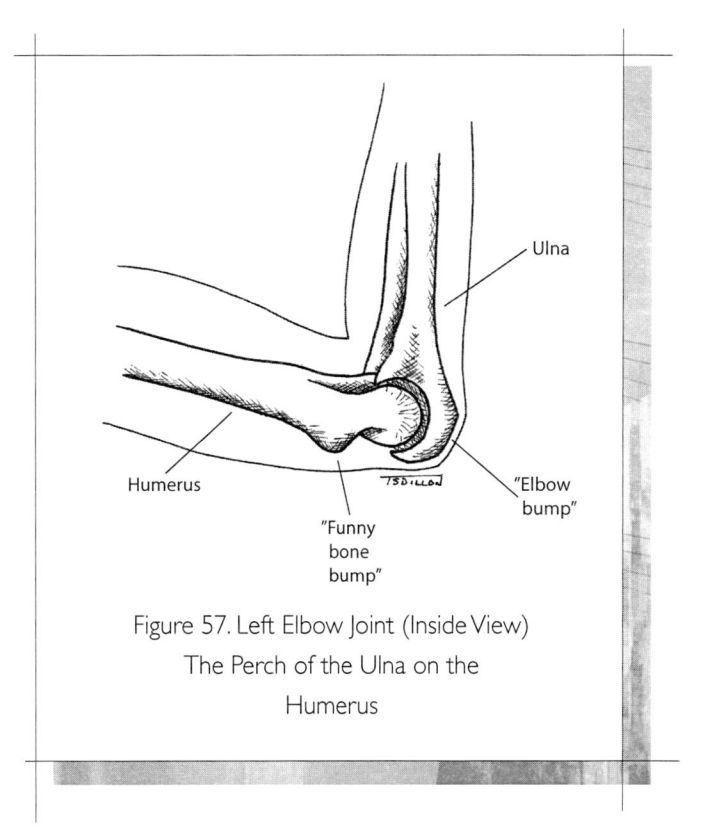

Figure 57. Left Elbow Joint (Inside View)
The Perch of the Ulna on the Humerus

Exploring the Bending Function of the Ulna with the Humerus

1. Raise your violin arm as if about to play and palpate alongside the notch on this arm.
2. Notice that the curved top of the notch is now hooked over the rounded end of the humerus that inserts into the notch, thus providing the upright forearm with a supported perch rather than requiring it to maintain its uprightness by purely muscular means.
3. To further experience this structural balance, hold your left forearm completely perpendicular to the floor.
4. Place the index finger of your right hand underneath the funny-bone bump on your left elbow joint.
5. Allow all of the weight of the left forearm to rest on top of the humerus, which in turn is supported by your finger.
6. Your right index finger now supports the bones of the left lower arm, wrist, and hand as they stack up, perched on the humerus below.
7. Slowly remove the support of the right hand but maintain the sense of connection and support the left humerus provides as the forearm perches on its bony fulcrum.
8. Explore the same connection in your right arm to discover how the notched end of the ulna swings freely at its joint with the humerus when you bow.

Perching one bone on top of another this way frees the upper arm muscles to perform their primary job, which is to *move* the lower arm rather than trying to do double the work of holding it in a bent position and then trying to move it. The very first movement required of the left arm after raising the violin is bending at the elbow. The biceps do the initial work of bending the forearm; however, the ulna must perch balanced on the humerus as playing begins or the biceps will continue to hold unnecessarily.

It is the upper arm muscles which move the lower arm to perform violinist tasks, such as shifting up and down the neck and setting the lower arm in motion for an elbow vibrato. These muscles will never move the lower arm freely to perform these tasks as long as they are bound up in holding the forearm in its bent position under the violin. (For a detailed account of the balance of the left forearm in violin playing, see "Weight Delivery of the Violinist's Left Forearm Arch" at the end of this chapter.)

A player who holds too many muscles in the arm often has mis-mapped the location of the elbow joint because of the *sensation* that it is elsewhere—often slightly up the ulna from the joint itself. Try tensing the muscles around the humerus and the forearm and then doing an "air vibrato." Notice that when this much muscular work happens in the arm that the sense of where the two bones meet is distorted. This mis-mapping of arm joint 3's location reinforces faulty movement patterns and causes even more unnecessary muscular work as the player tries to create movement from the middle of a bone rather than from the ends of bones.

Once again, inaccurate terminology is often responsible for violinists mis-mapping the location of left arm joint 3. The term "arm vibrato" is misleading because it does not label the true source of the movement. Because "arm" is such a general term, it draws attention away from the specific joint (the elbow) that provides the movement for this kind of vibrato.

A violinist trying to produce an "arm vibrato" frequently attempts to initiate movement from the humerus—after all, the humerus is part of the *arm*. This humeral interference from arm joint 2 causes a jiggling of the whole violin as the player tries to vibrate from too many joints and with too many muscles involved. This jiggling is an unmistakable sign that the violinist does not have the elbow joint mapped as the actual source of vibrato movement: a good reason to rename "arm vibrato" as "elbow vibrato" in our pedagogy. In an ironic reversal of this terminology and a good example of how a joint is often mislabeled as a "thing," Ivan Galamian writes, "The terminology 'wrist vibrato' is not accurate. It is as wrong to call the hand vibrato 'wrist vibrato,' as it would be to term the arm vibrato, 'elbow vibrato.'"[10]

His point is understood: it is not desirable to encourage the regions colloquially named as *wrist* or *elbow* to wobble around; the hand or lower arm (depending on which kind of vibrato is being used) is the moving body part in vibrato. However, inherent in Galamian's statement is a misunderstanding of the wrist and elbow as "things" rather than as joints or *places from which bones are moved*. As long as wrists and elbows are accurately mapped as joints, "wrist vibrato" and "elbow vibrato" are precisely the right terms to use. Because there are a myriad of ways to move individual body parts in harmful and inefficient ways, labeling must draw attention to the exact joints from which movement happens rather than to the body part being moved.

In a similar way, mis-mapping the location of the elbow joint in a violinist's bow arm will cause movement to be stiff. Moving the bow with accuracy at any great speed across the strings to produce a resonant sound is severely limited when forearm movement is stiff. When a violinist has problems with off-the-string strokes, it is frequently at least in part because the location of the elbow joint is mis-mapped due to efforts to muscularly stabilize the forearm under the mistaken impression that this frees the movements of the fingers and wrist.

Every single down bow, up bow, and pizzicato we play, requires free bending movement from the bow elbow joint. This is why it is essential for a violinist to know exactly how and where the ulna and the humerus meet. If the structure or exact location of the joint is mis-mapped, continually exploring the joint as outlined above will correct the map and restore a free and easy movement between these two bones.

Structure of the Radius and Humerus

The radius is the lower arm bone on the thumb side of the hand. Unlike the ulna, the radius does not form a deep joint with the humerus. The end of it is rounded, effectively providing it with a surface for swiveling against the humerus in its function of rotation.

Mis-mappings at the elbow joint in rotation are often responsible for tendonitis and carpal tunnel syndrome in violinists. If you have suffered from either of these, the following information may be the most important part of this book for you.

As discussed above, the ulna is responsible for bending and unbending at the elbow joint. By virtue of the ulna's deep notch into which the humerus fits, it is impossible for the ulna to make any other motion besides bending and unbending; and yet it is very common for violinists to mis-map the ulna as the bone which is responsible for rotating the lower arm from palm-down to palm-up (pronating and supinating.) Some violinists even make it look as if the ulna moves in rotation; but this illusion is caused by overstretching the tendons and other connective tissues at the elbow. The ulna itself cannot budge in a rotational movement inside its notch because the humerus does not allow it. Tendonitis, or "tennis elbow," is the diagnosis given when a violinist injures the tendons at the elbow by chronically attempting to rotate the ulna in the pronating and supinating movements from the elbow. Only one step away is the consequent mis-mapping that causes carpal tunnel pain in the wrist (covered in detail below).

Function of Rotation at Arm Joint 3
Exploring the Stationary Ulna and Rotating Radius

1. Walk the fingers of your left hand up the radius of your right arm to familiarize yourself with the shape of the bone.

Figure 59. The radius crosses over the stationary ulna.

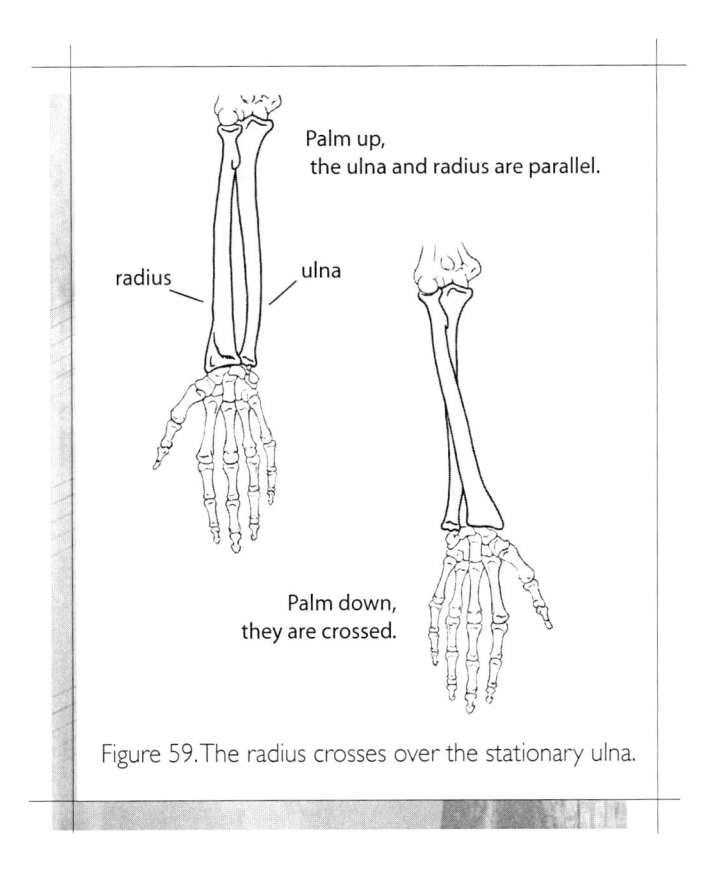

2. You will find it is much easier to palpate the radius at the wrist end because there is far less muscle tissue here than near the elbow end. However, with deep palpation it is possible to follow it right up to the elbow joint.
3. Now make three marks on your arm up the length of the radius with a washable pen or small stickers.
    a. Make the first mark at the end of the radius closest to the wrist.
    b. The second mark goes halfway up the bone.
    c. Put the third mark right at the top of the bone, just under the crease on the radius side of the elbow joint.
4. Next, turn your hand palm-down while watching how the marks move.
5. Notice that the mark nearest the wrist describes a trajectory of 180 degrees while the second mark only moves a quarter turn—about 90 degrees.
6. Watch the mark closest to the elbow joint carefully.
7. Notice that it does not move through space at all; the radial bone under this mark only swivels on its fulcrum with the humerus.
8. Repeat the pronating and supinating motions while holding the end of the ulna (the "elbow" bump) in the fingertips of the other hand.
9. Notice that the ulna is completely stationary—it only acts as an axis over which the radius rotates.

Unhealthy Rotation

The purpose of this exploration is to contrast unhealthy and healthy rotation at the elbow joint.
1. Place your hand and forearm palm-up on a piece of paper.
2. With a pen placed snug up against first the ulna and then the radius, draw a line on each side of the arm the full length of the forearm.
3. The following rotating movement is the unhealthy version, mimicking that of a mis-mapped person.
4. Watch the two bones move down at the wrist end as you attempt to "swap" the location of the two bones on your piece of paper.

a. To do this, turn your hand palm-down by moving your ulna over to the radius line you drew and your radius to your ulna line.
5. Can you feel the strain this places on the ulna where it meets the humerus on the pinkie side? You have just tried making the two bones crisscross over each other.
6. Now recall that the ulna bone's design does not allow for *any* rotational movement. The only way to move the ulna over to the radius line on your paper is by putting enormous stretch and strain on the tendons, muscles, and other connective tissue at the elbow joint.
7. Notice also the strain on the back of the hand and that the wrist is cocked in such a way that it causes the thumb to line up with the radius as opposed to the healthy neutral position of the pinkie lining up with the ulna (pinkie orientation).

This cocking of the hand is known as *ulnar deviation*. When the hand is chronically used this way due to mis-mapping rotation at the elbow joint it leads to the wrist problems known as *carpal tunnel syndrome*. Healthy rotation at the elbow allows a free motion of the hand swinging from side to side—a perfectly good movement. Violinists, in fact, require this side-to-side freedom in the bow wrist in combination with the up-and-down wrist movements of bowing. It is not moving the hand off to the side that causes problems in and of itself; it is how the hand is rotated palm-down that matters.

If pronation is attempted by trying to move the wrong forearm bone, the hand will always have this cocked appearance and side-to-side wrist movement will never be free because the hand does not begin the movement from a place of neutral. This mis-mapping is fairly easy to spot because the hand is habitually cocked to the side in many of daily activities, such as reaching for a doorknob or taking the steering wheel of a car. When this deviation from neutral becomes chronic, the eight wrist bones which form the arch known as the carpal tunnel are brought into a strained relationship with each other. In addition to impeding freedom of the wrist joint, the jammed wrist bones also put pressure on the median nerve that runs through the tunnel. The pain of carpal tunnel syndrome comes from this impinging of the median nerve.

Healthy Rotation
1. Take the paper used in the exploration of unhealthy rotation given above.
2. Put your forearm palm-up between the lines you drew to either side of your arm.
3. This time, as you turn your hand palm-down, ensure that you leave the ulna exactly where it was on its line.
4. You will find that the radius side of your arm now travels a long distance across the page from where you first drew the radius line.
5. Now draw a third line along the length of the radius once it has crossed over into its new location.

6. Note how far it has traveled from the first radius line.
7. Notice that the back of the hand is free from strain, the wrist is not cocked or jammed in any way, and the pinkie is lined up beautifully with the ulna side of the hand, leaving the thumb to be on the side of the hand by itself rather than lined up with the radius.
8. This is a hand at neutral.
9. Notice that the hand is pronated in this way only by *crossing* one bone over the other rather than a *crisscrossing* of two bones over and under each other.

Violinists need a healthy rotation at the elbow joint in both arms: pronation in the right forearm and supination in the left forearm.

A violinist's bow arm is in a state of continual pronation as long as the bow is on the strings. A healthy pronation is essential for the extra leverage needed to set a string vibrating where there is more resistance to the bow, such as on the thicker strings and on sounding points nearer the bridge. In addition to risking injury both at the elbow and wrist joints, a violinist who tries to pronate by moving the ulna is severely limited in all bowing techniques because of the loss of freedom at the wrist. Brush strokes, *spiccato,* and *sautillé* will be irregular and hard to control because of the stiffness in the wrist. Bow changes will not be smooth, and even getting to the extreme ends of the bow becomes difficult because of limited mobility in the wrist.

The rotation in the left forearm is in the opposite direction from that in bow arm and is called supination. Violinists need some supination in order to comfortably bring the fingertips around far enough to meet the strings, the first finger requiring less supination than the fourth finger. Cocking the hand off to the right is always a sign of an attempt to supinate the forearm by rotating with the ulna. This chronic ulnar deviation prevents the hand from being balanced over the strings and causes the fingers to approach the strings from the side instead of from directly above.

Playing this way requires much more muscular effort, since the mechanical advantage derived from the balanced stacking of finger and wrist bones over the ulna is lost. This loss of support almost always produces a complaint that the pinkie feels weak because it is now way over by itself on the side: the player has lost the strength of the arm that pinkie orientation provides.

When the pinkie finger is lined up with the ulna in neutral, the pinkie feels strong and is in no way the "weakest" finger on the hand, despite it being the shortest.

Players who try to rotate the ulna to supinate the left arm also experience difficulty in comfortably maneuvering up to the highest end of the fingerboard. Jamming the wrist bones caused by this ulnar deviation makes it very difficult to bend the wrist sufficiently to play freely up and over the shoulder of the instrument when in the highest positions.

Chronically jammed wrist bones sometimes lead to the development of ganglion cysts in the wrist. There are numerous tendons, blood vessels, and nerves that run through the carpal tunnel, and when the carpal bones are jammed together, these tendons are overcrowded and vulnerable to injury if excessive movement is required of them. Forming a liquid-filled cyst is the body's way of protecting from injury by preventing excessive movement in an overcrowded area. Remapping rotation movement at the elbow as well as carefully mapping the wrist itself frees the wrist bones so that they do not overcrowd the contents of the carpal tunnel.

Besides the chronically cocked hand, another distinctive sign that often indicates mis-mapped elbow rotation. When the hand becomes chronically tilted, the thumb is restricted in its ability to cross the palm to fulfill its role as the opposable digit. It winds up being pulled into the side of the hand beside the other fingers. In the left hand of a violinist with this mis-mapping, this pulled-in thumb is rigid at all three thumb joints and is pulled back on the violin neck considerably behind where the first finger makes contact on the other side.

In extreme cases of left-hand ulnar deviation, the thumb seems to want to wrap around the neck and sometimes over onto the G-string, as if the crooked hand is searching for a hook from which to hang. By contrast, a hand that is not skewed by mis-mapped elbow rotation displays a truly opposable thumb—the thumb makes contact on the neck across from the first finger and is free to move across from any of the fingers when necessary.

The right-hand thumb's appearance can also be a red flag for chronic ulnar deviation in the bow arm. The alignment of the bow thumb with its radius causes the index finger to make contact with the bow too close to the largest row of knuckles, causing it to wrap around the stick like a hook.

Violinists who suffer from tendonitis, carpal tunnel syndrome, or from ganglion cysts need to remap the functions of the two lower arm bones and re-learn how to rotate the forearm by moving the radius over the stationary ulna in order to regain full freedom in the elbow, wrist, and hand.

Nota bene!

Though less common than ulnar deviation, chronic radial deviation is also possible. This is a cocking of the hand out of neutral toward the thumb side. Occasionally, students who discover their ulnar deviation cause themselves equal misery by over-correcting. In an effort to line the pinkie up with the wrist bones directly beneath, they once again lose neutral position, jamming the wrist bones in the other direction. As can be seen in the figures in this chapter, when the hand is at neutral there is still a slight indentation where the wrist bones nestle between the pinkie hand bone and the ulna.

Arm Joint 4: Wrist

If you suffer from wrist injury or stiffness, make certain you have thoroughly read and absorbed the preceding section detailing elbow rotation mis-mappings. Most serious wrist problems

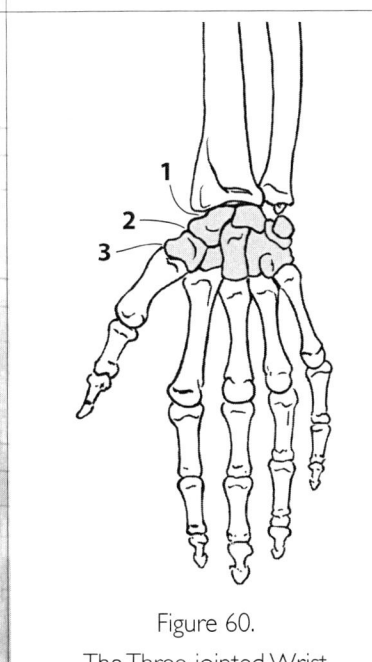

Figure 60.
The Three-jointed Wrist
Enjoy exploring the three-jointed wrist and then return it to an integrated whole arm.

violinists encounter stem from poor rotational movement at the *elbow*. Even when the problem does stem from a mis-mapping of the wrist itself, all previously described restrictions on the instrument caused by limited wrist mobility still apply.

These mis-mappings can originate from different joints, but the end result is the same: the eight little wrist bones are jammed together or moved out of right relationship to each other, restricting movement at the wrist. A player experiencing wrist problems needs to check how she has mapped the structure and function of *both* the elbow and wrist joints to discover the source of poor movement at the wrist.

The eight little carpal bones at the wrist are roughly arranged in two rows and are curved to form an arch—the "carpal tunnel" through which tendons, nerves, and blood vessels run.

As figure 60 illustrates, the wrist is made up of three joints rather than one hinge-like joint. The first joint is between the arm bones and first row of wrist bones; the second between the two rows of wrist bones; and the third between the second row of wrist bones and hand bones.

Locating Both Ends of the Wrist

1. Flex your wrist so that the fingertips are brought as close as possible to the inside of the forearm.
2. With the hand in this extreme flexed position, most people are able to see or at least feel the row of bumps across the back of the hand with the fingers of the other hand. These bumps delineate the ends of the hand bones.
3. In finding the ends of your hand bones you have also located one end of your wrist.
4. Next, walk your palpating fingers down the length of the wrist until you run into the large bump on the pinkie side of your forearm (which is the end of the ulna).
5. Palpate deeply on the hand-side of this bump, and you have found the other end of your wrist.
6. Mark the two ends of the wrist with a washable pen or stickers to guide you as you search for the middle wrist joint between the two rows of wrist bones.
7. Place the side of your palpating hand's index finger exactly midway between the two marks.
8. Now bend your wrist to its extremes.
9. You should be able to see how the movement of bending is shared across all three wrist joints.

10. If you are mis-mapped at the wrist and have only allowed your wrist to bend like a hinge from its joint with the forearm bones, you need to spend time exploring all the movement available to you from the other two wrist joints.

Common Wrist Mis-mappings

The most common way that violinists mis-map the wrist is to map it like a hinge. This dictates that wrist movement is restricted to just one joint rather than distributed across all three joints. If you point to the creases in the skin on the inside of your forearm when asked to point to your wrist, it is a good indication that you have mapped movement as coming only from the joint of the forearm bones with the first row of wrist bones. To correctly map your wrist you need to become very clear about its length—it is not just a crease in the skin.

Both left and right hands will suffer from not having full freedom in the wrist. If you do not know where the third wrist joint is, you also don't know where the beginning of the hand bones are. The hand bones must be free to move from their joints with the wrist bones (see "Structure of the Hand" below). Dexterity is limited in the left hand, and reaching the extreme ends of the bow with the right will be very difficult if the hand bones are not mapped as moving from this joint.

Sometimes a violinist will point to the bumps at the end of the forearm bones when asked to find her wrist. This mis-mapping is reinforced by where most of us wear our "wrist-watches." Look for any part of the wrist movement to come from here and there will be strain and a loss of freedom. Movement can come only at the ends of those two bones where they meet the first row of wrist bones; no bending movement is available along the shafts of the ulna and the radius.

A few violinists have not mapped their wrists at all. One version of this mis-mapping views the hand as a solid palm coming all the way down to butt right into the ends of the non-yielding forearm bones, leading to severe limitations in wrist mobility.

Sometimes the wrist is mapped as having three joints, but not curved in a tunnel-like structure. In order to fulfill the fantasy of a *flat* wrist, a great deal of muscular holding must be done by the same set of muscles designed to move the wrist.

It is not uncommon for violinists to mis-map supination and pronation of the hand at the wrist rather than at the elbow. For a violinist, this can lead to severe and painful tendonitis in the left hand by attempting to bring the left hand into supination to play by cranking it all around at the wrist.

Regardless of which mis-mapping causes wrist immobility, it is nearly impossible for a violinist's mis-mapped left hand to be comfortable playing in the highest registers on the instrument. The wrist must be able to move into a free and easy flexion, the movement distributed across all three wrist joints in order to reach the top register without strain. Often violinists develop ganglion cysts in the left wrist as a result of hours of practicing in the upper register while only allowing the wrist to bend at an imagined hinge, or while trying to bend the wrist while imagining that it is flat. A cyst forms to prevent excessive movement in an area where bones already overcrowd the tendons running through the carpal tunnel. Careful remapping of the wrist into a long, three-jointed, and curved structure with lots of easy movement between all of the eight little wrist bones is sometimes enough to alleviate pressure from the tendons and their sheaths, allowing the cysts to gradually subside.

Structure of the Hand

Mapping the Bones of the Hand

A hand is comprised of nineteen bones: four in each finger and three in the thumb. Figure 61 gives the Latin names for each bone and joint along with a numbering system. *WEV* uses this numbering system to avoid cumbersome Latin terminology.

Finger bones are labeled FB; joints, FJ; thumb bones are labeled TB; and thumb joints, TJ.

Finger joints are numbered from 1 (most proximal, or closest to the center of the body) to 4 (most distal, or farthest from the body's center), just as the arm joints are numbered from most proximal to most distal. For example: FJ1 is the joint where FB1 meets the wrist bones; FJ4 is the joint closest to the fingertips.

Note right at the outset that FB1 comprises what many call the hand or the palm of the hand. These labels (and any labeling system that makes a hand/finger distinction) can mislead some to map the hand as solid—an immovable plate of bone to which the moveable fingers attach at the largest row of knuckles. The skin covering the hand also suggests this, but underlying the skin and connective tissues, the hand's bony structure belies the truth.

Figure 61 shows that each finger extends all the way down to form individual joints with the wrist bones, which means that there is movement available to the fingers from these joints. In order to avoid reinforcing the palm/finger distinction, and because violin playing requires finger movement from these most proximal finger joints, these bones are called FB1 rather than "hand" bones, and their joints with the wrist are labeled FJ1 (with TB1 and TJ1 for the thumb).

Mapping the Location of the Finger Joints

Most have no trouble identifying the location of FJ3 and FJ4 because the palm-side creases in the skin clearly delineate where one bone ends and the next one begins. However, the location of FJ1 and FJ2 are commonly mis-mapped by violinists.

Locating FJ1

1. Look at the back of your hand.
2. Flex your hand downwards as if trying to touch the inside of your forearm with your fingertips.

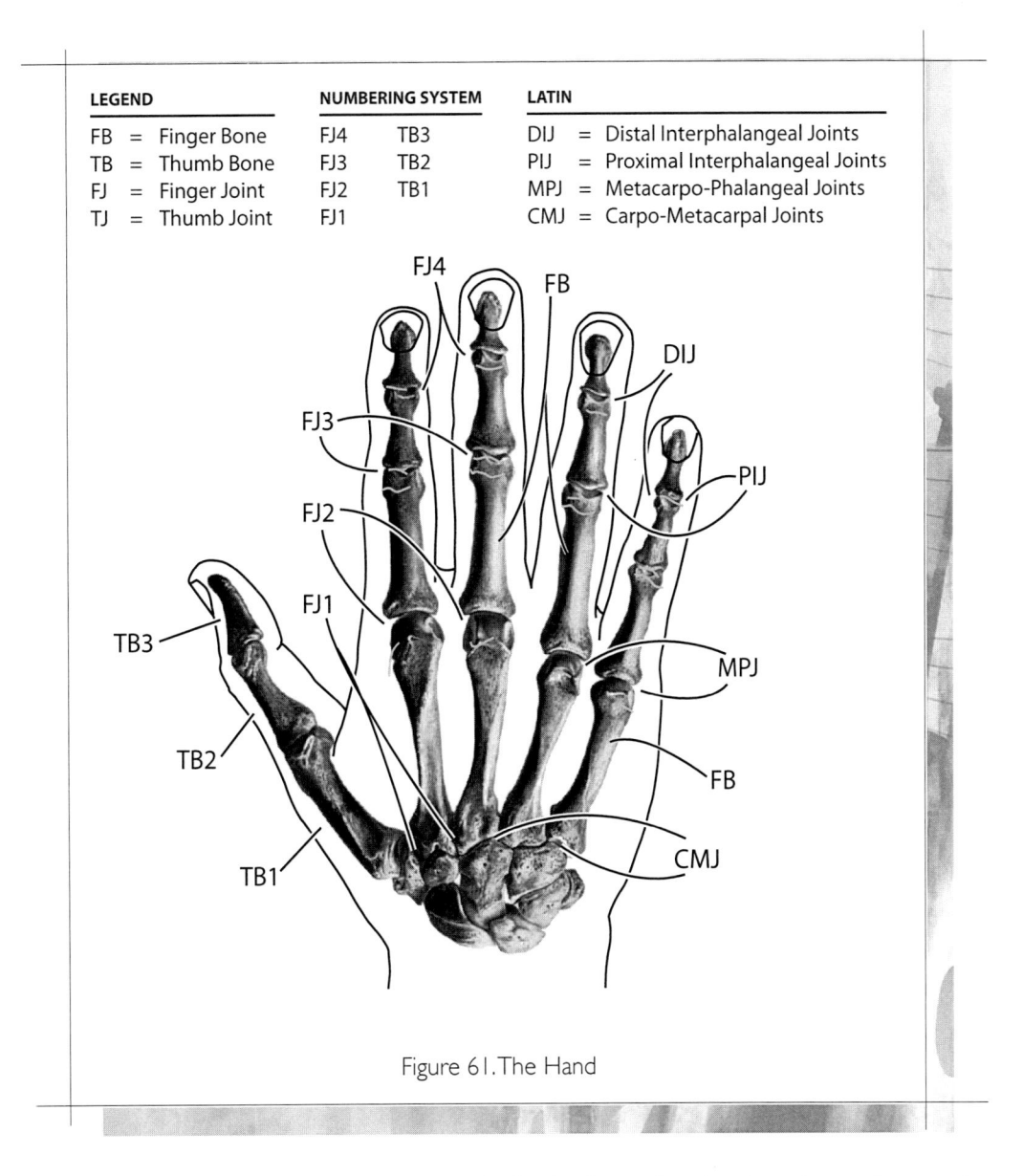

LEGEND		NUMBERING SYSTEM		LATIN		
FB	= Finger Bone	FJ4	TB3	DIJ	=	Distal Interphalangeal Joints
TB	= Thumb Bone	FJ3	TB2	PIJ	=	Proximal Interphalangeal Joints
FJ	= Finger Joint	FJ2	TB1	MPJ	=	Metacarpo-Phalangeal Joints
TJ	= Thumb Joint	FJ1		CMJ	=	Carpo-Metacarpal Joints

Figure 61. The Hand

3. With the skin stretched taut across the back of your hand, it is easier to discern where each FB1 ends and the wrist bones begin.
4. Beginning at the large knuckles, run the index finger of your other hand down the length of each FB1 toward the wrist until you reach the row of bumps running across the back of the hand.
5. These bumps identify the end of each FB1.
6. Next, follow this row of bumps across the width of the hand's back toward the thumb until you feel the bump that identifies the end of TB1.
7. Continue around to the palm without being misled by the location of the wrist creases lower down on the palm side of the hand.
8. Your index finger is now tracing the joint where the wrist bones end and each FB1 begins.

9. Players who map the wrist as ending at the skin creases will be surprised to find that the bottom inch of what they have always called their palm is actually comprised of wrist bones.

In addition to reinforcing the location of FJ1 and the wrist's length, this exploration also clearly establishes that there is nothing immovable about the palm of the hand. Mapping a separation between *fingers* emerging from the hand at the large row of knuckles and a solid, immobile *hand* or palm prevents the movements from FJ1 essential to free violin playing. By palpating each FB1 all the way down to the wrist bones (as we did above) it becomes clear that the palm is made up of finger bones that move at their joints with the wrist bones.

Locating FJ2

1. Locate the crease on your index finger closest to the fingertip.
2. This is the palm-side indicator of FJ4.
3. Explore the movement available at this crease by wiggling the tip of your finger.
4. Move to the next crease and experiment with movement here.
5. Finally, move to the third crease and play with movement at this place.
6. You will discover that movement is physically impossible at this crease.
7. Unlike the upper creases, which do indicate the location of an actual joint, the third crease is deceiving.
8. Follow the third crease around to the back of the hand.
9. It is immediately apparent that the actual joint where the two bones move in relation to one another is at the large row of knuckles—considerably lower down than the third crease.
10. Follow this FJ2 back around to the palm side.
11. You will discover that the crease corresponding to this joint is more than an inch lower into the palm than the third crease.
12. Flex all four fingers simultaneously to a 90-degree angle from FJ2.
13. Notice how movable this top portion of the palm is.

Functions of the Finger Joints in Violin Playing
Left-hand Up-and-Down Movements from FJ1

While most of the movement required to bring the fingers of the left hand to the violin strings happens at FJ2, it is essential for the freedom of the hand that the FB1s are allowed to move up and away from the top row of wrist bones upon which they stack. This cannot happen if the palm is mapped as a solid plate.

Exploring Up-and-Down Movements from the Left-hand FB1

1. Raise your left arm as if you were about to play.
2. Allow the hand to find its neutral balance on the wrist bones below. (Neutral is where the hand and wrist bones are free to jiggle on their perch on the forearm bones when you move the lower arm back and forth.)
3. Place your right-hand fingers on the back of your left hand.
4. "Air finger" a piece you have memorized, monitoring left-hand movement.
5. First, do this with the "solid plate" palm mis-mapping by purposely immobilizing the FB1s in your left hand.
6. Your right-hand fingers will feel holding and lack of movement in the left hand, and the left hand itself will experience fatigue.
7. Drop your left hand and shake it.
8. Next, "air finger" the same passage again, this time watching and feeling for the free vertical movements of FB1 originating from FJ1.
9. Your movement from FJ2 should also feel much freer.
10. It is this movement from FJ1 that prevents strain and limitations in the speed and the stamina of the left hand.

Left-hand Spreading Movements from FJ1

A violinist who maps the palm as immovable rather than as individual finger bones does not have any of the spreading movements that FJ1 makes available. Playing anything requiring large stretches in the left hand, such as fingered octaves or tenths, is very difficult and strained when trying to spread the fingers only from FJ2. The amount of spread that happens from FJ1 might appear to be negligible if you are only watching FB1. However, like a flashlight beam moving several feet across the wall by simply nudging the handle a half-inch, the fingertips travel a much greater distance than do the FB1s themselves.

Exploring Spreading Movements from the Left-hand FJ1

1. Turn the left hand palm down.
2. *Actively* bend all four fingers at a 90-degree angle at FJ2 so that the fingertips point straight down.
3. Put the fingertips of your right hand on top of the large row of knuckles on your left hand.
4. Monitor left-hand movement while trying to spread the left-hand fingers apart.
5. Notice that it is impossible to get any spreading from either FJ1 or FJ2 (see "The Interosseous Muscles of the Hand" below for details).

6. Repeat this exercise, this time, allowing the fingers to bend *passively* at FJ2—curving naturally—as opposed to actively bending at FJ2.
7. You should see the FB1s moving away from each other on the back of your hand.
8. You will also feel the movement with the fingers of your right hand.
9. Notice that, though there is not as much spreading of the fingers as there would be if your fingers were straightened, there is some capability of the finger bones to spread from FJ1 when passively curved that is not possible when actively bending the fingers at FJ2.

Left-hand Forward-and-Back Movements from FJ1

Violinists who hold the left-hand pinkie on the same plane as the other fingers when they play are trying to fulfill the false notion that the palm is a *flat*, solid plate. They will always feel limited in their ability to comfortably reach the fourth finger to the string. There is an additional forward movement of the fourth finger at FJ1 that is nature's way of compensating for the pinkie's limited reach due to its being shorter. If you do not allow the pinkie its forward movement, you will always feel the strain between the FB1s of the third and fourth fingers. You will find yourself frequently massaging the back of the hand between these bones.

The pinkie on the bow hand requires exactly the same freedom to move forward from FJ1 when you are at the frog of the bow and need the pinkie to provide extra counterbalance for the tip of the bow!

Exploring Forward Movement from the Left-hand Fourth-finger FJ1

1. Watch the back of your left hand as you straighten all four fingers as far as you can.
2. Notice how the largest row of knuckles—FJ2—line up with one another on the same plane.
3. Continue to watch the back of your hand while slowly closing your fingers into a firm fist.
4. You will notice immediately that the same row of knuckles now forms a diagonal line.
5. This is due to the forward movement of FB1 of the fourth finger and to a lesser degree, of the third finger.
6. Next, without losing the forward movement of the third and fourth FB1, release the fingertips from your fist at FJ2 as if about to play.
7. The distance the fourth finger FB1 must travel to make a fist is how far forward it must be allowed to travel when it is needed to reach the string.

Bow-hand Forward-and-Back Movements from FJ1

If you have not mapped movement from FJ1 in his bow hand you will always feel restricted as you approach the extreme ends of the bow, as well as in any off-the-string strokes requiring a lot of finger and wrist movement.

Exploring the Bow-hand FJ1

1. Earlier you traced the ends of FB1 of your left hand.
2. Now use your index finger to trace this same row of bumps on the back of your right hand until you have a good sense of where the finger bones end and the wrist bones begin.
3. Next, take your violin and bow and play on open strings.
4. Keep your eyes on FJ1 as you move from the frog to the tip.
5. Notice as you approach the tip and the wrist begins to extend that there is movement across all three wrist joints.
6. By the time you have reached the tip, the FB1s have passively moved back somewhat from their place of neutral with the top row of wrist bones (FJ1).
7. If you have mapped your palm as a solid unit, you may need to repeat this exercise many times before you begin feeling the free movement of FB1 in relation to the wrist bones.
8. Now approach the frog with your sounding point quite close to the fingerboard so that your bow hand is in its most suspended state.
9. Notice that the FB1s move passively again, but in the reverse direction in order to allow flexion at the wrist.
10. Movement happens at all three joints of the wrist.
11. In the hand's most suspended state, there is a slight passive forward movement of the FB1s from the FJ1 row of bumps.

Bow-hand Movements from TJ1

1. TB1 must be mapped as free to move in the same way as the FB1s in the bow hand.
2. The pedagogy which encourages an extremely bent TJ3 (tip joint) for the bow to "sit on like a shelf" contributes to the problem of this joint being left out of players' maps altogether.
3. When TB3 is extremely bent (some players bend it at nearly a right angle to TB2), both TJ2 and TJ1 are locked into immobility.
4. The other obvious signposts of this mis-mapping are an overdeveloped thumb muscle (the thenar muscle) and also an overdeveloped, bulbous TJ2.
5. When the thumb is mapped as one long, long digit all the way down to the wrist bones, it is free to passively bend and straighten at all three of its joints as the wrist actively flexes and extends.

Exploring Bow-hand Movements from TJ1 for a Freer Off-the-String Stroke

1. Find the natural curve of your hands with your hands at your sides.
2. Raise your right forearm so that it is parallel to the floor and allow your hand to dangle at the wrist, then raise your right arm as if you are about to start bowing.
   a. Your thumb should be at neutral, opposite your index finger rather than beside it.

b. You should be able to both see and feel how long your thumb is—that it does not end until it reaches its joint with the wrist bones.
3. Next, support the weight of the bow with your other hand.
4. Place the bow in between your fingers and thumb.
    a. Make sure that you do not lose the sense of the long thumb, right from its tip all the way down to its joint with the wrist, especially as you swing your thumb from neutral opposite the index finger over to its place opposite the middle two fingers of your bow hand. This swinging should happen almost entirely from TJ1.
5. Notice that when supporting the bow in this most neutral way your thumb does not contact the stick next to the nail. Instead, it is a bit more on the pad of the thumb rather than so close to the nail of the thumb.
6. You will feel that each of the three thumb joints is equally flexible, while at the same time equally sharing the work of supporting the bow.
7. If you have mapped the thumb as a digit with two instead of three joints, you probably have extremely over-developed muscles surrounding the thumb.
    a. This is because it is these muscles that are working to hold TB1 still as you try to move the rest of the thumb.
8. This new, more neutral way of supporting the bow should feel that it requires much less muscular work, especially in the thenar muscle and between TB1 and FB1—it will feel softer in both places.
9. With a cloth under the bow and the bow resting on your left collarbone, begin a slow *colle* stroke.
    a. An active wrist flexion for the down-bow stroke causes a passive extension of the fingers.
    b. This is all you need for this stroke as long as all other joints of the arm are free to help (see "Bow-hand Co-contraction" below).
    c. Keep watching your thumb so that it does not begin to take on the appearance of a shelf for the bow.
10. Maintain kinesthetic awareness of the softness of the muscles on either side of TB1.
11. Notice how much more movement there is in the hand and wrist to make down and up bow strokes, and therefore how much longer the stroke is as compared to playing *colle* with only a two-jointed thumb.
12. If you have always felt that your off-the-string strokes are slightly out of control, or that the bow never seems to move parallel enough with the bridge in these strokes, spend some time remapping your bow thumb into a long, three-jointed digit that supports the bow in a natural curve. This leads to full freedom of movement from TJ1.

Functions at FJ2, FJ3, and FJ4

The muscular workings of the fingers which provide the human hand with both its strength and its marvelous dexterity are necessarily complex. However, for our purposes, it suffices to say that though there are some muscles in the hand itself, the muscles that do most of the work of bending and straightening the fingers from FJ2, FJ3, and FJ4 are located in the forearm.

There are two groups of forearm muscles: the flexors, located on the underside of the forearm, *bend* the fingers when contracted; contract the extensor group of muscles, located on the top of the forearm, and the fingers *straighten*. Because the flexors and extensors move the fingers in opposite directions, they are called opposing muscles. As long as one group of opposing muscles releases out of contraction as the other group contracts, movement is free. However, when the flexors and extensors are mapped as needing to work simultaneously, there is strain and fatigue in the hand and the fingers are limited in how quickly they can move. This simultaneous contraction of opposing muscles is called *co-contraction*.

Left-hand Co-contraction

A few pieces of pedagogical advice can cause students to co-contract by bringing their fingers to the string *curled* at FJ3 and FJ4 rather than in their natural curved position.

If the left hand contacts the neck of the violin too close to FJ3 on the first finger, the fingers are forced to move to the string by bending FJ3 and FJ4 into an active *curl* since FJ2 has dropped too far below the level of the string to be an effective fulcrum.

Sometimes teachers ask students to play "right on the tips of the fingers," which requires the last two finger joints to actively *curl*. The fingertip always crosses the string through its center instead of the left-of-center point of contact that fingers have when *curved naturally*.[11]

Other times students curl the last two finger joints because they have been told to line the whites of the nails up with each other so that they all run parallel to the next string instead of allowing the fingernails to face the player. Sometimes this is taught to young students by drawing a happy face on the muscular side of the fourth-finger FB1 and saying that the happy face should always be looking at the student's face. Regardless of the cause, the result is the same: FJ3 and FJ4 have to actively flex or curl in order to reach the string, and having them this bent while trying to lift them off the string with the extensor muscles causes co-contraction and prevents easy movement.

Exploring Left-hand Co-contraction

1. Hang your left arm at your side.
2. Notice that the left-hand fingers have a slight natural curve.
    a. This is neutral for the hand when it hangs down.
3. Next, bring your left arm up as if you were about to play.

4. Take note of how the FB2s settle even further into their natural, passive curve when gravity acts on them as compared to when your hand hangs at your side.
    a. This is neutral for the hand when it is perched on top of an upright forearm.
    b. There is no muscular work from the flexors or extensors actively bending or straightening the fingers.
4. Quickly move the fingers up and down from FJ2.
5. Feel how free the movement is when FJ3 and FJ4 begin in neutral.
6. Bend FJ3 and FJ4 into a curl.
7. Now try to make the same quick up-and-down movements from FJ2.
8. Can you feel how much strain is placed on the fingers when you move them like this?
    a. When FJ3 and FJ4 are curled, it takes more effort to move them and they move much more slowly than when allowed to begin from their naturally curved neutral.
    b. This is because the flexors actively bending the FJ3s and FJ4s are working in direct opposition to the extensors, which are lifting the fingers from FJ2—a situation of co-contraction.
9. Take up your instrument and play a scale with vibrato while you curl at FJ3 and FJ4.
10. Notice that in addition to the extra effort it takes to move the fingers to and from the string, the FJ4s are not free to vibrate when they are actively curled.

Bow-hand Co-contraction

A similar mis-mapping can happen in the bow hand. When teaching students about the finger and wrist movements needed to play any off-the-string stroke in the lower half, a distinction is frequently made between active and passive fingers. The *colle* stroke at the frog, a forerunner to the faster strokes like *spiccato* and *sautillé,* is sometimes taught as requiring an active straightening of the fingers using the extensor muscles for the down-bow stroke. This, unfortunately, sets up a situation of co-contraction because the extensor muscles actively engage the fingers while the flexors actively engage the wrist and thumb. The only way to send the bow downward with the fingers when the wrist is flexing (bending toward the floor) without co-contraction is to allow the fingers to extend passively. This occurs naturally without active work from the extensor muscles when the wrist is flexed because the extensor tendons on the back of the hand (that attach to the fingers) are pulled taut.

Comparing Active and Passive Bow-hand Finger Movements

1. Actively flex your bow arm wrist toward the floor while trying to actively straighten your fingers.
2. Notice the feeling of strain as you do this.
3. This is the feeling of co-contraction.

4. Compare this with the passive straightening of the fingers.
5. Place your right forearm in an upright position, palm facing ahead, and your bow hand in its natural curve perched on top of the wrist bones.
6. Next, bend your wrist forward.
7. Notice that the natural tendency of the fingers is to straighten.
   a. This happens because the tendons which run from the extensor muscles in the back of the forearm down to the fingers are passively pulled taut.
   b. The only muscles actively working are the wrist flexors on the underside of the arm.
8. Now try the opposite movement by extending the wrist toward the back of the arm as far as you comfortably can.
9. Notice that the fingers have a natural tendency to bend or flex.
   a. This is because the active work of the wrist extensors passively pulls taut the flexor tendons of the fingers located on the inside of the forearm and in the palm.
10. When we allow the fingers to straighten and bend in this way, the forearm flexor and extensor muscles that operate the fingers are never in active contraction; they are simply passively pulled taut by the work of wrist flexion and extension, and so there is not a situation of co-contraction.
11. In addition to correctly mapping the thumb as three-jointed, this is one of the most important re-mappings for a violinist who is not happy with the consistency of her *spiccato* or other off-the-string strokes.

Interosseous Muscles of the Hand

The interosseous ("between the bones") muscles form one of the few finger-moving muscle groups found in the hand itself, and have two main functions: the *bending* of the fingers at FJ2 when FJ3 and FJ4 are not being bent; and the *spreading* from side to side of the fingers from FJ2. Note, however, that the interosseous muscles *cannot perform both the bending and the spreading movements from FJ2 at the same time.*

Recall that when the fingers actively bend at 90 degrees from FJ2, there is no spreading movement available to the fingers. We also saw that when the fingers bend passively at FJ2 there is a small amount of spreading afforded the fingers from FJ1. Now try this:

1. Spread your left-hand fingers while extending them straight out from FJ2.
2. Contrast how much spreading you achieve this way with how little movement is available when you try to spread them while *actively or passively* bending at FJ2.

This is important for any violinist who wants to increase the span of his left hand by doing stretching exercises. Any effort to stretch the fingers apart from FJ2 without first allowing these joints to come out of active flexion risks strain and injury to the left hand.

When the first finger, in particular, is required to make an extension back in tasks such as playing fingered octaves, tenths, or simply reaching a note lower than the neutral frame of the hand allows, it must first come *all the way* out of flexion (it must straighten) at FJ2 and then make its spreading movement away from the other fingers (reaching back). The other fingers can remain naturally curved at FJ2 and still benefit from the smaller amount of spread they are afforded from FJ1.

Ligaments Connecting the Fingers

In addition to mapping the muscles that actively control and co-ordinate finger movement, it is also necessary to map the elastic ligaments which connect one finger to the next and provide a springy rebound of the fingers as they depress and release a string.

At the base of the fingers at FJ1, the FB1s have bands of ligaments connecting them on the back side of the hand *(dorsal metacarpal ligaments)* and on the palm side of the hand *(palmar metacarpal ligaments.)* The joint capsules at FJ2 (where the FB1s connect to the FB2s) also connect to one another by bands of ligaments called the *deep transverse metacarpal ligaments.*

Map all three of these sets of ligaments as what they really are—bands of elastic—and you will experience your left hand as free and supple, and movement as facile—a left hand that can move like lightning without fatiguing because you now have an extra element of stretchy rebound that aids the muscles in moving your fingers: one finger springing back up from the string to release tension off the bands that can initiate the rebound impulse that sends another finger down to the string, sling-shot style.

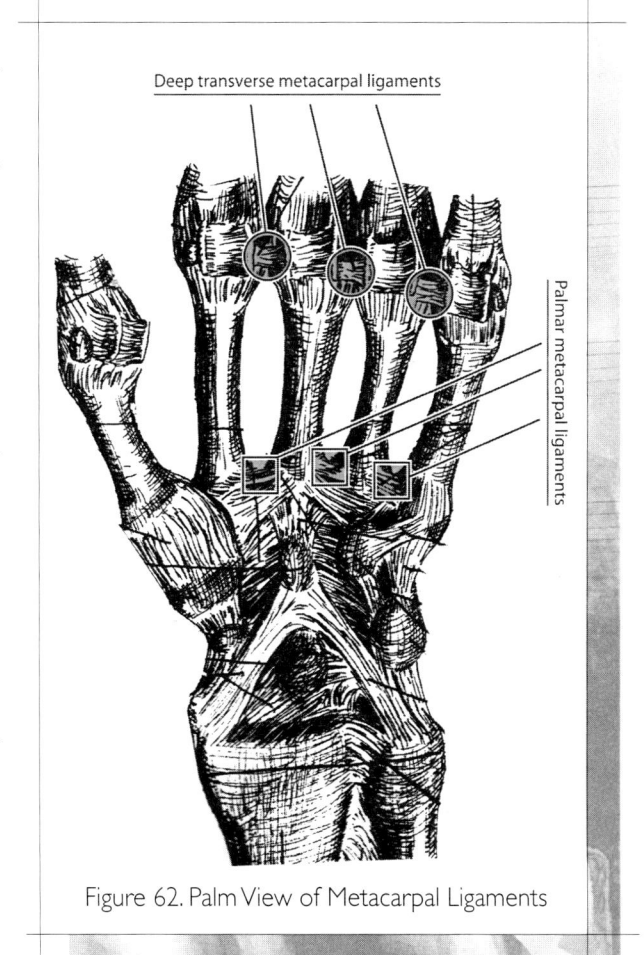

Figure 62. Palm View of Metacarpal Ligaments

Searching for Elastic Rebound: Rubber Mitt Exploration

1. Imagine wearing a snugly-fitted rubber mitt over your left hand—like a surgical glove, but without the fingers individuated.
2. With your fingers in their natural curve, slowly spread them apart as if your pinkie is depressing the A string in first position. Your first finger is off the string, but coming down in order to play a B.
3. Using your kinesthetic imagination, sense how the stretched rubber mitt encasing the hand creates an elastic pull between the first finger and pinkie.
4. When the stretch is released, the rubber mitt helps the pinkie rebound up while propelling the first finger down toward the string.
5. This sling-shot-like rebound is naturally at our disposal to support the muscular work of the fingers for fast and easy playing *as long as the elastic ligaments between the finger bones at both FJ1 and FJ2 are correctly mapped.*
6. The notion of a rubber mitt reinforces the mapping of the hand as an *integrated unit*, with the fingers attached to and affecting one another instead of individual, isolated fingers sprouting up from the top of the palm.
7. Just as it is possible to mis-map the arms as being in isolation, fingers can be mis-mapped in isolation as well. But we need integration rather than isolation in order to simultaneously find the greatest strength, speed, and freedom in our left hands.

Students of Pablo Casals, the great twentieth-century cellist, report that in his teaching he placed great emphasis on not only the elastic nature of the hand but also on how the angle of the hand in its approach to the fingerboard affects the amount of elasticity available. He taught that pronating the left forearm a small bit so that the fingers point slightly more toward the bridge provides much more freedom to stretch the hand.

Players experiencing left-hand elasticity for the first time might well wonder why they have not been taught this before. In many cases, this information is not taught because there are so many myths and mis-mappings that get in the way of experiencing the truth. For example, a person with her palm mapped as a solid unit or her fingers as beginning at the large row of knuckles never fully avails herself of the help that the stretchy, elastic ligaments between the finger bones can provide in moving them quickly and easily.

Casals' teaching on this matter really entails two different mapping issues.

Spreading apart the Finger Bones

Spreading of the fingers, which is necessary to put stretch on the elastic ligaments, is only permitted at FJ2 when the fingers are not already being *excessively actively bent* at FJ2—in other words, it is only permitted when the fingers are approaching the string in their *natural curve*.

At the risk of extrapolating too much from others' accounts of Casals' teaching, I believe that when he advocated the slight turning of the forearm so that the fingers point more toward the bridge, he knew that this releases the left hand into its natural curve, therefore enabling the fingers to spread apart better. This pointing the fingers toward the bridge translates into movement terminology as *less supination* of the forearm (radius) and applies equally well to violin playing.

The more the left forearm is supinated (so that the side of the pinkie faces the player), the more the left-hand fingers must curl (active bending) at FJ2, FJ3, and FJ4 to depress a string. In addition to the problems that co-contraction causes by doing this (discussed above), when the fingers are forced to primarily *actively bend* to the string from FJ2 (losing their *natural, passive curve*), they can no longer *spread* apart from FJ1 or FJ2 and the third and fourth fingers cannot *move forward* from FJ1.

Actively bending the fingers at FJ2 is in part caused by the contracting of the interosseous muscles, but when these muscles are already contracted they are not free to *spread* the fingers from FJ2. When the forearm is released from its extreme supination so that the fingernails can face the violinist more or point toward the bridge, the left-hand fingers *passively bend* at FJ2 to reach the string. This frees the interosseous muscles to do the work of *spreading* the fingers, especially when the first finger completely straightens at FJ2 to reach back. It also frees the muscles responsible for moving the fourth FB1 *forward*. This provides the largest possible span between the left-hand finger bones, which translates into the greatest amount of *stretch* on the inter-finger ligaments.

Stretching the Elastic Ligaments

I believe that Casals instinctively knew that if the left hand is free to *spread* more there is an *elastic rebound* that provides more facility in moving the fingers to and from the string. Put in mapping terms: once the greatest *spread* between finger bones is achieved by bending them to the string primarily *passively* at FJ2, there is more *stretch* on the ligaments. Once there is more stretch on the bands of ligaments, there is more lovely, elastic rebound for the fingers as they travel both to and from the string. Movement of the fingers becomes much faster and more facile. This is only possible, however, *if the elasticity of the hand is accurately mapped.*

It is worth repeating here that the body map does not have to be conscious to be accurate. In fact, most of the world's great players have the *spreading* and the *stretchy elasticity* of the hand very accurately mapped, but for many of them it is completely unconscious. They either never lost their accurate map from childhood or they were as well instructed as Casals' students.

If you have mis-mapped your palm as solid and therefore *not spreadable,* you need to remap in order to find the movement and springiness between the FB1s. Keep figure 61 in sight at all times, especially when you are practicing.

Exploring How to Stretch the Hand

1. Hold your left hand beside figure 61 and study both until you have no confusion about the truth of where your own finger bones end down by the wrist bones.
2. Massage and palpate the left-hand FB1s with your right hand, gently swinging the fourth and third finger FB1s forward and back.
3. Massage between each FB1 down to the FJ1s to experience the distance between the bones.
4. Watch great players whose left hands you admire.
5. Two of the freest and springiest left hands I have ever seen belong to Jascha Heifetz and Weigang Li (the first violinist of the Shanghai String Quartet).
6. To observe some up-close and slow-motion footage of Heifetz' left hand, view his performance of Wieniawski's *Scherzo-Tarantella*.[12] Fortunately Weigang Li is still performing, so if you ever have the chance to hear the marvelous Shanghai String Quartet play in concert, get front row seats so you can also enjoy watching Li's left hand.
    a. You will immediately see its natural curve the interconnected elastic rebound of his fingers to and from the string, and the strength and resilience this provides him.
    b. If you have mapped your palm as solid, you will probably be amazed by the speed and clarity Li's left hand is capable of while appearing to be doing no work at all!
7. As violinists we can only look at the *palm* of the left hand as we play, so it is advantageous to watch the back of your hand in a mirror or to record video[13] as you do some slow, large-interval practice.
8. Watch how the FB1s spread apart as you finger an octave, then a ninth, and finally a tenth on the fingerboard.
9. Sometimes it is even more helpful initially to go to a piano and watch the back of your hand as you slowly move the finger bones from the hand's natural curve into the spread of an octave. This also allows you to more easily feel the spreading with the right hand.
10. The slow, patient work necessary to achieve a remapping like this may seem daunting, but you will reap the rewards for the rest of your life once it is done!

Developing Awareness Along the Pinkie Side of the Arm

To experience optimal freedom and strength for the arms, we need to develop our kinesthetic awareness of the pinkie side of the arm.

Thumb- or Pinkie-oriented?

1. Run the fingers of your left hand slowly up the thumb side of your right arm.
2. Start at the thumb, move up the radius, over the bicep, and along the collarbone until you reach the sternoclavicular joint (arm joint 1).

3. When there is more awareness of this side of the arm and movement is initiated from this side, the arms feel heavy and stiff.
4. This is called "thumb orientation."
5. Now try the opposite. Extend your right arm straight up in the air so that your fingertips point to the ceiling.
6. Slowly palpate with the fingers of your left hand straight down the extended arm, beginning on the side of the pinkie, across the wrist, down the ulna and the humerus on the triceps side, through the back rim of the armpit, and ending at the tip of the shoulder blade.
7. When there is an awareness and an engagement of this side of the arm and movement is initiated from this side, the arms feel light and free because muscles from deep in the back are engaged.
8. This is called pinkie orientation.

All babies gripping their mother's finger and all of our primate cousins who hang from trees exhibit pinkie orientation in their arms. Why then, do so many of us become thumb-oriented? Place one hand in your lap and notice what side of the arm presents itself as you look down at it. You will see the thumb, the radius and the bicep. If you glance in a mirror you will see the collarbone half of your collarbone/shoulder blade unit. Already this side of your arm has more prominence in your awareness because you view it more frequently than the pinkie side of the arm.

Those who suffer from the good posture disease are prone to thumb orientation. When the shoulder blades are pulled back and down in the military fashion, the humerus rotates backward in its socket with the shoulder blade, causing the arms to hang at the side so that the palm of the hand faces the leg and the thumb faces toward the front. Those with thumb orientation believe that this is neutral position for the arms at rest rather than true neutral, which sees the thumb facing the leg and the palms facing *backward*. (If you doubt this, study the arms of the next toddler you see on the street!)

The good posture disease causes the thumb side of the arm to become more prominent because it is rotated into plain view with the thumb facing to the front. But conversely it obscures awareness of the pinkie side of the arm by tucking it away, close in to the side of the body. This tucking-in impedes awareness of the pinkie side of the arm by concealing the connection between the humerus and the shoulder blade in the armpit, preventing this side of the arm from being ready to engage in initiating movement.

Chronic backward rotation of the humerus caused by the good posture disease leads in turn to another mis-mapping which contributes to thumb orientation in the lower arm. Tucking the humerus into the side of the body draws the ulnar-humeral joint (elbow joint) too close into the side of the body. This produces a feeling of being crowded by the arms. Attempts to pronate the lower arm to turn the hand palm-down (which involves the hand moving closer *again* to the body) from this position usually result in sweeping the wrist end of the *ulna* out and away from the body in order to prevent the pronating movement from making things feel even more crowded.

But the *ulna* is not designed to make a rotating movement. Rotating the hand palm-up and palm-down is solely the job of the other lower arm bone—the *radius* (see "Unhealthy Rotation" under "Arm Joint 3: Elbow" above for a detailed description of this mis-mapping). Moving the ulna in any kind of rotation can only be done by stretching and straining the soft tissues around both ends of the ulna. In addition to causing tendonitis in the elbow, this strain in the soft tissue also pulls the hand off to one side so that the thumb lines up with the radius, causing the pinkie to lose its alignment with the ulna. When this happens we lose pinkie orientation and are forced to initiate movement from the thumb side.

Three Examples of Pinkie Orientation in Action
Example 1: Breaking a Board with the Side of the Hand

We have all seen karate black belts demonstrate this. It is always done with the pinkie side of the hand and the striking motion is always initiated from the pinkie side of the arm. As long as the hand is not tilted toward the ulna side, the pinkie side of the hand has a flat surface with which to strike—unlike the thumb side. There is also plenty of padding on this side which the thumb side does not offer.

Example 2: Hanging by One Arm

Most have experienced hanging by one arm, either in the gym or on monkey bars on the playground. We naturally become pinkie oriented when we hang, because hanging encourages a release of the good posture disease muscles which, when contracted, hold the shoulder blade back and down and rotate the humerus backward. If we do not release those muscles, we quickly tire and lose our grip.

Example 3: Babies Crawling

When a baby crawls, it is clear to the observant eye that the weight of the upper torso travelling down through the arms is primarily borne by the pinkie side of the arm, which only makes sense according to the arm's design. The ulna is thicker and stronger than the radius. It also forms a secure and supportive, deeply-notched joint with the humerus in contrast to the swivel joint that the radius forms with the humerus. Try crawling like babies do with pinkie orientation, then contrast this by crawling with thumb orientation. As soon as the pinkie orientation is lost, by either pulling the shoulder blades back or from twisting the ulna to rotate the forearm, you will feel that the arms are weaker and you will feel strain in the wrists.

Thumb- Versus Pinkie-orientation Movement Experiments
Experiment 1: Initiating Movement from the Thumb Versus the Pinkie

1. Stand with your arms hanging at your sides.
2. Run your left hand up the thumb side of your right arm from the thumb, over the radius, bicep, and collarbone.
    a. This orients you to this side of the arm.
3. Next, move your thumb upward so that it initiates the movement of the whole arm up toward the ceiling.
4. Lead with the thumb and let the arm follow until your arm is above your head.
5. Hold your arm above your head a few moments to absorb the sensation, then return it to your side.
6. Next, since you cannot see the pinkie side of the arm, heighten your awareness of it by raising your arm and running the other hand down it from pinkie, over ulna and triceps, and through the back rim of the armpit to the tip of the shoulder blade.
7. Begin again with your arms at your side.
8. Raise your arm above your head, leading the movement from your pinkie.
9. Can you feel how much lighter the arm is when it is pinkie oriented?
10. Repeat this experiment, alternating between initiating movement with the thumb and the pinkie until you are clear on the difference.

Experiment 2: Clumsy Versus Graceful Dancer Arms

Part 1

1. Face a mirror. Raise both arms out to the sides, a la ballet-dancer style, palms facing forward, leading with the thumb and radius.
2. Hold your arms parallel to the floor for a few moments.
3. Feel how the thumb, radius, and the whole edge of the arm behave as a beam or rod from which the width of the arm hangs down in the same way that a curtain hangs from a rod.
4. Can you feel the heavy drag on the top edge of the arm?
5. How awkward do your arms feel when you try to initiate movement?
6. Can you see in the mirror that your arms look clumsy?

Part 2

1. Again face a mirror. Raise both arms out to the sides, palms facing forward, but this time, initiate the movement with the pinkie so that you feel the pinkie side of the arm engaging all the way down to the tip of the shoulder blade and can sense support for the arms from the bottom edge rather than the top edge of the arm.

2. Can you feel how much easier the arms are to take into movement?
3. Can you see how graceful they appear in the mirror?
4. Do you feel the arms are light now because there is buoyant support coming from underneath?
    a. There are more than ten different arm-moving muscles that originate deep in the back as compared to a single arm-moving muscle group that originates on the front of the torso.

Thumb Versus Pinkie Orientation in Playing the Violin
1. Let your arms hang at your sides.
2. Check to see if your palms face your legs or are facing backwards.
3. If they face your legs, you know you still have some upper torso tension (the good posture disease) rotating your humerus away from neutral because at neutral, your palms face backwards.
4. Let your arms hang at your sides with the palms facing your legs.
5. Leading with the thumbs, pick up your instrument and play open strings with full bows.
7. Take note of the tone and sensations.
8. Does this feel easy or restricted? light or heavy?
9. Return your arms to your sides.
10. This time allow the upper torso tension to release so that your arms are in neutral with the palms facing backwards or get as close as you comfortably can at this time. (To release upper torso tension, repeat the lateral neutral explorations under "Place of Balance 2: The Whole Arm" in chapter 3.)
11. Notice that you can now see the pinkie side of your arm.
12. Wiggle your pinkies to heighten awareness of this side.
13. Now lead with your little fingers as you move to pick up your violin.
14. As before, play open strings with full bows.
15. Compare how this sounds and feels to playing with a thumb orientation.
    a. Can you hear an added depth of tone?
    b. Do both arms feel lighter?
    c. Does the violin itself actually feel lighter?
    d. Can you feel the power of the down-bow stroke?
    e. Doesn't it feel much easier to get to the frog because you are no longer crowding yourself with your own arms?
16. Repeat these experiments until you can sense a clear difference between thumb- and pinkie-oriented arm movement.

When you regain a pinkie orientation in the arms you will experience them as being stronger and more unified. This strength will not only be apparent in your sound, but also will aid you in claiming all of your space as you play. It will seem to an observer that you have expanded into your rightful amount of space in the rehearsal room or on stage rather than being squeezed into a smaller person than you actually are Orienting your arms in this expansive and ready-to-move fashion exudes a strength that provides the resilience necessary to not just withstand but to revel in the pressures of a performer's life.

1. Can you see that the arm's design makes pinkie orientation more logical than thumb orientation?
2. Can you see how a hand at neutral with the support of the strong ulna behind it greatly reduces the chance of a wrist injury like carpal tunnel syndrome?
3. Is it now obvious that the thrust of a down bow, like an arm striking to break a board, has much more momentum when the humerus is not tucked into the side of the body?
4. Does it make sense that arm movement must include the shoulder blade in order to support the violin for any length of time without experiencing fatigue in the arm?

These conclusions may not yet be self-evident, but they will begin to make more sense as you continue in your remapping work.

Core of the Arms

In the same way that it is possible to mis-map the back as the body's source of support instead of allowing the central core to do this work, it is also possible to mis-map the arms as back-oriented.

When a person who is back-oriented lies on the floor, even though his back muscles are not trying to hold him in an upright position they still work unnecessarily because he lacks the sense of the central organization through the body. In order to fully release the superficial layer of back muscles so that the full support of the floor can be experienced by the torso, the back-oriented person must map the core as the center around which the rest of the body is evenly distributed instead of organizing the body back to front—as something which is propped up at the back and from which everything in front of it hangs.

Organizing the torso from back to front means that the shoulder blades are involved as part of the overworked back. This loss of the sense of centrality is communicated down throughout the rest of the arm. The part of the upper arm touching the floor takes on a sense that it has a back *side*. Reflecting that sense, the muscle work will be unevenly distributed throughout the arm, causing the arm structure to be unbalanced.

1. Lie on the floor with legs bent at the knees, feet flat on the floor, arms slightly bent at the elbows, and palms down.
2. Kinesthetically locate the core of the torso and legs by mentally "connecting the dots" between your six places of balance.

3. In the same way as you just reorganized your body around a central core, now mentally allow the humerus bone to be the central organizing factor for your upper arms.
4. The floor is not the only firm surface providing support for the upper arm—you now have available the full length of the strong bony surface area of the humerus to which the flesh of the arm is attached and around which it can cluster.
5. As you sense the centrality of the humeral bone, you will probably feel a lively shifting of the soft tissues around it and perhaps even a widening between the shoulder blades.
6. It is very likely that your arms will feel lighter once you have organized them around the core.

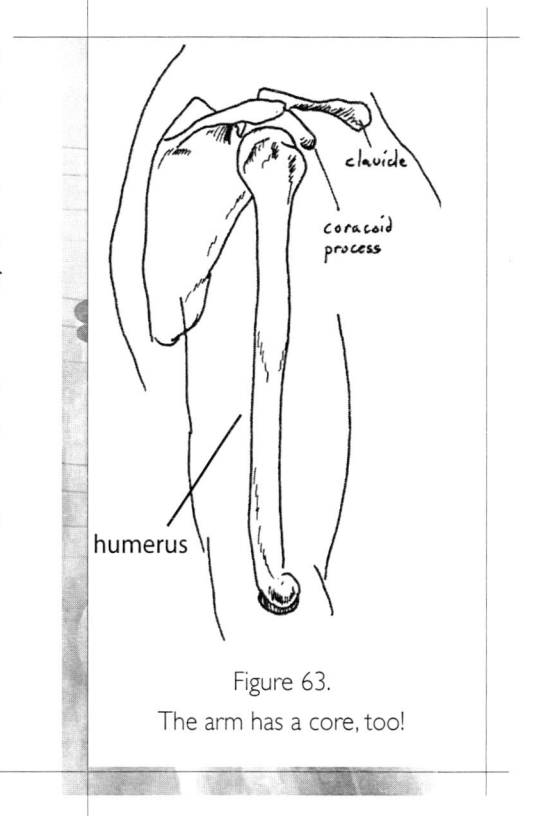

Sources of Arm Support
1. Direct Support in the Sense of "Helping to Hold Up"

Spine, Pelvis, and Legs

When the body is organized around its core, the head and upper torso, including the arm structure, receives support from the spine and pelvis if sitting, and the spine, pelvis, and legs if standing. The upper structures *deliver their weight* downward through the core, and conversely, the lower structures provide support (*bear the weight*) of those directly above. This primary source of support for the arms is lost as soon as unnecessary muscle tension interferes with the balance of the bony structure.

Sternum and Surrounding Connective Tissue

A small portion of the weight of the arms is directly supported by the sternum itself and the connective tissue attaching one collarbone to the other as well as to the ribs. These sources of support are lost however, if the shape of the sternoclavicular joint or the connective tissue is distorted by loss of balance on the bony structure.

Suspension

The suspension system (described in detail in chapter 4) plays an enormous role in supporting the arms from above by way of the interplay of the upper torso's connective tissues; namely the ligaments, tendons, and the great sheet of fascia that is part of the scalp. The suspension system is not available as a source of support if the bony structure is not in a state of balance, since the success of the suspension depends entirely on the arms being suspended in neutral *around the core from a balanced head*. The arms cannot be suspended in balance from the head directly above it if the head itself is imbalanced.

Figure 63.
The arm has a core, too!

2. Indirect Support in the Sense of "Aiding" or "Facilitating" Involuntary Muscle Support

The superficial layer of torso muscles (mostly on the back) are the voluntary muscles designed to move the arms. The two innermost layers of torso muscles (back, front, and sides) are the involuntary support muscles of the torso. When properly engaged, they *facilitate* arm movement by fully freeing the superficial layer of back muscles to move the arms. However, the engagement of these involuntary support muscles cannot be consciously or directly accessed and so are not available until balance is found on the bony structure, at which point they engage involuntarily. Only then are the voluntary, superficial back muscles able to stop their chronic, compensatory tensing and become available to move the arms freely.

The advantages to engaging the involuntary muscles do not, however, stop with simply freeing up the voluntary arm-moving muscles. The same kind of automatic postural patterns (APPs) which cause the reflexive spring in the step that aids in locomotion for the lower limbs is presumed to be what provides the experience of a springiness in the arms that well-balanced players regularly report. It's not just the *absence of holding* in the arm-moving muscles, but the added bonus of an involuntary, *springy buoyancy for the arms* that in all likelihood is caused by these marvelous and only recently researched automatic postural patterns.

Gathering and Lengthening of the Spine

The spine naturally gathers and lengthens due to the springy nature of its discs as long as it is not restricted by tensed, superficial back muscles. (See chapter 5 for more detail on gathering and lengthening of the spine.) The same superficial back muscles which, when tensed, inhibit free arm movement, also inhibit the free gathering and lengthening of the spine.

When the spine is left unhindered to alternately gather and lengthen, it coordinates the arms in repetitive actions such as bowing. When a free spine moves into its greatest length, the head moves up and away from the tailbone end of the spine. The arms, because they are suspended from the sheet of fascia that helps form the scalp of the head, will of course go along for the ride and experience a constantly renewed buoyancy, somewhat like a balloon being gently and repeatedly tapped upwards into the air with the palm of the hand to keep it airborne.

Some experiencing this spinal lengthening and the extra arm freedom that comes with it for the first time liken it to the sensation of changing out of a tight-fitting sweater that binds the arms in their extreme ranges of movement into an extra large size that allows the arms to freely perform even the most strenuous tasks. If you are tuned in to the rhythm of your spinal movement, you can synchronize the movements that require the most arm freedom (such as reaching right to the tip of the bow) with the lengthening of your spine. Remember, however, that the gathering and lengthening of the spine relies entirely on balance on the bony structure, because only then are the tensed, superficial back muscles able to release.

It can't be said often enough: freedom for the arms depends entirely on balance on the bony structure throughout the rest of the body!

Weight Delivery of the Violinist's Left Forearm Arch

Even though the *entire* left arm, right up to and including the collarbone, must be mapped as support for the violin, it is especially important to map the portion of the arm from the fingertips to the elbow and to sense how weight delivers through each end of this asymmetrical arch shape. The delivery of weight through the two ends of this arch is frequently imbalanced. Correctly mapping a balanced distribution of weight delivery is essential for optimal left-arm freedom and left-hand facility.

Balancing a Candy Cane

Imagine balancing the tip of the short end of a candy cane on the edge of a table while balancing the long end on your fingertip. Most can instinctively sense how much of the candy cane's weight to allow the table to support at the short end and how much support to provide for the long end to prevent the candy cane from toppling over. When the candy cane balances easily on both supporting surfaces, its weight delivery is distributed through both ends. Take too much support away from the long end, however, and it either immediately topples over or hangs from the edge of the table. In hanging, it is supported but is not in a state of *balanced* support.

Push up too hard with your fingertip from under the long end and you upset the precarious balance of the candy cane's weight delivery, winding up with a candy cane shattered on the floor.

When there is too much weight delivery through the short end of the arch and not enough through the long end:

If there is not enough sense of upward support coming from the elbow joint where the ulna perches on the humerus, the whole arm can hang from the violin neck like a dead weight, dragging the neck down with the hand. In this situation, the first finger always contacts the side of the violin neck far too close to FJ3, causing extreme limitations for the mobility of the left-hand fingers. The hand grips the neck to avoid the feeling that the fingers are going to slip off the strings. This causes the left hand to feel heavy and cumbersome. The fingers are not free to be easily jiggled in any kind of vibrato.

When there is more weight delivery through the long end of the arch and not enough through the short end:

When there is not enough weight of the unit delivered through the fingers, and too much weight delivered down through the ulna into its perch on the humerus, the whole upper arm structure is dragged down from its state of buoyant, suspended balance. It causes an unnecessary muscular holding through the whole arm, particularly in the muscles controlling the fingers, since their weight is not allowed to release into the strings. When there is unnecessary work in the muscles controlling the fingers, the fingers cannot move easily or quickly. Vibrato suffers because the weight of the fingers themselves needs to be released into the string before they can jiggle freely.

When there is no weight delivery through either end of the arch:

If you do not sense any support through the ulna or the fingertips, the only way the forearm can stay upright to support the violin is through purely muscular means. There is too much muscular work in the biceps and around the elbow joint itself in an effort to keep the forearm in an upright position (see chapter 4—Arm Joint 3.) Vibrato becomes impossible. There is also too much muscular holding in the forearm muscles, causing the fingers to feel that they have to work in isolation from the rest of the arm. They have no sense of support from the ulna and the wrist bones on one side, or the violin fingerboard on the other side. This is akin to gripping a candy cane in the middle and holding the short end just above the surface of the table, not allowing it to be supported at either end. This method of support has nothing to do with balance.

When there is a balanced weight delivery through both ends of the arch:

Allow the weight of the finger bones themselves to release into the string at the short end of the arch. When this weight is counterbalanced at the other end of the arch by the ulna releasing onto the perch that the humerus provides, you will experience simultaneous support at *both* ends of the arch. The fingers experience a lovely upwards support that the fingerboard and the string provide for them, and this facilitates free movement in the fingers. The ulna experiences a lovely, upwards support that make the violin and the arm seem very light and easy to move.

Experiencing the balance of the forearm arch can be learned by going in search of the same simultaneous weight delivery/weight bearing that we feel through the whole body when we stand on balance around the core. Remember the definitions of weight delivery and weight-bearing from the glossary at the beginning of this book:

Weight Bearing

Experienced in the body as the support any given lower structure supplies to the structure resting above it. It is felt as an upward force.

Weight Delivery

Experienced in the human body as the release of any given structure into a state of rest onto the structure directly below. It is felt as a downward force and it is the subjective sensation of gravity.

Candy Cane Exercise

1. Stand on balance with your left side facing a mirror and your arms hanging at your sides.
2. Your fingers should be slightly bent in their natural curve.
3. Notice that the candy-cane-shaped arch of your left forearm is naturally present as you stand.
4. With your eyes, trace the arch shape that you see in the mirror from the tip of your pinkie up to the elbow.
5. This heightens the kinesthetic experience of the unified sweep of the forearm's arched shape.
6. Next, with the violin in place, bring that unified arch-shape to the neck of the violin as if to play.
7. You should feel both the downward release of the arch's two ends into the structures below them and the simultaneous upward support that those structures below provide (i.e., the strings and fingerboard at the short end and the humerus at the long end).
8. Repeat this experiment many times, each time bringing the hand onto the violin in a different position so you can sense the integrity of the arch equally well in twelfth position as you can in first position.
9. Once you find this easy balance the candy cane analogy has outlived it usefulness, since your arch (unlike a candy cane) is alive and free to move at all of the joints between its two ends.
10. However, that free and easy movement is only possible if your forearm arch is in a state of balance.
11. Finding a balanced weight delivery through the two ends of this asymmetrical arch also allows the upper arm structure to remain balanced and provide the *whole* left arm with a sense of lightness and buoyancy and the left hand with optimal facility.

Chapter 5
Breathing

"Cultural ideas of beauty such as a flat stomach also contribute to the tightening of the lower torso muscles."

It is true that violinists do not need as *refined* a map of breathing structures as do singers or wind and brass players, However, *inaccurately* mapped breathing structures can prevent violinists from discovering both balance around the core and also freedom for the arms. The breathing structures lie along the core of the torso and are therefore inextricably connected to the state of balance around the core.

Remapping the breathing structures is not just for singers anymore! Rather, it is *essential* to any violinist looking for balance and freedom of movement. Here, then, we explore breathing mis-mappings in the context of violinists' most frequent myths regarding balance around the core.

Myth 1: A Violinist Needs Good Posture to Play
Resulting Breathing Distortions

1. A distortion in the structure and functioning in the breathing structures of the upper torso (*ribs, sternum, lungs and diaphragm*) and the lower torso (*abdominal wall and pelvic floor*) due to a flattened thoracic spine, overarched lumbar spine, and tilted pelvis that comes with the good posture disease.

Upper-torso[14] Breathing Structures
Structure and Function of the Ribs and Sternum

We have discussed at length the implications for the arms and the spine of a violinist who is attempting to play with good posture. However, because the ribs attach to the spine in the back at joints and then reach around to join to the sternum in the front by means of cartilage, the

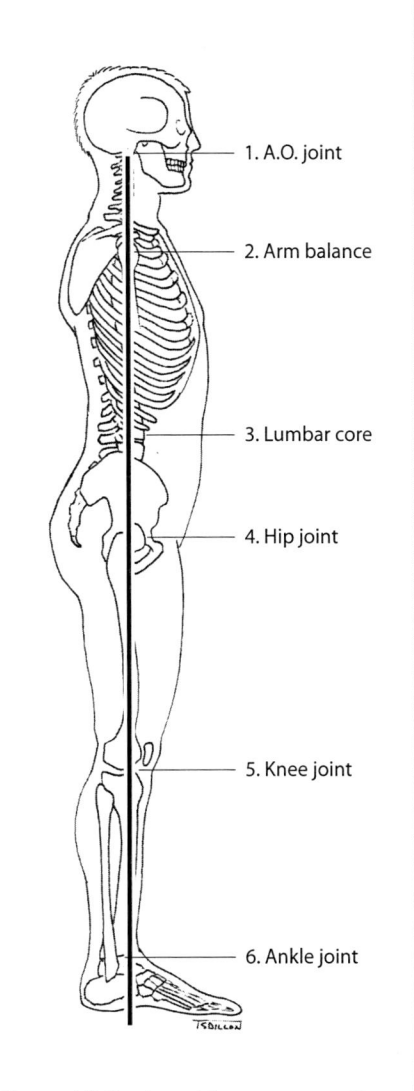

1. A.O. joint
2. Arm balance
3. Lumbar core
4. Hip joint
5. Knee joint
6. Ankle joint

Figure 64. The breathing structures lie along the core between Places of Balance 1 and 4. Enjoy exploring the breathing structures and then return them to the integrated whole.

shape of the ribs and sternum are also distorted by altering the shape of the spine by trying to sit up straight. The artificial lifting of the ribs that the good posture disease causes restricts the ability to move, which in turn restricts the amount of air able to flow into the lungs. Note the emphasis on ribs rather than the ribcage, since a cage generally implies an immovable structure. Ribs are designed to be moveable and therefore the term ribcage is a misnomer.

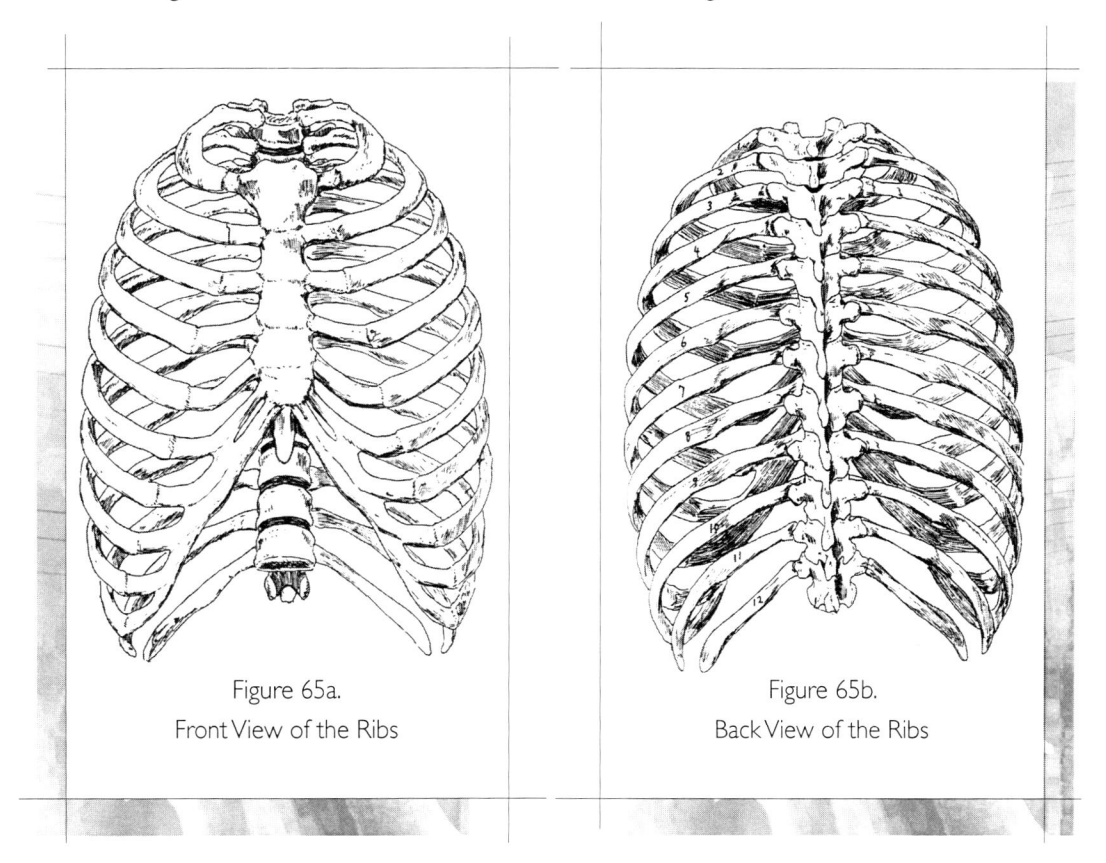

Figure 65a.
Front View of the Ribs

Figure 65b.
Back View of the Ribs

There are twenty-four ribs which form joints on either side of the twelve thoracic vertebrae in the back. Only twenty of the twenty-four ribs attach in the front; the four bottom ribs—two on each side—are called floating ribs because they only attach to the spine in the back. The ribs that do attach in the front join with the sternum by way of springy cartilage. With joints in the back and stretchy cartilage in the front, ribs are extremely mobile bones. It is the excursion of the ribs swinging up and out that gives us our *only* voluntary control over how much air enters the lungs. Therefore, for easy and free breathing, we must learn to take full advantage of rib mobility.

Two sets of intercostal muscles lie between the ribs. One is responsible for swinging the ribs up and out on inhalation, and a second set is responsible for returning them to neutral on exhalation. Violinists frequently map the rib-moving muscles as one and the same as the arm-moving, superficial torso muscles which are exterior to the ribs. It is important for full-arm freedom that the rib-moving muscles are clearly mapped as being *between* the ribs.

The farther you move your ribs up and out on inhalation, the more the walls of the lungs expand. The lungs are obliged to follow the movement of the ribs because there is a thin layer of vacuum space between the lungs and the inside of the ribs. Expanding the lung walls causes air pressure inside the lungs to drop. Similar to the operating principle of a vacuum, the lower the air pressure becomes inside, the more air must rush into the lungs from outside the body where air pressure is higher to equalize the pressure inside and out. However, when a violinist with the good posture disease juts out his sternum and his upper ribs, he leaves his ribs, particularly the upper ones, with very little or no mobility. This lack of mobility of the ribs results in a feeling of breathlessness, since it prevents sufficient air from reaching the lungs.

To overcome the feeling of breathlessness, some try to suck in the air, which causes the pharyngeal muscles to tighten. (For a discussion of pharyngeal muscles, see myth 4 below.) However, this sucking in also leads to mis-mapping rib movement as being the *consequence* of air filling the lungs as opposed to being the *cause*. Violinists who map the ribs as moving only as a consequence of the lungs filling with air suffer tension in the upper torso, because the upper ribs do not make a full excursion and are therefore in a state of holding. This point is of such importance to the freedom of the upper torso and arm moving muscles that it bears repeating!

> *It is the voluntary up-and-out movement of the ribs that allows the lungs to fill with air.*

Some violinists who first experience the movement of the ribs as the *cause* of breathing and the lungs being filled and then emptied of air as a *consequence* of rib movement, describe the sensation as "being breathed."

Rib Movement

How would you breathe if someone asked you to take a deep breath? Would you thrust your chest out in an effort to get more air into your lungs? This kind of hauling up and out of the upper torso is actually a spinal movement caused by the good posture disease rather moving the ribs. Overarching the lumbar spine and the thoracic spine thrusts out the thorax. Inhaling in this way restricts rib movement and diaphragm descent.

1. Inhale.
2. As you exhale, keep your neck free, allowing the cartilage at the front of all of your ribs to spring all the way back to neutral.
3. This guarantees that you moved your ribs all the way back down to complete their excursion and that the old, stale air is released from the lungs.

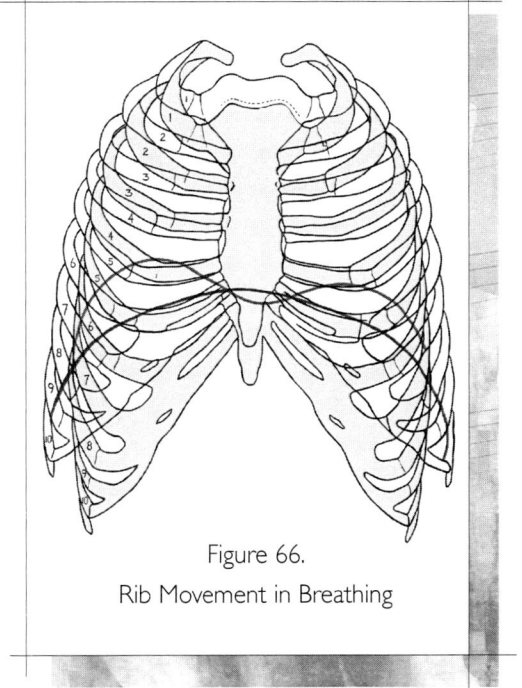

Figure 66.
Rib Movement in Breathing

4. Now, without arching your lower spine, move your ribs up and out—front, back and sides.
5. Can you feel the air rush into your lungs?
6. Do you notice that your breath is less noisy?

Rib Slope

The good posture disease causes the upper thorax to jut forward, unnaturally flattening the natural curve of the thoracic spine. The cartilage attaching the ribs to the sternum then becomes overstretched as the fronts of the ribs are chronically held up and out. Pushing up the ribs in the front this way leads to mis-mapping the shape of each rib as *horizontal* to the ground rather than higher in the back and sloping down in the front to where the cartilage attaches each rib to the sternum.

1. Choose one rib in figure 65a.
2. Place your index finger on this rib where it forms its joint with the spine at the back.
3. Trace the rib's swooping trajectory from the back all the way to the front where it meets the cartilage.
4. Are you surprised at how much farther down at the front the rib is than its origin at the back?
5. If so, you have some remapping work to do.
6. You need to trace your own ribs with your fingers until your body map is absolutely clear about their shape.

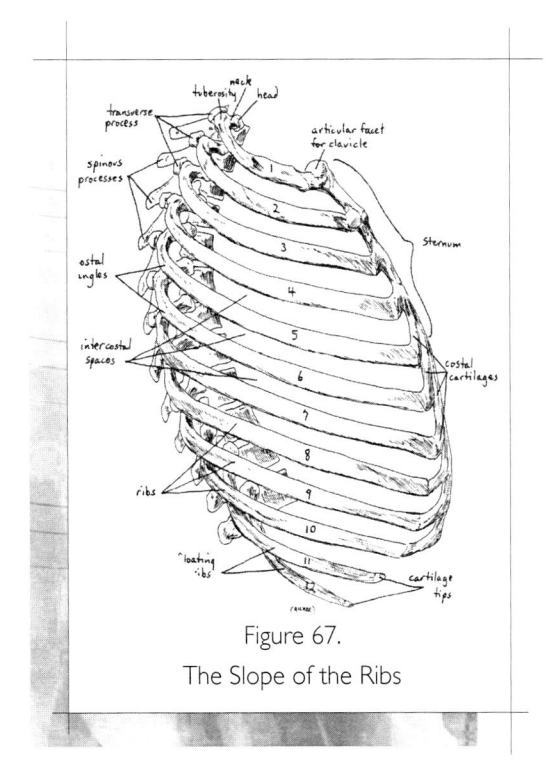

Figure 67.
The Slope of the Ribs

Sternum Slope

When the good posture disease causes the sternum to thrust out, more than the shape of the ribs is mis-mapped; the slant of the sternum is mis-mapped as well. Whereas the relaxation disease leads to mis-mapping the sternum as *vertical,* the good posture disease encourages mis-mapping it as *nearly approaching the horizontal* plane rather than gently angled down and away. Until the angles of both ribs and sternum are correctly mapped, finding an easy balance around the core is impossible and breathing will continue to be restricted.

1. Place your fingertips on the top and bottom of your sternum as you study figure 67.
2. Go into a full relaxation disease slump.
3. Feel how the sternum becomes nearly vertical.
4. Notice how your breathing feels.
5. Next, thrust out your sternum as in the good posture disease.

6. Notice how different the sternum's angle is as compared to figure 67.
7. Notice how your ribs feel as you breathe.
8. Finally, release your neck muscles.
9. Find balance at all places of balance.
10. Allow your sternum to return to a place of rest as you see it in figure 67.
11. You will immediately notice that the ribs swing much more easily from the sternum as you breathe.

Upper-torso Depth

The good posture disease's horizontal ribs and sternum mis-mapping is reinforced by the notion of a "front" and "back" of the body, as if we were flat or only two dimensional. The thoracic ribs are long, curved bones that reach a long way around from their joints with the vertebrae at the back to the sternum's cartilage at front to enclose and protect the heart and the lungs, and as such they afford a *depth* through the upper torso from the curved back thoracic spine to the angled out sternum that many people with the good posture disease have not mapped. (When this depth is restored, many are surprised to find as much rib curving up and back behind the arms hanging at neutral as rib curving down in front of the arms.) Recovering depth in the upper torso often helps in returning the ribs, sternum, and thoracic spine to their neutral shape. Doing so restores balance around the core as well as optimal rib movement, permitting the lungs to fill to the requirement of the moment. The impact that mis-mapping depth in the *lower* torso has on breathing is discussed below.

The Back of the Lungs

Those who have lost the sense of the full depth of the thorax from the good posture disease often think that the lungs exist only in front of the spine. One can see from figure 68 that half of the lungs' surface area resides beside and behind the weight-bearing portion of the spine. Frequently massage therapists and chiropractors ask their clients to "breathe into the back." This of course, can be misleading, since air must move into the lungs—the back itself cannot contain air. However, the benefit of this advice is that attention is brought to rib movement in the back, and to the fact that air does go back there.

Although it is true that the only *voluntary* part we play in breathing is in moving our ribs, rib movement accounts for only twenty-five percent of the work of inhalation. The other seventy-five percent of this muscular work is almost entirely *involuntary* and is achieved by the diaphragm.

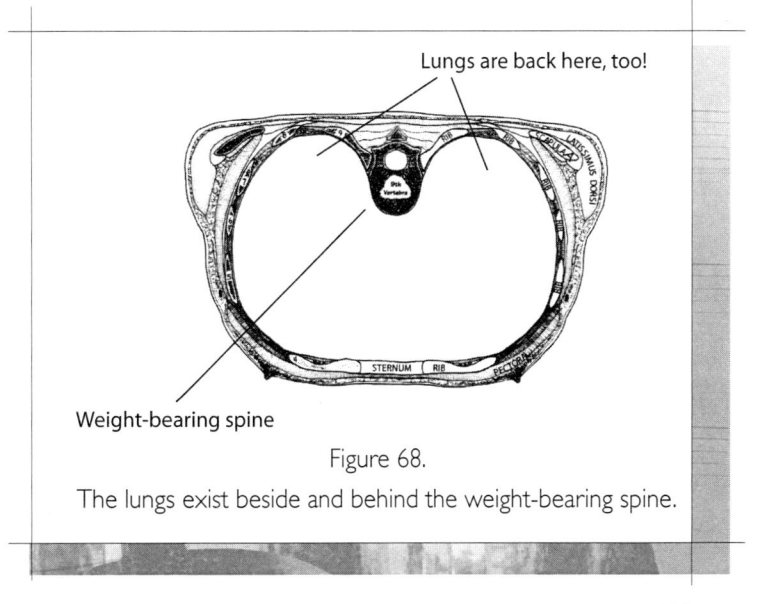

Figure 68.
The lungs exist beside and behind the weight-bearing spine.

Diaphragm Structure and Function

The diaphragm is the great dome-shaped muscle which separates the thoracic cavity above, which contains the lungs and heart, from the abdominal cavity below, where the abdominal organs are. On inhalation, the strong diaphragm pushes down into a slightly flatter dome; on exhalation it releases out of contraction and springs back into its highly-domed shape. When the diaphragm descends, it drags the base of the lungs down with it. The extra space created in the lungs by this descent in conjunction with the up-and-out rib movement leads to lower pressure in the lungs, causing air to rush in.

We cannot sense the movement of the diaphragm directly because it contains very few sense receptors. However, we *can* sense its movement indirectly because of all the movement throughout the abdomen and pelvis that occurs as the diaphragm descends and ascends *as long as there is no tightening in the abdominal wall and pelvic floor muscles.*

On the diaphragm's descent all of the abdominal organs are pushed out and down, and in turn, the muscular abdominal wall and the muscular pelvic floor are pushed out and down by the movement of the organs, as long as they are not restricted. On the diaphragm's ascent, the elastic tissue of the abdominal wall and pelvic floor will, if allowed, spring back into neutral.

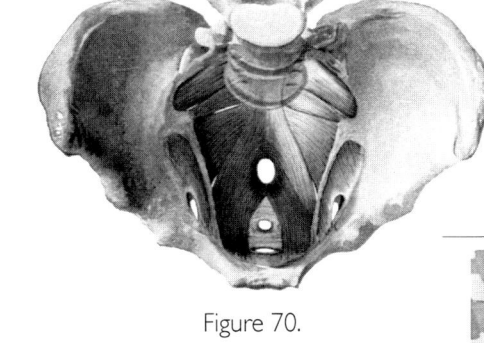

However, if the abdomen and pelvis are not mapped to their full depth, there can be unnecessary muscular holding that prevents this springy response to the diaphragm's movement.

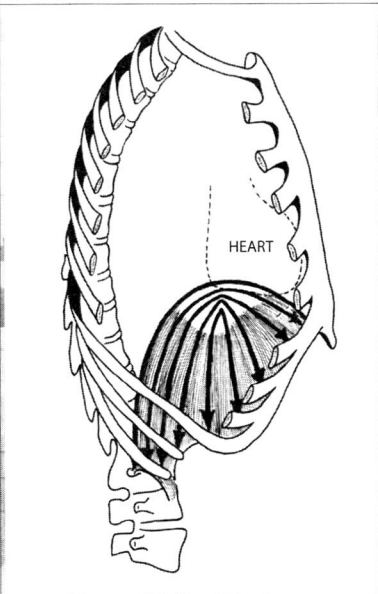

Figure 69. The Diaphragm

Figure 70.
The muscular pelvic floor must remain springy to aid in breathing.

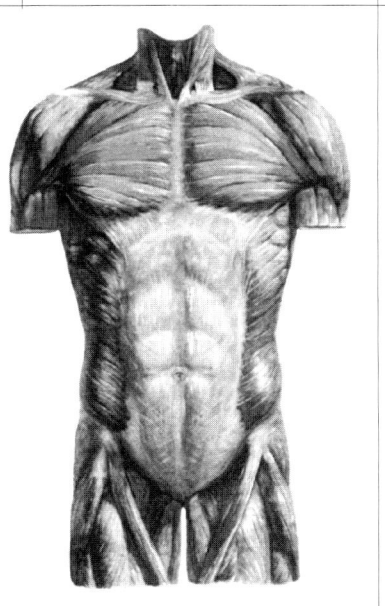

Figure 71.
The muscular abdominal wall must remain springy to aid in breathing.

Lower-torso Breathing Structures

Lower-torso Depth

The good posture disease (among other cultural myths) also prevents accurate mapping of the full depth of the *lower* torso, which in turn restricts movement that passively supports the active work of breathing. The springiness of the muscular abdominal wall and pelvic floor plays an important support role in the movement of breathing, but this springiness is forfeited when we try to "sit up straight" or "suck in the tummy," because both of these actions involve holding in the muscles we need to remain springy. Cultural ideas of beauty such as a flat stomach also contribute to the tightening of the lower torso muscles, causing depth to disappear from the body map.

Pelvis Depth

In the same way that depth needs to be mapped in the upper torso from the sternum through to the thoracic ribs in the back, the full depth of the pelvis also needs to be mapped. Mapping this depth is easiest to do by palpating from one bony point of reference to another.

Figure 72. Depth of the Pelvis

Finding Front-to-Back Pelvis Depth from the Pubic Bones to the Tailbone

1. Sit in a chair.
2. Place the fingers of one hand on your sacrum in the back.
3. Palpate down to the end of the tailbone.
4. Remember that the tailbone is not part of the pelvis. As the tail end of the sacrum, it is sandwiched right between the two pelvic bones in the back.
5. With your other hand, palpate the front of your pelvis (commonly known as the pubic bone, even though it is actually the place where the *two* pelvic bones meet at the front).
6. Keeping one hand on the pubis at front and the other on the tailbone at back, rock slightly on your rocker bones to heighten awareness of their location in the body.
7. Can you sense the distance from your pubic bones to your rockers?
    a. Note that the pubic bone is continuous with the rocker; it is just the front and highest point of the same bony curve.
8. From your rockers to your tailbone?
    a. Note that these are two different bones.
9. The rockers are much lower than the pubic bones and the tailbone, but they are still

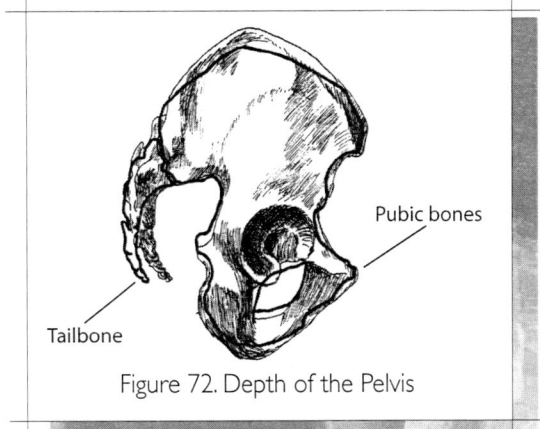

central to the bony front and back you feel with your fingertips.

10. If you have not mapped sufficient depth here you will likely feel some muscular release as you mentally trace the distance from your bony front to your bony back with the sit bones as a central reference point.

11. It is these muscles which need to be released into neutral to allow the springy abdominal muscles to be moved out on inhalation and rebound on exhalation in response to the diaphragm's movement.

In addition to helping to free the lower torso muscles, the above exploration also aids in finding balance on the rockers. It is necessary to sense the rockers as central in order to balance on them, and the only way to discover centrality is to sense the equal distances on either side of center (i.e., the distance from center to tailbone as equaling center to pubic bones). Centrality for the rockers is lost if the lower torso muscles are working to hold the body up, because contraction in these muscles alters the distance between the tailbone and the rockers, upsetting the balance between the back, center, and front points.

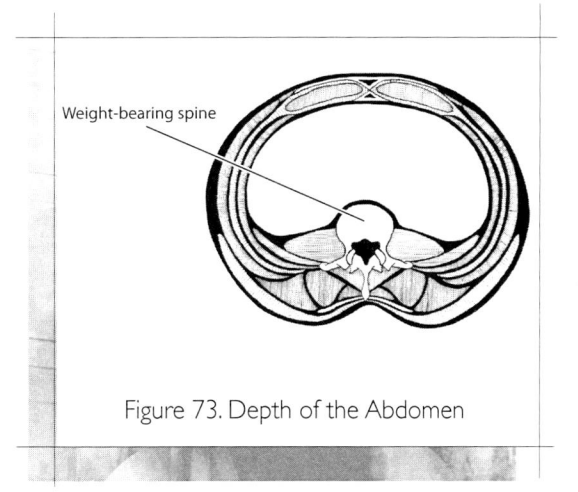

Figure 73. Depth of the Abdomen

Abdomen Depth

For anyone who has fallen prey to the flat stomach myth, it is important for balance and freedom of breathing to accurately map the depth and shape of the abdominal wall. The muscular abdominal wall is cylindrical in shape; there is nothing flat about it. It is this cylindrical shape which makes it possible to balance around and be organized around the body's core in the same way that an apple is organized around its core. Ease of balance disappears the flatter something becomes.

Compare the impossible task of balancing a flat piece of paper on its edge with the much easier task of balancing it on the same edge after it has been curved and taped into a cylindrical shape, gaining the dimension of depth. Inherent in the word *flat* is the notion of only two dimensions. We are gloriously three-dimensional creatures!

Mapping the full depth of this muscular cylinder is also essential for free breathing. By not holding in the abdominal muscles to create the impression of a flat stomach or in an effort to sit up straight, an equal distribution of stretch and rebound is allowed all the way around the lower torso in response to the diaphragm's movement. The internal abdominal organs also benefit because they receive an ongoing massage when the abdominal wall is free to respond to the diaphragm's movement. A chronic knot in the stomach can sometimes be eased by allowing more of this internal massage.

Myth 2: Violinists Must Keep the Shoulders Down
Resulting Breathing Mis-mapping

1. The lungs are mapped too low.

Trying to hold the shoulders down frequently indicates that the collarbones are mapped too low or as actually resting on the top ribs. This prevents the top ribs from moving and leads to mapping the lungs as lower than they actually are in the torso.

As you look at figure 74, ask yourself if there is anything that surprises you about the location of the lungs. To those who map the lungs as reaching right down to the bottom ribs, this image might just look wrong. In reality, the lower boundary of the lungs is marked by the bottom of the sternum and *the very top lobe of the lungs reaches above the collarbone in the front and to the top rib in the back*. In order for the lungs to fill to capacity, the top ribs need to be free of the weight of the arms to make their full excursion. When the arms are in balanced suspension (see chapter 4), they are neither hoisted up on inhalation nor hauled down in a muscular attempt to keep the shoulders down. Instead, they gently ride the wave of movement provided by the upper ribs.

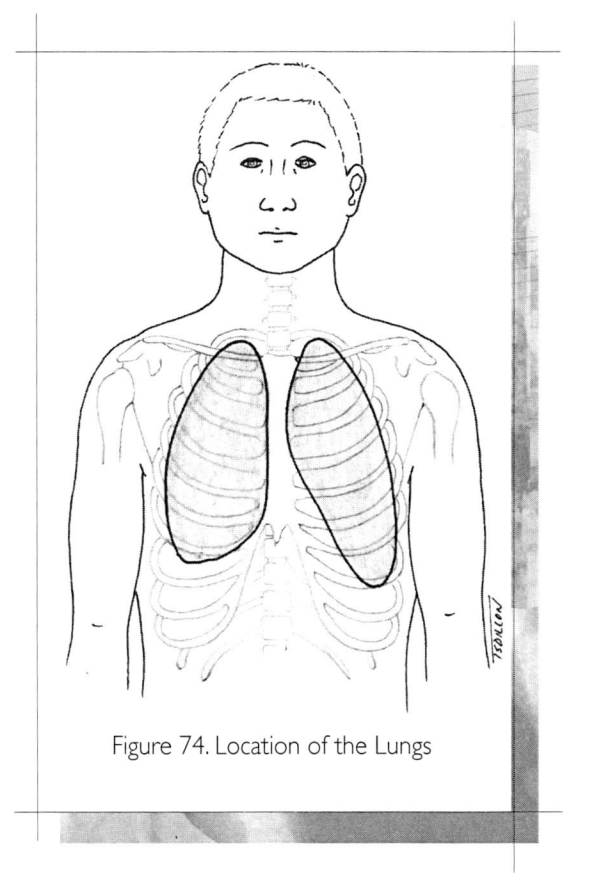

Figure 74. Location of the Lungs

Consistently hauling the arms down on top of the ribs for a very long time destroys the collective tapered or beehive shape[15] of the upper five ribs in the body map. Because they are unable to move much, there is little or no kinesthetic feedback from these topmost ribs; the crucial fact that the top rib is so much shorter than the lower ones is thereby lost in the map.

But find more of a suspended balance for the arms and then go looking for sensation from a moving top rib and you will discover the sensation much closer in to the sides of the neck than you might expect—conveniently right under the trapezius muscles that are so often tight and overdeveloped on violinists! In addition to finding freer arms and freer breathing, the bonus to restoring upper rib movement by remapping the suspension of the arms from above is a pleasurable massage with each breath. The freer the upper ribs, the more the upper torso muscles are massaged by those moving ribs on each breath.

Myth 3: The Spine Moves Only from Front-to-Back, Side-to-Side, and into Spiral Movements

(And, you might ask, does spinal movement really matter for violin playing, anyway?!)

Resulting Breathing Mis-mapping

1. The spine is mapped as remaining one consistent length.
    a. The consequences of this are a spine restricted in its natural gathering and lengthening that free breathing co-ordinates.
    b. This prevents the ribs from completing a full excursion on exhalation and natural rib excursion on inhalation.
    c. *Most importantly, it prevents us from experiencing arms at their lightest and freest.*

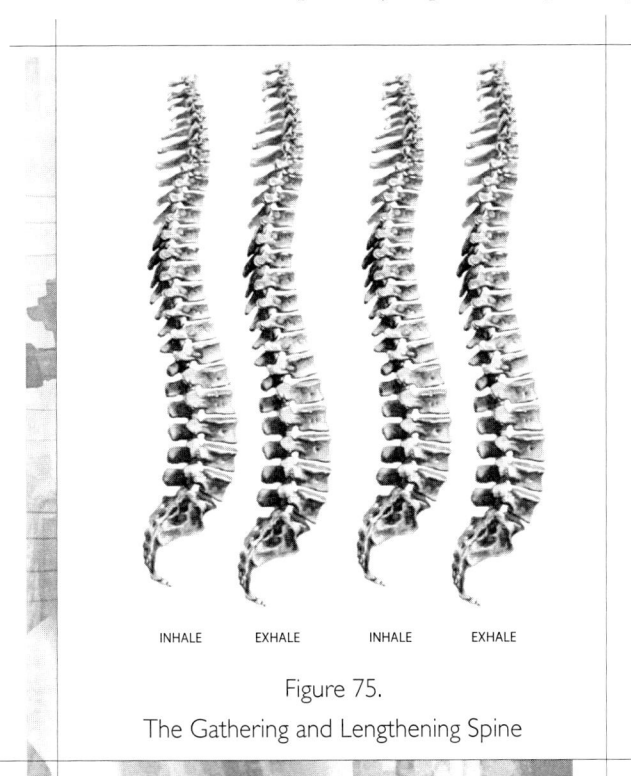

Figure 75.
The Gathering and Lengthening Spine

INHALE   EXHALE   INHALE   EXHALE

As we discussed in chapter 4, we can learn to allow the spine to move into greater length on an inhalation *or* an exhalation, and to synchronize it with arm movement so that the arms are permitted the greatest freedom in their most vigorous and extreme work. However, for those who have lost the kinesthetic perception of the spine's gathering and lengthening, the best way to recover this awareness is to observe the subtle gathering movement that happens naturally on every inhalation and the subtle lengthening movement on every exhalation.

Observing Spinal Gathering and Lengthening as Coordinated by Breathing

On the floor

1. Lie belly-down in front of a ground-level mirror with two medium sized pillows under your torso and the backs of your hands touching the floor, elbows slightly bent.
2. Inhale, focusing on moving all of the ribs up and out to achieve a silent intake of air.
3. Put special attention on the swinging up of the upper ribs in the back and you will enjoy the massage they provide for the trapezius muscles.

4. Notice, both kinesthetically and by watching, how your spine naturally gathers into itself so that it is slightly shorter on the inhalation.
5. Next, watch in the mirror as you exhale.
6. Make sure you allow the ribs their full excursion back down, taking special notice to permit all the stretchy cartilage connecting the ribs to the sternum to fully spring back to neutral.
7. The distance the ribs travel on their excursion down is a direct correlate to the length the spine is allowed, since the ribs attach to the spine in the back.
8. Allow all of the abdominal and pelvic floor muscles to spring back as far as possible.
9. Watch in the mirror. You will see a lengthening through the entire spine as you exhale.
10. As your head moves up and away from the other end of your spine, you will experience a lightness of the arms as they also move up and away from the torso (as long as you are not actively pulling the arms down with the muscles of your back).
11. This is the kind of lengthening you want to foster and absorb into daily activities as well as your violin playing.

As discussed in chapter 4, the most common mapping error preventing the spine from gathering and lengthening is mapping the superficial back muscles as support muscles rather than as arm-moving muscles. When the superficial back muscles are chronically tensed in an effort to hold us up, arm movement and freedom, as well as the gathering and lengthening of the spine, are compromised.

We established in chapter 4 that the arms are suspended above the ribs by the sheet of springy connective tissue which runs from the collarbone and shoulder blade up the neck to the top of the head. As the spine lengthens, the head, because it sits on top of the spine, naturally moves up and away from the lower vertebrae. Because the arms are attached to the head and cervical vertebrae, they move in the same direction as the head. This extra loft the arms receive from a lengthening spine provides them an extra freedom that make especially challenging tasks feel much more facile.

Many great players and teachers instinctively know that breathing out at the beginning of a long shift or during a slow, sustained down bow aids in executing the task at hand by providing a sense of ease. This ease is felt because the spine is naturally afforded a small bit of lengthening on each exhalation.

Observing Spinal Gathering and Lengthening with the Violin

Watch yourself in a mirror for this exploration.

Part 1

1. Before raising your violin to play, find balance around your core.
2. Nod your head from the A.O. joint, checking to see if you are tensing in the neck muscles or surrounding regions like the jaw or tongue.
   a. If you notice that you are tensing muscles it means you are capable of finding an alternative!
3. Take a step back to check that you are on balance around the lumbar core.
4. Make sure you are not locking at the hip, knee, or ankle joints.
5. Check the depth of your upper and lower torso.
6. Spinal lengthening will not be available to you if you are muscularly pulling yourself down off balance.
7. Breathe in deeply by moving all of your ribs up and out.
8. Feel the expansion equally at the front, sides, and back.
9. Breathe out and make sure that you are allowing the cartilage at the front of your ribs to spring fully back to neutral.
10. Because the ribs attach to the spine in the back, they will impede the spine in finding its fullest length if they do not complete their downward excursion and return fully to neutral.
11. On the next several inhalations put your attention on the outward and downward movement you feel in the springy abdominal walls and pelvic floor as the diaphragm descends and gently pushes down on all of the internal organs.
12. Allow all to spring back into place on exhalation until you feel and see in the mirror the slight lengthening between your vertebrae and the reflexive need for more air to rush in for the next inhalation.

Part 2

1. When you are ready to play, bring the violin and bow into playing readiness from above your head to renew the suspension of the arms from above.
2. Begin playing at the tip of the bow on the open A string.
3. Breathe in as you travel toward the frog.
4. Begin your exhalation a moment before you start the down bow.
5. Observe the top of your head in the mirror passively moving up and away from the lower vertebrae.
6. Play to the very tip of the bow without losing balance around your core.

7. Notice that the lengthening of your spine gives you extra freedom for the arms to reach the tip.
    a. You may especially feel this in the collarbone and shoulder blade.

Part 3

1. Repeat this exercise, this time, air-bowing past the tip.
2. How much farther could you reach if you had an especially long bow?
3. Repeat this extra-long reach past the tip again, but now remain for a moment with your bow arm fully extended as you begin to inhale.
4. Notice how the slight gathering of the spine facilitates the beginning of the up-bow.
5. If you are successfully allowing the gathering and lengthening of the spine, you will feel how your arm is aided in moving the bow both down and up.

Part 4

1. Now reverse directions.
2. This time play on the open G string.
3. Begin at the tip on an *exhalation*.
4. Change to the down bow at the frog *before* you begin the inhalation.
5. Does the lengthening of the spine help you sense the extra buoyant suspension and freedom of the bow arm as you play near the frog?

Nota bene!

We begin teaching the gathering and lengthening of the spine by observing it happening as breathing naturally coordinates it for us because this is the simplest way to bring a student's awareness to it. However, it is extremely important to emphasize that it is possible to allow the spine to move into length on the inhalation as well as on the exhalation.

One of the main purposes of WEV is to promote the freedom that results from finding a balanced relationship for the bones and consequently a balanced distribution of muscle work through the body through correcting body mapping errors.

Once a player is regularly releasing the muscles providing this balance, the spine naturally moves into even greater length, in turn providing more freedom for the arms. (The amount it lengthens from balancing the body's muscular work is much greater than that caused by simply exhaling!) Therefore lengthening is not dependent on the breath but can be enhanced just that little bit more by an exhalation, and watching it happen on an exhalation is the best place for a student to begin exploring the lengthwise movement of the spine.

Myth 4: Neck Muscles Work to Hold the Violin
Resulting Mis-mappings in the Structures Related to Breathing

1. The muscles of the *pharynx, tongue, hyoid bone, soft palate, jaw* and *face* become mis-mapped in their functions.

Throughout *WEV,* the importance of having a free neck is repeatedly emphasized because it is impossible to find freedom at the other major joints of the body if the neck is tense. A violinist who tenses his neck muscles to hold the violin will undoubtedly have unnecessary tension in the surrounding muscular areas. The pharyngeal muscles, tongue, muscles of the hyoid bone, soft palate, jaw and face muscles are all prone to overworking when the neck is tight. Remapping these structures produces greater freedom in them and simultaneously provides more awareness of the state of the neck, leading to more release of the neck muscles and in turn restoring balance through the whole body.

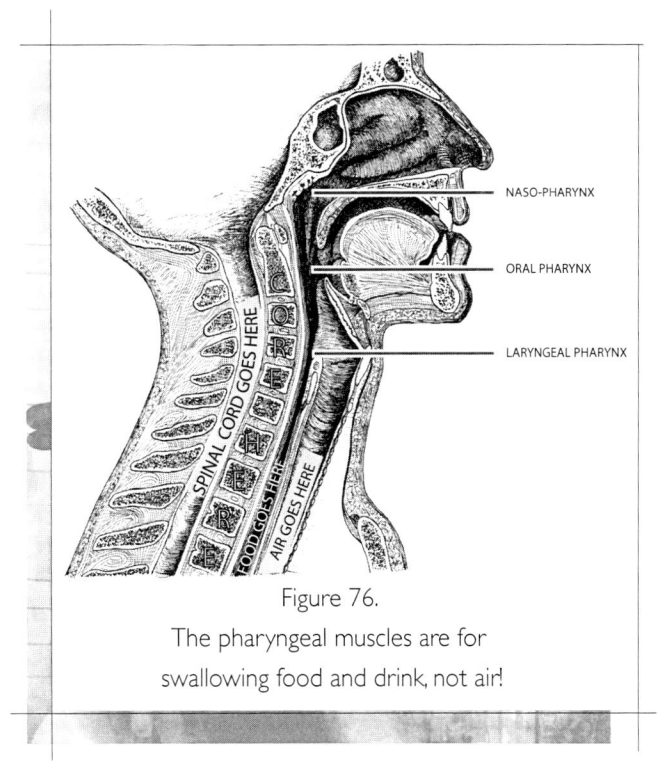

Figure 76.
The pharyngeal muscles are for swallowing food and drink, not air!

The Pharynx

The most important thing to know about the pharynx is that even though the pharyngeal *space* is shared by both the digestive system (*food* travels through it) and the respiratory system (*air* travels through it), the pharyngeal *muscles* belong solely to the digestive system. In other words, the muscles that comprise the throat are only there to swallow food and drink, not to swallow, suck, or gulp air. If your breathing is audible as you play, you are unnecessarily tensing your throat muscles, making it impossible to free the all-important neck muscles.

Frequently students learn at an early age to cue fellow musicians by constricting the pharynx in order to produce a clearly audible breath. While it is possible to use this as a tool, much good body mapping work would need to be done to prevent it from leading to a mis-mapping of the function of the pharyngeal muscles and to chronically noisy breathing. It seems a much easier solution to simply teach students to cue through beautiful movement rather than relying on noisy, constricted breathing.

Chronically noisy breathers are sometimes seriously mis-mapped with regard to the location of the esophagus and the trachea. If you are convinced that the trachea is behind the esophagus, then you may be attempting to suck air in muscularly to ensure it reaches the back of the throat. As figure 76 shows, the trachea is in *front* of the esophagus, which allows for an effortless flow of air through to the lungs.

Finding Your Pharyngeal Muscles

Swallow a few times and notice the muscular work you feel in your throat. These are your pharyngeal muscles and their only purpose is to swallow food and drink. They have nothing to do with the work of breathing.

The Soft Palate

A head chronically pulled off balance by the neck muscles often affects the group of muscles in the back of the roof of the mouth, called the soft palate. If you are using too many neck muscles to hold the violin with the head, you are likely hauling down on the soft palate as well. The soft palate can also be chronically held too high but like all muscles in the body, it has a place of neutral that it returns to as balance for the head on the spine is restored.

Finding Neutral for the Soft Palate

Unless you have had vocal training, it is possible that, as a violinist, you have never been required to find your soft palate.

1. Run your tongue over the roof of the mouth.
2. Notice the place near the back where the hard roof becomes softer. This is the soft palate.
3. The easiest way to learn about its movement is to yawn.
4. Try yawning.
5. Notice how the soft palate is drawn up into its most open position.
6. Now try the reverse, drawing the soft palate down as far as you can as you push the tongue up into it.
7. This is its most closed position.
8. Allow the soft palate to spring back between these two extremes into its slightly domed neutral.

In singing and in speaking, the soft palate constantly moves between these extremes. For instance, compare its closure when saying the consonant "p" with how open it is when saying "ah." In order to prevent the necessary muscular work of the soft palate from triggering unnecessary neck and throat tension, singers must carefully train to dissociate palate work with neck and throat work. It is not necessary to tense the neck for either the lifting or the lowering of the soft palate.

When you play the violin, however, if you notice that the palate is chronically pulled closed or makes contact with the tongue in the back of the mouth, then you have mapped the soft palate's neutral position as closed and probably have some unnecessary neck tension.

If you find that you chronically haul up on it, then you have neutral mapped as too high or open and probably still have some unnecessary neck tension! In either case, along with continuing your search for a freer neck, you need to play with the two extremes of the soft palate until it naturally settles into its released, domed neutral.

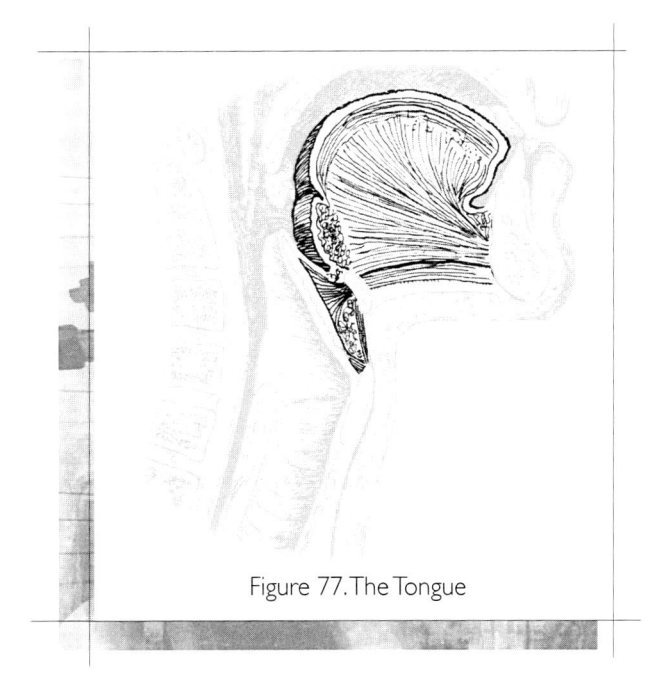

Figure 77. The Tongue

The Tongue

The tongue is a composite muscle made up of many smaller muscles that are capable of working independently of one another. Many have the tongue mapped as only horizontal in the mouth and do not realize that the back third of the tongue is vertical. Because this vertical section helps to form the top portion of the front wall of the oral pharynx, any unnecessary tension in the tongue compromises the freedom of the pharyngeal and neck muscles. Many who hold in the neck muscles also hold tension in the tongue. The tongue, however, is not required to work in any way to play the violin, unless one is playing contemporary repertoire requiring vocalizations. The place for a violinist's tongue is at neutral.

Finding Neutral for the Tongue

Often, violinists who close down the soft palate also brace the tongue against the roof of the mouth. If the tongue is accustomed to tensing against the roof of the mouth, it may feel very strange at first to release it to a place of neutral. Neutral for the tongue is where its front and central portions are resting between the lower teeth.

It is possible for the tip of the tongue to rest inside the lower front teeth while the center of the tongue continues to push up, so it is important to be aware that your very back molar teeth provide the boundaries between which the central portion of the tongue should settle down. It is extremely important to make sure that the base of the tongue is not tensed. (This is addressed in detail in the following section.)

As you go about your everyday activities, check in frequently to see where your tongue is. Is it pushing against the roof of the mouth or tensing or curling in any other way? If it is, it is likely this is also happening as you play.

The Hyoid Bone

Frequently, excessive neck tension from trying to hold onto the violin can lead to a total omission of the hyoid bone from the body map. It is one of the few bones in the body which does not articulate with another bone. It is suspended from the base of the skull by the stylohyoid ligaments, one on each side of the skull, and provides support and shape for the neck muscles in the front. One of its most important functions is to anchor the base of the tongue. The neck muscles and the tongue will never be free if the hyoid bone is not included in your body map because these muscles will try to do all of the work that this sturdy little bone is designed to do.

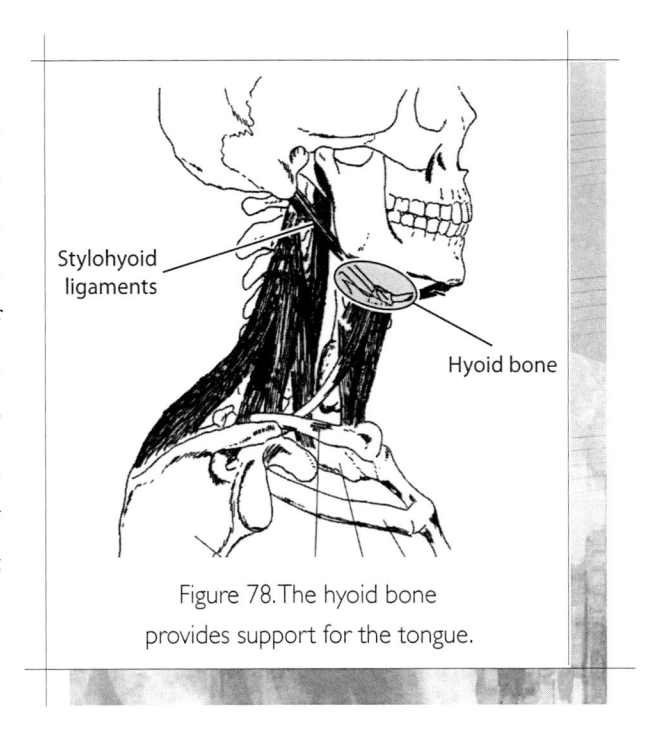

Figure 78. The hyoid bone provides support for the tongue.

Locating the Hyoid Bone

1. Place the thumb and fingers of one hand on either side of your jawbone.
2. While palpating carefully, slide them down just under the jawbone until you find the horseshoe-shaped bone shown in figure 78.
    a. Make sure you have not gone so far down that you palpate the Adam's apple.
3. This is the hyoid bone, suspended from the styloid processes on the base of the skull which are *directly beside* the all-important condyles that form the head/neck joint with the atlas.
4. With your fingers still palpating, tighten the tongue and bunch it up so it pushes into the roof of the mouth.
5. Next, push the tongue down into the floor of the mouth.
6. If you are palpating deeply but gently enough, you should be able to feel the hyoid bone move under your fingers.
7. When neck and tongue muscles try to take over the job of the hyoid bone, or when they work too hard to hold a violin, the hyoid bone's position is displaced.
8. This has a direct effect on the balance of the head, since the hyoid bone is suspended from the very place where we search for balance for our heads.

The Jaw

Chronic muscular holding in the neck while playing inevitably creates some unnecessary holding in the jaw muscles because of the proximity of the neck to the face, and because of the consequences for the face and jaw when the head is dragged off balance by tightened neck muscles. If this holding becomes chronic from repeated instruction to hold the violin with the jaw, it will lead to jaw mis-mappings.

As mentioned in chapter 3, the jaw is not part of the skull; it is only an appendage to the skull in the same way that the limbs are appendages to the torso. One frequently hears the jaw referred to as the "lower jaw" as if the bottom of the skull comprised an "upper jaw." Those who have mapped two jaws in their internal representation of the body open their mouths as if the upper row of teeth actually have to move up and away from the lower teeth in order to chew or sing. This reinforces the head's loss of balance at the A.O. joint, since the neck muscles in the back have to contract in order to make this movement. In truth, the jaw only has to swing down and away from the skull at the temporomandibular joints to open the mouth.

Actors and singers need to be very clear about where their jaw joints (temporomandibular joints or TMJs) are located because their profession depends on being able to open their mouths freely. Violinists need to be just as clear about where their TMJs are because it is the jaw that makes contact with the "chinrest" (another misnomer, since it is the jaw, not the chin that rests in it.)

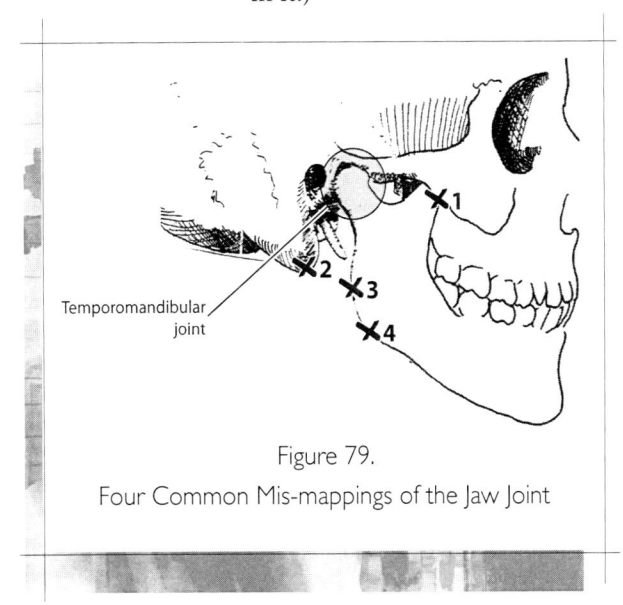

Figure 79.
Four Common Mis-mappings of the Jaw Joint

Just as we have one jaw, we have two TMJs: one on each side of the head. We want and need to have TMJs. What we do not want to experience is the pain of TMJ syndrome. TMJ pain occurs when chronic strain is placed on the joint from mis-mapping its location. The longer the joint is under strain, the more wear there is on the soft, cushiony cartilage designed to prevent friction between the two bones. When violinists suffer from TMJ syndrome, it is because this cartilage has either worn away or has popped out of its central location between the two bones. The result is that the jaw becomes offset from center and one bone begins to make painful contact with the other.

Finding the Temporomandibular Joints
1. Place both index fingers in front of your ears, directly in front of the little flaps of cartilage right above the ear lobes.
2. Open your mouth slowly two or three times.
3. Note that a hollow opens up as the jaw descends.
4. This hollow is the space created as the jaw bone moves down and away from the skull.
5. Keep your fingers in the hollow and close your mouth.
6. Notice that, if you palpate deeply enough, you can still feel where these two bones meet.
7. These are your temporomandibular joints.

8. As you open your mouth, if one of the hollows feels more shallow than the other, then there has been enough chronic pressure placed on one side of the jaw in holding the violin to cause it to be slightly off-set.

Figure 79 shows four places commonly mis-mapped as the location of the TMJ. Try opening your mouth according to these mis-mappings while watching your face in a mirror.
1. Try opening the jaw as if its joint was at X1 and you will notice that it gives your lips a fishy look.
2. The X2 mis-mapping forces the jaw to jut out while it opens.
3. Mis-mapping at X3 tenses all face muscles.
4. Opening with the TMJ mapped at X4 promotes mumbling, since the jaw can only open a very small bit, barely parting the lips.
5. Does one of these mis-mappings feel familiar to you?
6. Are you surprised to find out where the TMJ actually is?
7. Does one of the hollows at the TMJ feel deeper to you than the other?
8. If so, you want to spend time every day for a few weeks allowing the jaw to swing down and out while you monitor the movement with your fingertips in front of your ears, making certain that you are clear on what is jawbone and what is skull.

There are four possible conditions for a violinist's jaw while playing:
1. Teeth tightly clenched.
2. Teeth touching lightly.
3. Lips closed, teeth slightly apart.
4. Lips and teeth parted.

If your jaw is adequately mapped you probably alternate between the last three possible conditions as you play. If you find yourself using the first condition predominantly as you play, you are at risk of TMJ problems. This is a red flag that there may be excessive neck tension as well. You need to carefully remap the location of the TMJs, practicing primarily with the fourth condition until it is clear that the most released place for a jaw in neutral is with the teeth parted.

Face Muscles

As stated earlier, tension in the neck is always accompanied by chronic tightening of facial muscles.

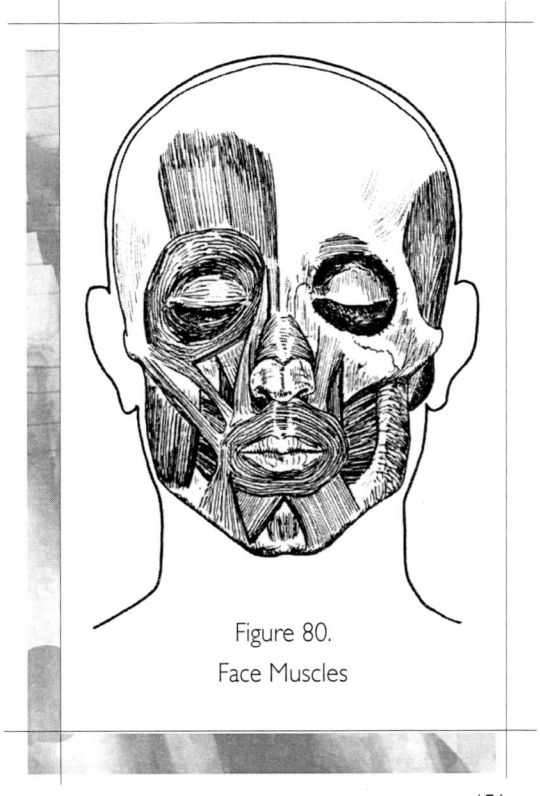

Figure 80.
Face Muscles

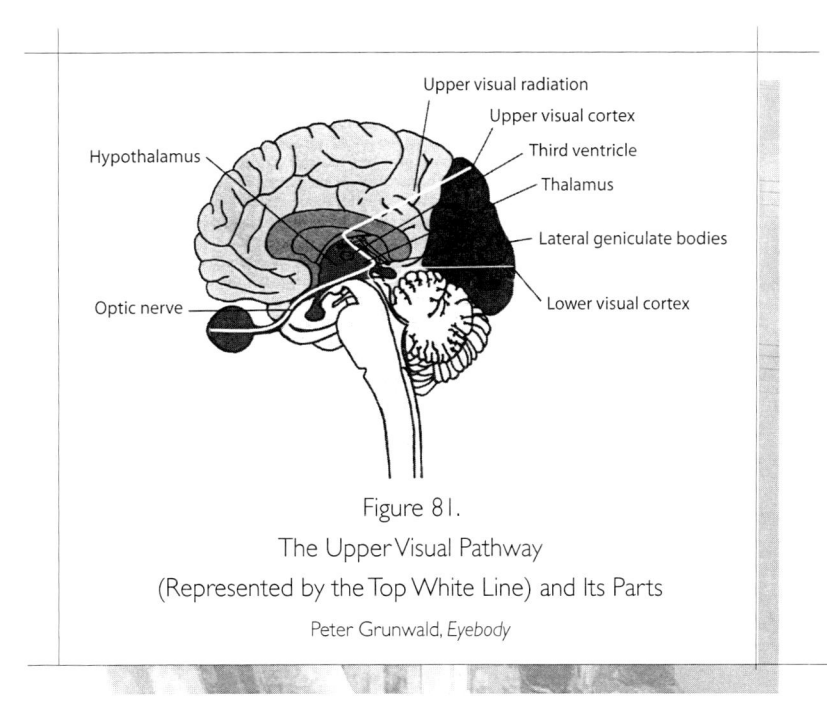

Figure 81.
The Upper Visual Pathway
(Represented by the Top White Line) and Its Parts
Peter Grunwald, *Eyebody*

Figure 80 shows that there are many face muscles of which most of us are unaware. When they are frozen in chronic holding, they are unavailable to be fully expressive as we play.

Frequently, chronic holding in the jaw leads to holding in the muscles around the nose and mouth. A personal story about my own experimenting with releasing chronic holding in these muscles might be illuminating:

I had just finished six weeks of daily Alexander Technique lessons with Pedro de Alcantara in Paris and was returning to London to complete my six months of Alexander Technique sabbatical. During one of my last lessons with Pedro, he placed two fingers on either side of his own nose and gently gestured up with them. He said little about it but I immediately felt that I was pulling down and in around my nostrils. As soon as I softened the muscles in that area, I felt my nostrils opening more (as if they were flaring) and more air rush into my lungs. I also felt a corresponding release in my TMJs and around my eyes.

At first, even though it was an empowering new sense, it also felt as if I was snarling when I allowed this release. So, for the next few days, I experimented in front of a mirror to make sure that it didn't appear this way. It didn't.

On the flight back to London, I spent my time on the plane reviewing my notes I had taken after each lesson with Pedro and was especially experimenting with this new release in my face. As I walked to the luggage belt to collect my bags at Heathrow Airport, a very kind gentleman stopped me in my tracks and said "I just have to tell you what a beautiful smile you have," and gesturing to each of his ears (actually at his TM joints), he said, "It goes right from here to here!" I was delighted that someone had noticed something pleasing enough about my countenance that he felt it was worthy of comment!

Eye Muscles

Of all the facial muscles, violinists most often unnecessarily tighten those surrounding the eyes. If you find yourself squeezing these muscles when reading music, it is likely that you have mapped your eyes as the point of vision and you are trying to "see with your eyes." In truth, the eyes are only windows to the brain that allow the image of what we look at to reach the part of the brain that actually does the seeing. The true point of vision is in the back third of the brain and is called the visual cortex.

Once again we are brought to a depth mapping issue. We mapped the depth of the upper torso from sternum through to the thoracic spine to allow the lungs their fullest capacity of air intake. We mapped the depth of the lower torso from pubic bones to tailbone to aid in freeing the abdominal wall and pelvic floor muscles. When the depth and the completely round shape of the eyeball itself is correctly mapped, and the depth of the skull (and therefore the brain) is incorporated by mapping the point of vision in the *back* of the brain rather than at the eyes themselves (or even worse, at the page of music itself!), the many chronically tensed muscles around the eyes and forehead automatically release.

Finding the Point of Vision While Playing
Part 1
1. Choose a familiar piece of music which is not too difficult to read.
2. Begin sight-reading the piece.
3. Notice what happens to the muscles around your eyes as you move into the faster passages.
4. Do you habitually squint or furrow your eyebrows?
5. If your eyes are not mis-mapped and your reading is usually fluid and easy, try reading with tension around your eyes anyway, since you will surely, at some point, encounter a student who does have the point of vision mapped at the eyes.
6. Next, cup a hand on the back of your head.
7. The visual cortex part of your brain is right under the part of the skull your hand is resting on.

Part 2
1. Play again, this time allowing the image of the notes to travel from the page through your eyes, through the mid-brain, where the optic nerves come together to integrate the image, and on to the visual cortex at the back of your brain where the work of interpreting the image is done.
2. This process of interpretation in the visual cortex is what we call "seeing." As long as your eyes are open and you are paying attention to what is around you, (daydreaming is an example of having your eyes open and not seeing your surroundings), there is no muscular work required in the face to allow images through the optic nerves to be interpreted by the brain.
3. Notice how much more of the page you can see at once, how much farther ahead your eyes can travel from the notes you are presently playing.
    a. "Look ahead" is common advice from teachers, but many students cannot do this because they are trying to "concentrate," craning their necks to peer at the music so they can get the eyes closer to the surface of the page.

    b. Assuming you have been to see your optometrist recently and whatever corrective lenses you may use are still appropriate, it is not necessary to take your eyes closer to the page.[16]

Part 3

1. Let the image travel to *you*. Not just to the surface of your eyes, but all the way back into the brain.
2. Can you sense other muscles releasing?
    a. In your neck, perhaps?
    b. Maybe down through the length of your spine?
3. Do you also begin to sense the greater depth of space in which you exist?
4. Not just behind the music stand in front of you; not just beside yourself where your stand partner sits; but also behind yourself.
5. Practicing sensing where the back of your skull is helps increase this awareness of your personal space.
6. There is a huge amount of space on all sides of you available for your whole being to expand into if you are able to sense and acknowledge it. Our world does not just exist in front of us!

This brings us nearly full circle back to the discussion in chapter 1 on training an *inclusive awareness* rather than training *concentration*. Students who are told to "concentrate" nearly always map their eyes or even the page of music as the point of vision rather than the visual cortex. Training yourself to see at the true point of vision simultaneously releases the muscles around your eyes as well as helps you retrain the quality of your attention. You may reach a whole new level of understanding of inclusive awareness if you now return to the exploration at the end of chapter 1 and apply your new knowledge regarding the point of vision.

Chapter 6
The Five Places of Support for the Violin

"Of the five places of support, the collarbone is the primary one."

The Collarbone

When the collarbone is not pulled back or down as a result of a mis-mapping in the upper arm structure, it is available in all of its length to provide a shelf-like support for the violin to sit on, or the shoulder-rest to sit on if one is used. The collarbone is the primary place of support for the violin and the only one that is constant, especially for players using a shoulder rest who choose to use the left hand minimally as a means of support. The collarbone as a place of support is essential for baroque violinists who choose to use little or no weight of the head in supporting the instrument.

The Head

A small portion of the head's weight can be lightly released onto the jaw-rest or "head-rest" (it is not a *chinrest!*) in order to prevent the violin from rocking side to side with each sweep of the bow across the strings as long as the head's perch is accurately mapped at the A.O. joint. When more stability is needed (such as in a downshift from a higher position), more head weight can be temporarily nodded onto the violin.

The Left Hand

Some players do not avail themselves of this source of support for the instrument at all, and consequently their neck and upper back muscles are overworked in an effort to hold up the violin at one end only. Some use the left hand optimally, in which case the head is much freer to move as they play; others use the left hand minimally, but enough to successfully relieve the head and neck muscles from the full-time job of supporting the violin. Use the left hand optimally and you will have many hundreds more places for the left thumb on the neck of the violin than those who do most of the support work at the other end of the instrument.

The Side of the Neck

Using the left hand optimally for supporting the violin requires contact and support from the side of the neck. Players using no shoulder rest or only a small amount of padding find large downshifts in particular are only possible if the scroll is higher than the other end, so that the weight of the instrument is allowed to fall right into and nestle against the side of the neck.

It is important to be very clear that the support from the side of the neck advocated here is *not* the same as *jamming* the violin into the side of the neck in search for security, nor is it the same as *squeezing* it between the collarbone and jawbone by tightening the neck muscles. Proper support from the side of the neck is simply allowing gravity to bring the instrument into contact.

Violinists who suffer from inflamed skin and sores on the sides of the neck often push or jam the instrument toward the neck rather than allowing gravity to bring it in. Occasionally, however, the inflammation is from an allergic reaction to the materials used to make the jaw-rest (usually the metal attachments) and this can be alleviated by switching to a hypoallergenic brand.

Many who use a shoulder rest find that they do not need to make use of the side of the neck as a source of support at all.

The Bow

The bow as a source of support for the violin is frequently overlooked, since support is often conceived as being something that must come from below. Think of supporting a book on the palm of your left hand. If you started tilting your hand, the book would begin to slip off; but if you placed your right hand lightly over the book, the book would stop slipping. It would not be necessary to apply a great force with your right hand to help support the book. The book only needs another surface to come into contact with it from above to provide that extra bit of support required to stabilize it. The bow functions in the same manner to help stabilize the violin, which at times can be nearly parallel to the floor, while at others on a fairly steep slope, depending on how much movement a player uses from her left sternoclavicular joint and what kind of rest or sponge she uses.

Interplay among the Five Places of Support

Of the five places of support, the collarbone is the primary one, since it is the only constant place of support and must be used by all violinists whether they use a shoulder rest, the left hand for support, or next to no support from the head as baroque players sometimes do. Even if you use all five places of support optimally, the other four places will be in a constant state of flux as the bow changes contact points, the head moves around, the left hand shifts up and down, and the changing height of the scroll changes the violin's contact with the side of the neck. Because the collarbone is essential as a place of support for the violin, it is necessary to have it accurately mapped (see chapter 4).

Chapter 7
Choices a Violinist Must Make

"Jaw and neck muscles are closely related."

Should I Use a Shoulder Rest?

This may well be one of the most contentious issues in violin pedagogy. Teachers who advocate using only a thin sponge or cloth insist that manufactured shoulder rests are too big, clunky, and rigid, and encourage a rigid response from the body. There are an equal number of teachers who believe that playing with a shoulder rest is just fine because they have used one their whole lives and have never encountered any problems. Playing the violin with superb artistry and freedom can be achieved both with and without a shoulder rest.

If you have been using a shoulder rest and the combination of its inflexibility, size, and *especially its misplacement* has already contributed to mis-mapping the collarbone as immobile and rigid, the first step in remapping the mobility of the left collarbone is to experiment with using shaped sponges or no rest at all. This often requires experimenting with more support from the left hand than perhaps you are accustomed to.

Some will decide to continue playing without a shoulder rest or with something much smaller. As discussed at length in chapter 4, if you pull your collarbones down in an effort to "keep the shoulders down," and if you rotate head back because of tightened neck muscles, you will discover that once you do the mapping work to find the suspended neutral of the arm structure the distance from collarbone to the bottom of the jaw is a much smaller distance. Often playing with an old shoulder rest is very uncomfortable once the head and arm structure are returned to neutral. It may be that something lower than first thought is needed to fill in the gap.

Still others decide to continue using a shoulder rest, but once remapping work produces mobility in the collarbone, they need to make sure that the shoulder rest sits primarily on *bone* rather than on *muscle*. Many encounter tension problems when using a shoulder rest because the shoulder rest is sitting on muscle—either the muscles in front of the collarbone (the pectorals) or on the muscles behind the collarbone (the trapezius.) Placing the shoulder rest so that it rests primarily on either of these muscle groups makes supporting the violin more difficult. It also makes freedom of the upper arm structure impossible, since a shoulder rest that exerts pressure on the muscles contributes to the notion of an immobile collarbone and also elicits a rigid response from the muscles.

If, however, the shoulder rest *crosses* the collarbone, it is supported almost entirely by the collarbone itself and is able to move with the collarbone when movement here is desired. Each player needs to experiment with the exact angle of this cross to find the most comfortable arrangement.

Finally, remapping work reveals to some players that they need to move in the other direction—from the sponge or small pad they were using to a *higher* shoulder rest. If neutral for the arm structure is mapped as higher than its place of balanced suspension, and this is combined with *squeezing* the violin with the neck and upper arm muscles, remapping may reveal that something larger is needed to fill the space between the collarbone and jawbone. Remember that the shoulder rest needs to cross over the collarbone itself and not rest on the surrounding muscles. For more ideas on custom-fitting a shoulder rest, see the excellent article by Phillip Pan at www.bodymap.org

Left-hand Support: Maximal or Minimal?

The left hand is one of the five places of support for a balanced violin and should be used to some degree in a role of support. Decide to use it optimally as a source of support and you will find a continually changing place for the thumb along the neck and in relation to the rest of the hand, depending on what finger is played, hand position, and the string depressed. This requires a precise and accurate body map of a three-jointed thumb so that the thumb is free enough to be this malleable.

If the left hand is used minimally as a source of support the thumb has fewer places of contact against the neck, but must be equally well-mapped for the very reason that it is *not* moving very much. If the thumb's base is not clearly felt as located next to the wrist bones, it will likely migrate up to the TJ2 in the body map and become locked at all three thumb joints.

Points of Contact between the Jaw and Jaw-rest: Many or One?

Some players heads are so beautifully balanced on top of the spine that they can play for hours and never feel the need to move the head one bit because the neck muscles are just so free! Others, however, do not move their heads when they play because the neck muscles are so hard at work in squeezing, tucking, dropping, or lodging the violin into place.

If your head is immobile and neck muscles are tense when you play, begin by playing slow scales in front of a mirror and see how often you can move your head from one contact point along your jaw to another. Also try taking your head right off the instrument at times. You may find you do not need it as much as you think. Being able to make contact along several points on the jaw frees you to easily turn your head to look from the conductor to the music and then over to watch the piano soloist.

Teeth Parted with Lips Closed (Neutral); Both Slightly Parted; or Teeth Lightly Closed?

If you do not make a conscious choice about how your teeth relate to each other in the mouth, you will be unconscious about what is happening in the jaw muscles. Jaw and neck muscles are closely related; any clenching of the teeth while playing leads to unnecessary neck tension. Choosing to play with any one of the three options outlined above prevents clenching in the jaw muscles. If you are a "clencher," it is best to start with muscular neutral: teeth parted and lips closed.

Will the Bow do all of the Moving, or Will the Violin Sometimes Move to the Bow?

There are numerous examples of great players (Heifetz comes to mind) who primarily move the bow across the strings but are still obviously very free in all four joints of the left arm. Sometimes, however, a player does not move the violin at all. This is because the collarbone is not mapped as part of a free and moveable arm.

If your left arm feels restricted, practice moving the violin *into* the bow on up bows and back to a neutral position on down bows. This is one of the easiest ways to awaken some sensation from arm joint 1. Once movement at the left sternoclavicular joint is mapped as a possibility, you can choose to what degree you wish to use it in performance. You may decide that you will only move the violin into the bow in dramatic gestures, such as at the beginning of a *fortissimo* down-bow chord. However, after doing the work required to remap this joint you will not likely ever again try to hold the sternoclavicular joint still. The movement from there may not be overt, but there is a felt resilience at arm joint 1, and you will never lose your awareness of the whole, four-jointed arm and the freedom afforded at all arm joints right down to the fingertips.

Chapter 8
Common Mis-mappings and Myths in Violin Playing

"Unlike a hinge, the wrist has three joints."

Mis-mappings Affecting the Violin Side
Raising the Violin

Violin-side Mis-mapping 1: Our Back Muscles Hold Us Up
Related Myths

1. The good posture disease.
2. It is necessary to lean back in order to counterbalance the weight of the violin in front.
3. Don't lock your knees back.

Fact

As part of the good posture disease, this mis-mapping leads directly to overarching the lumbar spine and indirectly to pushing the hip joints forward and locking the knees. The superficial back muscles (top layer) are designed primarily to move the arms, *not hold the body up*!

The support muscles (inner two layers) which *do* help to hold up the body are involuntary and much deeper and closer to the spine. These muscles automatically engage when the bones are brought into a balanced relationship with one another.

In order to play on balance around the core, places of balance 3 and 4 (the weight-bearing part of the lumbar spine and the hip joints respectively) must be over balanced knees and ankles when standing, and directly above the sit bones when seated.

When the good posture disease or leaning back in a misguided effort to balance the violin disrupts this balance when standing, the knees lock back in an effort to provide stability and protect the lower back muscles. Asking a person to unlock the knees before he finds balance for the structures above only causes his lower back muscles to contract further.

When the advice to "stop locking your knees back" is given without first correcting the balance issues above, diligent students frequently resort to locking the knees in a *bent* position. Easy balance at the knee joint is found between the locked back and "locked bent" positions. The sensations caused by chronically locked knees leads to mis-mapping 2.

Violin-side Mis-mapping 2: The Kneecap Is the Knee
Related Myth

1. Knees are only at the front.

Fact

When the knees are chronically locked back, the overwhelming sensation of the kneecap being driven backward into the thigh bone produces a hyper-awareness of the kneecap itself, and so leads to the kneecap-as-knee fantasy. Bending at the knee then becomes strained because the joint is mapped up where the kneecap is rather than just below it. A knee is not a thing; it is a place where two bones meet—specifically where the thigh bone meets and balances on top of the large lower-leg bone. Mapping the meeting of these bones from the back and the sides is as important as mapping them from the front.

Supporting the Violin to Play

Violin-side Mis-mapping 3: The A.O. Joint Is Lower and Farther Back than It Really Is
Related Myths

1. You must hold the violin entirely with your head so your left hand will be free.
2. Drop your head onto the violin like you would on a pillow.
3. Neck muscles must work to hold the violin.

Fact

Mis-mapping the location of the A.O. joint as too far back or too low results in a tightening of neck muscles which leads to the head, chin, or jaw holding the violin in place by *squeezing, lodging, tucking,* or *dropping* onto the chinrest. Try to balance your head anywhere but at the true A.O. joint, and your neck muscles are already working, even before a violin is introduced into the picture.

A small portion of the head's weight *is* one of the five sources of support for the instrument, but it can fulfill its role in helping to support the violin without losing its balance on the spine and without the neck muscles working to *hold* onto the instrument in any way.

Both *squeezing* and *lodging* usually entail the head/neck joint mapped too low and too far back.

Squeezing occurs when the neck is jutted out with the collarbone/shoulder blade pushed up to squeeze from underneath.

Rotate your head back and down and lift your chin, and you are *lodging*. It will appear that the chin, instead of the upper teeth, is on the same horizontal plane as the base of the skull, and the collarbone will also be pushed down too low. *Lodging* results from mis-mapping the head/

neck joint as only at the back rather than centrally located—right between the ears—and mis-mapping the collarbones as resting on the ribs. The huge gap this creates between the jaw and collarbone leads some to think they have an "excessively long neck," and therefore need more height in their shoulder rests.

Dropping the weight of the head onto the chinrest "like onto your pillow" is frequently connected to having the top of the neck mis-mapped as ending just under the jaw. The head (typically twelve pounds) is tilted forward or sideways right off its balance on the A.O. joint. Try to move the head from such a low place—from under the jaw—and several neck vertebrae are dragged along with the head. *Dropping* the head also results in the collarbone being pushed down too low from excessive head weight driving down onto the violin.

Tucking also results from mis-mapping the top of the neck as being just under the jaw instead of much higher between the ears. When the jaw is mapped as being part of the skull rather than as an appendage, the violin is pulled in close by the chin gripping the edge of the chinrest and tucking in. *Tucking* is one of the good posture disease mis-mappings and causes the cervical spine to flatten.

For healthy support from the head, *all five places of support* need to be used to some degree: head, left hand, collarbone, side of the neck, and contact of the bow on the string. The head should balance on the top of the *spine* and turn slightly until the jaw makes contact with the chinrest (chinrests are for jaws not for chins). This is sufficient support from the head for much of what we do as violinists.

When more security is needed, the head can rotate forward lightly on the A.O. fulcrum to make a firmer contact with the violin. In this way it is still perched on top of the spine, *releasing only a small portion of its weight* onto the violin. This allows the spine to release into its full length because the neck muscles are still free. A head that helps support the violin in this way is free to move in all directions, sometimes even bringing the jaw off the chinrest entirely. In so doing there are several contact points all along the length of the jaw bone.

Violin-side Mis-mapping 4: The Collarbone/Shoulder-blade Unit Rests on the Ribs
Related Myth

1. Keep the shoulders down and still.
    a. Consequent myth: The violin should not move, only the bow moves.

Fact

The collarbone is one of the five places of support for the violin and the only constant one. In order to fulfill this role, it must be balanced in suspension over the torso, not pushed down on top of the ribs. When the violin sits on a suspended collarbone it feels light and quite high, even without a shoulder rest.

When a collarbone is not pushed down on top of the ribs, it is free to take the violin into movement as well as the bow. Great players frequently take the violin right across the torso in dramatic gesture.

Violin-side Mis-mapping 5: The Ball of the Humerus Forms a Joint with Some Imagined Structure instead of the Shoulder Blade

Violin-side Mis-mapping 6: The Shoulder Blade Belongs on the Back
Related Myths

1. Sit up straight.
2. Get your shoulders back.

Fact

The socket is in the shoulder blade itself, and in neutral is at the side of the body, just like the ear directly above it—not yanked around somewhere on the back. In this way the humerus, and in turn all of the lower arm bones receive the balanced support they need from the upper arm structure when supporting the violin.

Violin-side Mis-mapping 7: The Elbow Bends an Inch Farther up the Forearm than Where the Joint Is Actually Located

See mis-mapping and myth under "Elbow Vibrato" below.

Fact

If the location of the elbow's bending joint in the left arm is mis-mapped, unnecessary forearm muscles work in an effort to support the violin. If the trochlear notch of the ulna and its perch on the humerus is accurately mapped, the forearm is brought to its bent position by the biceps and requires little muscular effort to stay upright. Unnecessary tension in the left forearm in an effort to support the instrument causes muscular sensation up the forearm from where the joint actually is—this reinforces the mis-mapping, creating a vicious circle.

Violin-side Mis-mapping 8: The Hand Supinates to the String by Rotating the Ulna at the Elbow

Related Myth

1. Bring the pinkie right over the strings.

Fact

The design of the elbow joint allows no rotation (supination or pronation) from the place where the *ulna* meets the humerus. It is the other forearm bone, the *radius*, that provides rotation for the forearm. The wrist and hand bones attach to the radius, and so the hand can be supinated safely and easily when the radius is the bone mapped for the movement.

It is true that we want the pinkie curved and poised over the string, but when a teacher mentions only the pinkie in an effort to correct a left hand, the student's attention is brought to the wrong side of the arm. In reality the rotating movement happens on the thumb side of the arm, not the pinkie side.

Violin-side Mis-mapping 9: The Hand Supinates to the String by Rotating at the Wrist

Fact

The hand cannot supinate or pronate by moving at the wrist. The tiny amount of movement available in a rotational direction from the eight little bones that comprise the wrist is negligible. Again, rotation happens from the *radius* swiveling at its joint with the humerus.

Violin-side Mis-mapping 10: The Wrist is a Single Joint Located at the Skin Crease between the Forearm Bones and the Palm

Related Myth

1. The wrist is a hinge.

Fact

The wrist has three joints, not just one joint as a hinge does, and the third joint (between FB1 and the top row of wrist bones) must be mapped high enough into the hand so that the FB1s in the left hand feel supported as they perch on top of the wrist bones. The freedom of the left-hand fingers depends on sensing this structural security for the finger bones and on sensing the available movement for the fingers from this joint.

Violin-side Mis-mapping 11: A Violinist's Fingers Move apart from the Large Row of Knuckles

Related Myth

1. The fingers begin at the large row of knuckles or base knuckles.

Fact

The large row of knuckles (FJ2) does provide a small amount of spreading, *but only when the fingers are straight.* Therefore, most of the spreading in the left hand that happens when playing originates from FJ1. (Exception: when the first finger straightens at FJ2 to extend back, as in playing tenths.)

Violin-side Mis-mapping 12: The Wrist Is at Neutral When the Back of the Hand Forms a Flat Surface with the Back of the Forearm

Related Myth

1. No pancake hands!

Fact

When the wrist is at neutral (no muscular work) and perched on an upright forearm, there is a slight backwards slope to the hand so that the FB1s do *not* form a flat surface with the surface of the back of the forearm. Frequently teachers disallow any of the natural curve at the back of a wrist in neutral in an effort to prevent students from trying to support the neck or shoulders of the violin with an extremely extended wrist ("pancake hands").

Violin-side Mis-mapping 13: The Thumb Is a Two-jointed Digit and Joins the Hand at TJ2

Related Myth

1. The palm myth.
2. The head holds the violin so that the left hand can be free.

Fact

The "palm" of the hand is comprised of four FB1s and one TB1, all of which form joints with the top row of wrist bones. It is not, as some violinists have it mapped, a solid piece of flat bone or flesh, so there is plenty of movement available in many directions from these base finger bones. If the left thumb is mapped as only two-jointed, it will pull into the side of the hand at TJ2 to take on the appearance that this is where it joins the hand. This leaves only a V-shaped "crotch" for the violin neck to rest in.

Because pulling in TB1 crowds and impedes free movement of *all* of FB1s, the whole hand is left feeling tense, and therefore fatigues quickly. This leads some to try to relieve the hand entirely from its shared role of supporting the violin. Having lost support for the violin at one end, they then resort to *squeezing, lodging, tucking, or dropping* the head to increase a sense of security at the other end of the instrument. The left hand *is* one of the five sources of support for the violin, and when it is not used at all in this role, the other four sources of support must share too much of the work.

If the thumb is mis-mapped as a two-jointed, rather than three-jointed digit, using the left hand to help support the violin will still produce limitations in left hand dexterity. The three-jointed thumb joins the hand at its joint with the wrist bones (TJ1), and is therefore long and opposable to all the other fingers rather than pulled in and forced onto the same plane as the fingers. A free, three-jointed thumb is sometimes opposite the first finger, other times opposite the second or even third finger, depending on where it is most needed for the task of the moment.

Depressing the Strings

Violin-side Mis-mapping 14: Most of the Bending from FJ2 to Sufficiently Depress the String Is from an Active, Muscular Flexing

Fact

If the first finger contacts the neck at or below FJ2, there is enough gravity acting on the finger bones themselves to take them into a full, passive, natural curve, which is sufficient to begin depressing the string. Only a tiny amount of active flexing work is required from FJ2 to depress the string for a clear tone. Excessive active bending at FJ2 prevents the important spreading movements between FB1s. (See "Playing Large Intervals" below.)

Violin-side Mis-mapping 15: The Fingers Move from the Third Skin Crease Down from the Tip (as Viewed from the Palm)

Related Myth

1. Each crease on the palm demarcates the location of a joint.

Fact

This is an example of a "false joint" that comes from mapping the structure of the hand from the palm-side rather than from the back of the hand. When traced to the back of the hand, it becomes clear that there is no joint at this crease. The real joint (FJ2) is about an inch lower into the palm. This mis-mapping is easy to spot because the first finger always contacts the violin neck either *at* the false joint or even further up the finger (in the direction of the fingertip.) This too-high contact point frequently leads to the mis-mapping 16.

Violin-side Mis-mapping 16: Active Bending or Curling at the Tip Joints (FJ3–4) Aids in Bending FJ2

Related Myths

1. The left hand must stand tall and be highly arched.
2. The fingers should meet the string right on their tips.
3. The fingernails should face the wall.

Fact

Highly arching the fingers by actively bending or *curling* them at the tip joints (FJ3 and FJ4) prevents an easy and free movement of the fingers up and down from FJ2 because it sets up the co-contraction of two opposing muscle groups. *It is not possible* to move the fingers up and down quickly from FJ2 when FJ3 and FJ4 are tightly curled. An easy and fast up-and-down movement results from allowing FJ3 and FJ4 to remain in their *natural curve* rather than being *curled*.

When the left forearm is constantly over-supinated so that the fingernails face the wall (to the player's left) instead of the player's face, the tip joints are forced into a curl in order to depress the string.

Violin-side Mis-mapping 17: Each Finger Has Only Three Joints

Related Myths

1. The palm is a solid unit of bone or flesh.
2. Drop the fingers to the string from the base knuckles (the large row of knuckles).

Fact

It is true that the majority of finger movement to the string comes from bending at FJ2; however, in reality each finger has *four joints,* and free movement of the fingers in all directions depends on mapping movement at *all four* of these joints, including the movement of the FB1s (in the base of the "palm") up and away from the wrist bones from FJ1.

Violin-side Mis-mapping 18: The Only Function of the Fingers When Depressing Strings Is an Up-and-Down Movement

Related Myth

1. The fingers are like little hammers.

Fact

In addition to moving up and down, the fingers, especially the third and fourth, need *forward movement from FJ1* to depress the string. The first, second, and third fingers also need some *spreading movement from FJ1 and FJ2 (known as reaching back)* to depress the strings and play in tune in first position. They also need quite a bit of spreading movement in any passage requiring backward extensions. Remember: it is not just FJ2 that allows the fingers to travel to and from the string, forward and back, and to spread apart from one another: *equally important is the movement in all of these directions from FJ1!*

Violin-side Mis-mapping 19: Only the Finger Joints Are Involved in Depressing the Strings

Related Myth

1. Drop or throw your fingers to the string from the base joints (large row of knuckles).

Fact

To move the third and especially the fourth finger to the lower strings, particularly in chord playing when the first and second fingers reach back to play pitches on the A or E strings, there is extra supination from the elbow joint (radius) required as well as movement across the whole wrist.

Moving the Fingers across from the Highest to Lowest Strings

Violin-side Mis-mapping 20: It Is the Elbow That Enables the Left Hand to Move from the E to G String

Related Myth

1. Get the elbow under.

Fact

This complex movement requires freedom at all four arm joints, including *a small bit* of extra rotation from the radius at the elbow joint. However, it is primarily rotation at the humeroscapular and sternoclavicular joints that is responsible for this movement. Drawing attention only to the elbow is misleading and can cause the upper two arm joints to lose mobility. Thinking only about the elbow "getting under" also draws too much attention to the ulna side of the arm, sometimes leading to mis-mapping the supination as happening from the ulna instead of the radius.

Shifting up the Strings into the Highest Positions

Violin-side Mis-mapping 21: Shifting up the Strings Occurs Only by Bending at the Elbow

Fact

Free movement must be mapped at *all four arm joints* in order for facile shifting into the higher positions. If it is mapped as happening only at the elbow joint, freedom at all three of the other arm joints is compromised. Shifting up and down the fingerboard requires as much movement side to side (mostly from arm joint 2 and a bit from arm joint 1, since the elbow joint cannot provide movement in this direction) as the in/out direction the bending elbow provides. Trying to shift up and down by using only the bending elbow joint leaves the wrist in particular vulnerable to strain, and problems like ganglion cysts can result.

Violin-side Mis-mapping 22: The Wrist Has Only One Joint

Related Myth

1. Bend your wrist like a hinge.

Fact

In addition to movement from the first three arm joints, movement across all three joints of the wrist must be explicitly taught as part of shifting into high positions. Frequently, it is long hours of practicing in the high registers with a wrist mis-mapped as a one-jointed hinge which causes wrist inflammation and pain. Remapping the wrist from a hinge joint to a long, three-jointed wrist usually returns the eight wrist bones to their right relationship with one another and relieves pressure on the tendon sheath.

Elbow Vibrato

Violin-side Mis-mapping 23: Elbow Vibrato Is Initiated by Moving the Arm

Related Myth

1. Arm vibrato.

Fact

Describing this as an "arm" vibrato does not specify the exact joint of the arm at which the movement occurs and is therefore too vague to be useful. But vibrato is often instantly freed when we understand that the movement originates at the bending joint of the elbow and accurately map how the humerus fits into the trochlear notch of the ulna, allowing support for the ulna from its perch on top of the humerus. Without the specific understanding of this bony balance, we can easily mis-map the joint somewhere else along the ulna (usually an inch or so toward the wrist; *see mis-mapping 5)*, which produces a tight and narrow vibrato.

Wrist Vibrato

Violin-side Mis-mapping 24: The One-jointed Wrist Is Located at the Skin Crease between the Forearm and Palm

Related Myth

1. Wave your hand at its hinge.

Fact

Unlike a hinge, the wrist has three joints: where the radius meets the first row of wrist bones, where the two rows of wrist bones meet, and where the second row of wrist bones meets the hand bones. If any of these bones are jammed together, a wrist vibrato will be clumsy, laborious, and eventually injury-producing.

Playing Large Intervals Such as Tenths and Fingered Octaves

Violin-side Mis-mapping 25: Spreading Movement Must Occur at the Large Row of Knuckles because This Is Where the Fingers Begin

Related Myth

1. Bring your fingers to the string from the base joint (large knuckles).

Fact

The finger bones *begin* where they form a joint with the wrist bones; therefore, when playing large intervals most of the fingers' spreading movements are allowed from the FJ1s. The fourth finger moves primarily *forward* from FJ1, while the first, second, and third fingers *spread apart* from FJ1. (It may seem impossible that FJ1 allows enough spreading to make a difference, but like all long levers, a little movement at the base where it pivots creates much more movement at the tip.)

Violin-side Mis-mapping 26: Fingers Can Spread While Actively Bending from FJ2

Related Myth

1. My hand is too small to play tenths.

Fact

Excessive active bending at FJ2 precludes an easy spreading of the fingers at FJ1 and FJ2 and creates the impression that the hand is too small to play tenths or fingered octaves:

Spreading at FJ1

If there is excessive active bending at FJ2, none of the FB1s are able to move in any direction. If the fourth finger cannot move forward at FJ1 and the other fingers cannot spread at FJ1, playing tenths is impossible. Remember that the string can be depressed nearly enough to make a clear tone by only the *passive* bending (natural curve) at FJ2. Only a very small amount of active muscular flexion at FJ2 is needed to finish depressing the string.

Spreading at FJ2

Active *or* passive *bending* at FJ2 precludes the possibility of the fingers from spreading from FJ2. This is why, when playing tenths, we need to straighten the first finger at FJ2 so that it can *spread* (reach back) from FJ2. The same holds true for the second finger reaching back to play fingered octaves.

When the minimal required amount of active bending is used at FJ2 to finish depressing the string, the hand is afforded a much greater degree of spread between the fingers at both FJ1 and FJ2.

Mis-mappings Affecting the Bow Side
Supporting the Bow

Bow-side Mis-mapping 1: Finger Muscles Are Located in the Hand
Related Myths

1. The bow is held.
2. In order to hold the bow, the muscles of the hand must be strengthened.

Fact

Most of the muscles that move the fingers are in the forearm. What is often mapped as muscle around FB2, FB3, and FB4 is actually fat, though there is some attachment of muscle (tendons) at FJ2. The thumb and pinkie muscles (on the palm side of hand) perform minimal work and do not need exercises to strengthen them. The bow is *supported* by the right hand balanced between the fingers and the thumb and the violin string.

Bow-side Mis-mapping 2: The Collarbone/Shoulder-blade Unit Rests on the Ribs
Related Myth

1. The right shoulder should be kept down.

Fact

When the arm structure is in a balanced neutral, it is in a state of suspension, suspended from the bony structures above by a sheet of elastic connective tissue. This balanced, springy neutral allows the bow arm to freely and easily move in any direction needed.

Bow-side Mis-mapping 3: The Top of the Arm Is at the "Shoulder Joint"

Related Myth

1. The "shoulder" is an anatomical unit separate from the arm.

Fact

The word "shoulder" describes only a region, and therefore is not specific enough. The whole arm includes the collarbone and the shoulder blade. For a free bow arm, it is necessary to map the arm as moving from the sternoclavicular joint.

Bow-side Mis-mapping 4: There Is an Arm Socket at the Side Separate from the Shoulder Blade, Which Must Stay on the Back

Related Myths

1. Keep your bowing shoulder back and down.
2. Stabilize your bow shoulder.

Fact

The arm socket is contained in the form of the shoulder blade, right in its side. Huge strain is placed on the upper arm structure when the humerus tries to move in one direction while its socket is yanked in another.

Bow-side Mis-mapping 5: The Arm Socket Is Large Enough to Encompass the Ball of the Humerus

Related Myth

1. Placing the fist of one hand in the enclosed fingers of the other hand demonstrates the arm's ball and socket.

Fact

The socket is only as large as the thumb's pad, and does not include the overhanging portion of the shoulder blade. The humerus can move in the myriad directions needed for bowing because the socket is small relative to the size of the ball.

Bow-side Mis-mapping 6: The Ulna Turns the Hand Palm Down in Order to Pronate the Bow Hand

Bow-side Mis-mapping 7: Pronation Happens When Both Bones Crisscross to Swap Places

Bow-side Mis-mapping 8: The Wrist Contributes to the Hand's Pronation

Bow-side Mis-mapping 9: There Is Only One Bone Running down the Center of the Forearm, around Which the Forearm Muscles Radiate

Fact

There are *two* bones in the forearm with completely different functions. The *radius* bone rotates; the ulna is stationary. The radius swivels at its joint with the humerus (at the elbow) to cross over the ulna. The whole hand moves with the radius to cross over the stationary ulna. The wrist is incapable of making a rotational movement to pronate the hand. This movement comes entirely from the elbow joint.

Bow-side Mis-mapping 10: The Bow Wrist Is a Hinge or Crease Found Only at the End of the Forearm Bones

Related Myth

1. Wrist creases mark the bottom of a solid palm.

Fact

For a free right hand as it supports the bow, all three wrist joints must provide movement. The joint where the wrist bones meet the ends of the finger bones can be seen and felt way up into the palm area; freedom at this joint is essential to having free thumb mobility in the bow hand.

Bow-side Mis-mapping 11: The Thumb Has Only Two Joints

Related Myths

1. The tip of the thumb is "a shelf" for the bow to sit on.
2. Bend the end joint of the thumb.

Fact

The thumb has three joints. Extreme bending of the thumb at TJ3 rather than leaving it in its natural curve locks both of the joints under it and contributes to the two-jointed thumb fantasy. When the thumb is immobilized at its base joint with the wrist, the wrist bones can jam, sometimes leading to numbness and always leading to an overdeveloped thumb (thenar) muscle and a bony, overdeveloped TJ2.

Playing from Frog to Tip

Bow-side Mis-mapping 12: A Down-bow Is Primarily an Unbending at the Elbow

Related Myth

1. A down bow means the arm moves down and out.

Fact

Moving the bow across the string in a down bow is a highly complex movement involving all four arm joints moving in multiple directions.

1. After following the humerus forward and up at the end of the up bow, the collarbone releases down to its balanced place of suspension.
2. The humerus moves in three different directions: down, back, and in rotation.
3. The elbow joint unbends and pronates the forearm as the bow reaches the tip.
4. The wrist extends by using all three of its joints.
5. The collarbone/shoulder-blade unit is allowed some forward movement as the bow approaches the tip, especially for short-armed players.

And then all of this happens in reverse for an up bow.

Playing from Tip To Frog

Bow-side Mis-mapping 13: The Collarbone/Shoulder-blade Unit Rests on the Ribs

Related Myth

1. The right shoulder must stay down as the player approaches the frog.

Fact

Trying to keep the shoulder region down when approaching the frog destroys humeroscapular rhythm. As the humerus rises and approaches a closer proximity to the torso, the scapula must be allowed to follow or great strain is placed on the humeroscapular joint and the muscles of the upper torso region. Breathing is also restricted because the upper ribs cannot move when the arm structure hauls down on top of them.

Crossing Strings

Bow-side Mis-mapping 14: The Collarbone/Shoulder-blade Unit Rests on the Ribs

Related Myth

1. If the shoulder rises as the arm moves the bow toward the G string, you are tense.

Fact

To cross from the E string to the G string, the humerus must simultaneously move up and rotate as the collarbone and shoulder blade follow in both the upward and rotational directions. Much injury, including bursitis in the humeroscapular joint and rotator cuff tears, occurs from not allowing the collarbone and shoulder blade to follow in a healthy humeroscapular rhythm. Violinists who play second violin in an opera orchestra are particularly vulnerable to injury if they have lost their humeroscapular rhythm because of the amount of time they spend on the lower strings at the frog.

Playing off the String

Bow-side Mis-mapping 15: The Collarbone/Shoulder-blade Unit Rests on the Ribs

Related Myth

1. The wrist and fingers make the bow bounce.
2. The shoulder must be stabilized.

Fact

It is not just the wrist and fingers—not just the wrist, fingers, and elbow—not just the wrist, fingers, elbow, and humerus—but the fingers plus all four arm joints, including the sternoclavicular joint, that are involved in producing an easy and clear off-the-string stroke. Even players who have mapped humeroscapular rhythm in their legato playing sometimes believe that they must "stabilize the shoulder" in order to play *collé,* brush, *spiccato* or *sautillé* strokes.

Bow-side Mis-mapping 16: The Fingers Can Extend Only through Muscular Effort

Related Myth

1. The *colle* stroke should be played with active finger movement.

Fact

Muscularly extending the fingers while flexing the wrist (e.g., for a down-bow *colle* stroke) causes co-contraction of the extensor and flexor muscles in the forearm. The fingers naturally extend when the wrist is flexed because the tendons of the fingers are pulled taut passively as a *result* of the wrist bending.

Playing over the Fingerboard

Bow-side Mis-mapping 17: Only the Flexion at the Wrist Joint Provides the Necessary Suspension of the Bow

Related Myth

1. Suspend the bow from the wrist.

Fact

In order to suspend some of the weight of the bow when playing on this more pliant contact point, all four arm joints are involved.

1. The wrist flexes.
2. The elbow joint unbends to move the bow farther away from the body.
3. The humerus moves forward and rotates upward.
4. The scapula follows the humerus in a healthy humeroscapular rhythm.

Playing Close to the Bridge

Bow-side Mis-mapping 18: The Collarbone/Shoulder-blade Unit Is Supported by Resting on the Ribs Rather than Being Suspended from Above

Bow-side Mis-mapping 19 (a Consequence of Bow-side Mis-mapping 18): The Arm Stops at the Shoulder Joint and Is Capable of "Hanging" from Its Socket

Related Myths

1. Make the arm heavy.
2. Hang the weight of the arm from the bow.
    a. Or drop the weight of the arm into the string.

Fact

The string is stiffer by the bridge and therefore requires more friction to set it vibrating. However, dropping arm weight drags the arm structure down from its suspended balance, which leads to mis-mapping the collarbone as resting on the ribs. When arm weight is dropped, most of it does not travel into the string, but rather down into the torso through the ribs, which are not designed to bear weight.

With the loss of suspension of the arms comes loss of humeroscapular rhythm because the scapula is not free to move when being dragged down onto the ribs. When arms work from a place of balance, the sensation is one of lightness, floating, and buoyancy—not one of heaviness.

Getting the string vibrating at this stiffer contact point is achieved by producing sufficient *friction* as the bow is drawn across the string. Producing sufficient friction is accomplished by rotating the balanced arm into the bow using an even distribution of muscle use throughout the entire arm structure rather than hanging or dropping arm weight into the bow.

Practicing and Performing

Practicing and Performing Mis-mapping 1: Violin Playing Requires Movement Only from Joints in the Upper Half of the Body

Related Myths

1. Put your feet in playing position.
2. Place your feet in the proper spaces on your foot chart.

Fact

Many children are taught to keep their feet in an exact position on a foot chart while they play. This immobility of the feet and legs contributes to locking in the knee and hip joints. Encouraging stepping into high points of phrases and moving the feet in musically dramatic moments helps to maintain balance by preventing locking in the leg joints.

Practicing and Performing Mis-mapping 2: The Legs Meet the Torso at the Front, not the Sides

Related Myths

1. Put your feet together when you bow after your performance.
2. Rest position feet on your foot chart.

Fact

The thigh bones meet their sockets in the pelvis at the *sides* of the body and then come down to meet the lower leg bone at the knee on a diagonal slant. Putting the feet together reinforces the fantasy that thigh bones come straight down from the front to meet the lower leg bone. For balance when bowing, the feet should be wide enough apart that they are under the hip joints.

Practicing and Performing Mis-mapping 3: Removing Everything from Awareness Except the Task of Playing Makes the Body Freer to Perform

Related Myth

1. Concentrate, Johnnie!

Fact

Concentration is a narrowing of the field of attention. When attention is narrowed, the body narrows. Inclusive awareness is the alternative. By including everything around you somewhere within your field of attention, nothing can take you by surprise. This reduces your feeling of vulnerability and therefore is a very effective strategy for dealing with stage fright. It also teaches the body that there is a great deal of available space to expand into.

Practicing and Performing Mis-mapping 4: The Eyes Must Look at What the Hands Are Doing at All Times in Order to Prevent Distraction

Related Myth

1. Keep your eyes on the bow or string.
2. Keep your eyes on your left-hand fingers.

Fact

This is related to concentrating. While there is information to be obtained from watching the bow, it is not healthy to keep the eyes anywhere while playing. Staring or fixing the eyes is a sure sign of loss of inclusive awareness and will cause the body to fix in position. Teaching peripheral vision and easy movement of the eyes to where they are most needed—from instrument to music to conductor to fellow musicians to audience—helps the player move away from concentrating toward a healthy inclusive awareness.

Acknowledgments

There are many people to whom I am grateful for making the writing of this book possible. I owe a huge debt of gratitude to my first Alexander Technique teacher and good friend, Trevor Allan Davies for bringing such integrity and care to the Alexander work and for his uncanny insight and eloquence when teaching it. I want to thank all of the other many wonderful Alexander Technique teachers with whom I've had the good fortune to study: Pedro de Alcantara, John Crawford, Diana Dantes, Alex and Joan Murray, and Peter and Ellie Ribeaux. Five years later, I continue to draw from the bank of your combined inspiration and wisdom in my teaching and writing.

I am grateful to the Canada Council for the Arts for granting the funding that provided me the opportunity to study the Alexander Technique abroad with all of these marvelous teachers and to Peter Gardner for his invaluable advice on securing funding. Thank you to Helen Brunner for welcoming me into her home during my intensive Alexander Technique study period in London.

This book could not have come to fruition without the talent and generosity of David Gorman. His wealth of knowledge of human anatomy and movement along with his beautifully detailed illustrations from *The Body Moveable* were constant companions of mine during the writing of this book. He generously permitted the reprinting of many of those images for *What Every Violinist Needs to Know about the Body (WEV)*. A huge thanks also to Ben Conable for allowing the reprinting of his beautiful illustrations from *What Every Musician Needs to Know about the Body* and to Tracy Dillon for all of her time, talent, and patience while creating the custom-made illustrations for *WEV*. Also thanks to Peter Grunwald for granting permission to reprint an illustration from his ground-breaking book, *Eyebody*.

An enormous thank you goes to Gregg Sewell, my editor, whose wonderful ability and careful attention to detail I so appreciate.

Thank you to William Conable, Nancy Dahn, Mark Latham, Marilyn McDonald, Christina Smith, and Donald Weilerstein for reading part or all of the manuscript and providing valuable feedback.

Love and thanks to Boyd and Sydney, for your constant encouragement, support and inspiration. Love and thanks to my mother, Joy Cehovin, for all your hours of babysitting during every stage of writing this book!

And finally, I cannot adequately express my gratitude to Barbara Conable for all she has given in her numerous roles as teacher, trainer, mentor, editor, and friend. This book would never have materialized without her. She initiated the project and provided continuous support and input throughout the writing of it. I am extremely grateful for the invaluable information she has provided all musicians by developing and writing about Body Mapping. Beyond that however, I am most grateful for the scrupulous integrity she brings to the subject and for her unwavering belief in human potential. Thank you so much, Barbara.

—Jennifer Johnson

Appendix A
Origins and Theory of Body Mapping[18] by William Conable
Professor Emeritus
at Ohio State University

Introduction

Our ideas about body mapping are not central to understanding the Technique, nor do they substitute for its essential teachings: primary control, inhibition, orders, and the like; but they can be important pedagogical tools. They are also not wholly original with us. They are clearly implied in Alexander's writings; both of our principal teachers, Marjorie Barstow and Frank Pierce Jones, occasionally used them in teaching us. They are suggested in David Gorman's work and in the pedagogy of many of our colleagues. What this chapter hopes to contribute is systematic exploration and a theoretical framework.

In trying to understand the difficulties people have in learning the Alexander Technique it is useful to observe that the words by which we refer to the parts of our bodies do not mean the same thing to all of us. This being true, what we do to carry out intentions related to the parts of our bodies is not consistent among all of us. This can easily be demonstrated in any group of people by asking them to point to their *shoulders* or their *hips*. Even among people very sophisticated in their appreciation of the human body (such as Alexander teachers) there is often a wide range of answers to such a question. It is noteworthy that in general all of these answers will be correct—that is, they will each refer to what people sometimes agree that these words mean.

Alexander frequently referred to what he called people's "imperfect sensory appreciation." What did he mean by this term? Although sometimes he maintains that he is referring to all the senses, the main thrust of his discussion refers to kinesthesis. There are two possible sources of the distortion Alexander describes. The first is that undue pressure on or tension in the kinesthetic receptors leads to a distortion of the information they send back to the brain; or perhaps that by the phenomenon of sensory accommodation the information they send is screened out. This is, in other words, the transmission of an imperfect or "debauched" kinesthetic message to the centers where it is interpreted.

The second possibility is that the information sent to the brain is indeed accurate, but is misinterpreted in experience. This would lay the emphasis in Alexander's statement on the word *appreciation*. This second possibility is the subject of this chapter.

Body Maps

We all seem to have in our minds *maps* of our bodies and their workings. They include size, shape, and mechanics. These maps are what we use to interpret our kinesthetic and visceral sensations; at least to some extent, we also guide our movement by them. This is not the same thing as the well-known neurological correspondence of various parts of the brain to various parts of the body. That is simply physiological; the map being discussed here is something constructed in consciousness.

The function of creating these maps may be in some way innate, but their contents are not. It is easy to understand that this must be so. Our bodies change in size and shape so radically and so continually throughout the course of our lives that if our maps of them could not change, the maps would almost always be erroneous.

Because the maps must be able to be changed, they must be learned. They are created from the experience of movement, of touching and being touched, and maybe from other things as well. They are our memories of our *interpretations* of our experience. But because these interpretations may not be accurate, the maps based on them may also not be accurate.

Indeed, inaccuracy in this regard seems almost inevitable. Knowledge of the complex details of the structure and function of the human body is not available to an infant mapping his or her body. Misunderstood or erroneous verbal and pictorial information, imitation of others' idiosyncrasies, and emotional charging or rejection of various body parts may play a distorting role. Fantasy and simple guessing are important sources for the details of the map. Details may be mistaken; neither is there any guarantee that the map will be consistent. Since it is formed out of many experiences over a long period of time and on the basis of an incomplete awareness of the totality of the body (or indeed, of the self) it is quite usual for different aspects of the body map to be, if not grossly contradictory, at least subtly inconsistent.

It also seems to be true that the interpretations forming the basis of the map are often unconsciously performed. They often take place early in life, well before the development of a sophisticated adult consciousness. Therefore the map based on them is often at least partly unconscious and often initially accessible to adult scrutiny only with some difficulty. Once this difficulty is overcome, it is possible to learn to change the map with surprising ease and with surprisingly powerful results.

An Example

The following story is a good introduction to the use of the mapping concept (in fact the incident led me to develop the idea) and illustrates a number of its implications. Some years ago a colleague asked me to observe a violin student who was having difficulty bending her bow arm at the elbow. Nothing the student or the teacher could think of was effective in helping her to solve this problem. Watching her play, I asked myself what I would have to think in order to move that way. It looked to me as if a possible answer was that she was thinking of her elbow joint about two inches higher on her arm than it really was. I thought that a plausible reason for this would be that that was the distance of her elbow from her shoulder when she started the violin as a child and that perhaps she had not changed her thinking as she grew.* When I proposed this to her and showed her where her elbow joint really moved, she said, "Oh, I can do that," and immediately proceeded to play with a freely moving elbow.

This story is significant in several ways. First is the issue of how the student's map influenced her behavior. Because she felt her elbow joint to be located where in truth there was nothing but solid bone, when she tried to bend it there no movement could occur. Further, since she interpreted the sensations from the area where the joint actually existed as being in the middle of her forearm, it became important for her to prevent any movement *there*—if you bend in the middle of a bone, something is broken! *Yet the moment she was made aware of these unconscious assumptions and revised them, she was able to move in a very different way.* This reveals an important underlying principle which seems to operate consistently: if there is a conflict between the way the body is mapped and the way it actually is, people will behave as if the map were true. I believe that this is because the map is the interface between conscious awareness and the bodily mechanisms: it is literally how we know ourselves. Although it is amenable to observation on a meta-level of consciousness, most of the time we simply accept it. And yet such is the power of the mapping function that simply changing the map can effect an instantaneous change in experience and behavior.

Next it is interesting that although this student was apparently unable to bend her elbow when playing the violin, she bent it over and over again in other activities of her life: eating, combing her hair, driving a car, and so on. This illustrates the apparent fact that the body map need not be internally consistent. In this it is no different from any other mental representation that people make of the world. Indeed, by its very nature any mental representation of the world is not the same as what it represents, and thus is necessarily flawed. Much of the time this is insignificant and even beneficial; sometimes it leads to difficulties.

Types of Mis-mapping

There are various common types of mapping errors. People map their bodies erroneously as regards size, structure, and function; they leave things out; and they are prone to vagueness and blankness. Illustrating these sorts of problems allows the discussion of a number of interesting examples without the necessity of offering a detailed description of the complete map.

Size is one of the most widespread inaccuracies in the map. A particularly prevalent mis-mapping is a result of the adolescent growth spurt. At the very time when rapid changes are occurring in the size, shape, and proportions of the body (and thus when the map is in strong need of revision) typical American students spend hours sitting still in school. The map is unconsciously revised through experience of movement and contact: the two things least likely to happen in junior high school. If this were not enough, children of this age are likely to feel awkward or self-conscious about their bodies and bewildered by their changing sexuality, as it affects both their internal and their social experience. Small wonder that many of us responded by saying in effect "Body? What body? I don't want to know about it!" and thus interfered with the automatic re-mapping process at a crucial developmental moment.

This can be observed in the demeanor of gawky adolescents of both sexes, awkwardly trying to operate an adult-sized body on the basis of a child-sized map. Sometimes they try to force the body down to the size their self-concept tells them it is—we often try to adjust the territory to fit the map!—stooping to get the head down to the level of smaller peers, or pulling the shoulders down in a way that gives the impression of a huge long neck on a spindly body. The hip joints are often operated as if they were the old distance from the head, and there seems to be no right place for the arms. Strange distortions are imposed in an effort to increase or decrease the size of the body as a whole or of various parts which are considered too large or too small. Many of these awkward-nesses are gradually eliminated as the map is unconsciously revised; but many adults manifest the discomforts of early adolescence in their body maps through life.

Other examples of sizing errors have other sources. We have found that most people greatly underestimate the diameter of the spine. When asked to demonstrate the size of one of their own cervical vertebrae, people will typically show diameters ranging from two to four centimeters. Rarely will anyone get close to the true dimension (a minimum of five cm. for a small adult) and almost everyone is astonished when shown how to feel the transverse processes of his or her own atlas. Realizing the true size of the spinal column gives almost anyone an increased sense of strength and stability.

The most frequent example of structural mis-mapping is the wrong location of joints. The story of the violin student above is an instance of this problem. Another common example which effects musicians and others who depend on finger dexterity is the mis-location of the joint between the proximal phalanges of the fingers and their respective metacarpals. This is not placed at the line at the base of the fingers (on the palm side) but from one to two centimeters further down into the palm. Going back in forth in one's mind between these two maps and wiggling the fingers is a highly revealing experiment in the power of the map.

The words *hip* and *shoulder* each have several meanings in English, and it is quite common for people to think of the hip and shoulder *joints* in ways which combine several of these meanings. People often try to move their arms as if there were no sternoclavicular or glenohumeral joints but at a notional joint at the inner border of the deltoid muscle (see the drawing on page 53). Similarly, they try to move their legs from the very top of the pelvis, or from an imagined joint at the bottom of the ischia or at the pelvic attachment of the gracilis muscle. Each of these misconceptions has its own characteristically distorted gait. There are dozens more of these confusions about joint placement.

Functional misconceptions also abound. One very common one is important for people who practice manual skills. When the forearm is rotated, the ulna is stable, while the radius rotates around it. This creates an axis of rotation approximately in line with the little finger. Few people realize this, but instead try to stabilize the radius and rotate the ulna on a putative axis in line with the thumb, the first finger, or the middle finger. This mistake can cause severe problems of awkwardness and even tendinitis.

The last kind of mapping errors which I will mention are those of vagueness, blankness, or absence of a part of the body in the map. These lacunae can come from simple ignorance or imitation. Frequently, however, they are the result of withdrawing from an injury and never entirely re-establishing contact with the injured part. Also, unfortunately, they can be the result of physical or psychological abuse which leads the sufferer to disown or distort part of the body. In such cases there may be a resistance to correcting the map, or there may be a resurfacing of repressed traumatic experiences which requires emotional support or treatment as an adjunct to the work of the teacher.

Appendix B
What to Do about Performance Anxiety[19]
by Barbara Conable

Our students come to us with physical discomfort and with emotional discomfort related to playing. Performance anxiety is the worst of the emotional discomfort. Here is what to do about it.

There are four distinct phenomena that go by the name performance anxiety. Each requires a different response, so it is important to name all four and distinguish them from each other so that the appropriate response may be chosen. Mixing responses guarantees failure.

FOUR KINDS OF PERFORMANCE ANXIETY

1. Butterflies
2. Self-consciousness
3. Emotions associated with inadequate preparation
4. Debilitating fear, terror, dread, and panic

DEFINITIONS
Butterflies
The fluttery sensations, sometimes intense, that precede performance and disappear as performance begins, often regarded by seasoned performers as indicative of readiness to perform but often mistaken for performance anxiety by inexperienced performers. Normal, not pathological.

Self-consciousness
Defined in my dictionary as "morbidly aware of oneself as an object of attention for others." A brilliant definition. I'd like to shake the hand of the person who wrote it. Self-consciousness is a pathology, but rather easily remedied. To call it performance anxiety is a misnomer because anxiety is not involved, as you will learn if you carefully question a self-conscious person. He or she will say, "Oh, I don't feel any fear; I'm just so self-conscious."

Emotions Associated with Inadequate Preparation

A witches' brew of shame, confusion, avoidance, and fear, not pathological, just human, often mistaken for number four by those who don't want to acknowledge the truth that they are not ready to perform. Shame predominates in this mix.

Debilitating Fear, Terror, Dread, and Panic

Intense emotion, coming in waves, usually expressed physically as sweating, shaking or other involuntary movement, rapid breathing, dry mouth, senses distorted or diminished, e.g., " It sounded like the piano was a quarter of mile away."

TIME OF OCCURRENCE

Butterflies

Occurs in the hours immediately preceding performance.

Self-consciousness

Occurs whenever the performance is thought about.

Emotions Associated with Inadequate Preparation

Pretty constant in the weeks preceding performance. Usually low grade because of the avoidance factor.

Debilitating Fear, Terror, Dread, and Panic

Grandly episodic throughout the entire period of preparation. Middle of the night. While driving one's car. At a party. Walking past the concert hall. Talking with one's accompanist on the phone. Taking a walk. Sudden. Unpredictable. Subsides, only to reappear another time.

EFFECT ON PERFORMANCE

Butterflies

Enhances performance.

Self-consciousness

Compromises the whole performance, start to finish. "I always play better in practice than in performance." Emotional expression and meaning are compromised.

Emotions Associated with Inadequate Preparation

Performance spotty and substandard because of the inadequate preparation, not because of the associated emotions.

Debilitating Fear, Terror, Dread, and Panic

May stop performance altogether. Performers may refuse to play or sing at the last minute or they walk off stage mid concert. If they play or sing the whole concert, the fear and its physical manifestation are episodic throughout. The sweating and shaking may be visible and result in wrong notes. The sensory distortion may interfere with ability to read the notation or to hear the other players so that performance has to be stopped and started again. Often results in "memory slips" or rhythmic distortion. Rarely if ever compromises expressiveness. In fact, some performers claim they are not expressive unless they are filled with fear, terror, dread, panic.

REMEDIES
Butterflies
Learn to enjoy them. Begin the performance and they disappear.

Self-consciousness
Being self-consciousness, morbidly aware of oneself as an object of observation for others, requires a two step remedy. First, get clear about the fact that the audience pays money and comes to the concert hall to make the music the object of attention. If the audience paid money and came to the concert hall to make *you* the object of attention, you wouldn't have to play the music. You could just sit there and let them look at you. Second step in the remedy, develop self-awareness. True self-awareness (kinesthetic, tactile, emotional) is the great, reliable remedy for self-consciousness. This two-step remedy can work literally overnight and solve the problem forever if the first step is truly comprehended. The music is what it's all about. The music is the object of observation for the audience and for the performer, who have a mutual interest in the music.

Emotions Associated with Inadequate Preparation
Cancel or postpone the performance or the audition, or get a sub. No other response is appropriate. Then, get yourself adequately prepared. If you don't know how to prepare, find someone who will teach you. Never, never use performance anxiety as an excuse when it was inadequate preparation that compromised the quality of your performance. Teachers, don't let your students get by with this, either. Nail them. Call them on it. It's your job. Don't let them perform unprepared.

Debilitating Fear, Terror, Dread, and Panic
The remedy for this is strenuous, demanding, difficult, uncompromising, but it works. The remedy will be described in great detail later in this essay, but, first, I believe it is important to understand that this type of performance anxiety happens in a context. In my experience, the context must be credited in order for the sufferer to do the work of liberation.

THE CONTEXT

Performance fear, terror, dread, panic is not purely personal and cannot be remedied without some understanding of its cultural context. In order for musicians to exert themselves to genuine change, they need to sense they are changing not just themselves but also the musical culture. In other words, they are doing it for everyone.

Let's look at the problem from the perspective of circumstances in which performance anxiety rarely or never occurs. Then, let's examine some unusual factors in the way music is taught and heard in our culture. Third, please consider the status of musicians in our culture as a factor in the fear musicians feel.

Let's look first at the circumstances in which performance anxiety rarely or never occurs in order to shine some light on the circumstances in which it does occur. Performance anxiety rarely occurs among pro-ams, as they are now fondly called, that is, amateurs who play at a professional level. It rarely occurs among church musicians, especially those who regard themselves as having a vocation for music, and it rarely occurs among Indian classical musicians (those who play the traditional ragas), though their music is at least as complex and demanding as western classical music, and it rarely occurs among African drummers, though their music is far more complex rhythmically than is western music. I have the impression that performance anxiety is less frequent among western jazz and rock musicians than among western classical musicians. Pro-ams tell me they feel eager anticipation when they perform. One said it is like preparing a fine meal for friends.

Pro-ams play a lot of chamber music, and the music itself is the motivating factor, the joy of hearing it, the joy of playing it, the joy of discovering something new about it. For these highly skilled amateurs there are no bad consequences in their imagination if they don't for some reason play well, no loss of job, no scorn from colleagues, and the like.

Church musicians tell me they attribute their absence of fear to the fact that even their very finest performances are not ends in themselves but rather dedicated to the overall effect of the celebration. Organists sometimes tell me it helps them that they are not seen by the congregation, or not watched as a concert pianist is.

Indian classical musicians tend to attribute their comfort in playing to the communal nature of their training and to the fact that they usually live with their teachers, who teach them every day, not every week, and offer the ongoing nurture and support in supervised daily practice. The students never experience the isolation so many young musicians experience in our culture.

One of the great African drummers at a Percussive Arts Society convention, when asked about performance anxiety, said he had never met anyone who suffered from it. Laughing, he said, "We are not afraid of music." Then he became serious and named some elements in the training of drummers that may prevent performance anxiety. First, he said, "We never ever name a mistake. Naming mistakes seems silly to us," he said, "like naming the mistakes" in a young child's talking or walking." He went on to say that young children are kept at the same level of playing for a long time and not allowed to go to the next level of complexity until they are practically bursting to do so. Then, when they do go to the next level, they can achieve it easily, they have so long anticipated it in their minds and because they have heard it and seen it for so long from others. In addition, African teachers play with their students or for their students all or most of the time, and there are no competitions, only performances.

Rock musicians, in my experience, are free of performance anxiety. When I ask them about this, they generally attribute it to the connection they feel to their audience. They are deeply, profoundly aware of their audience as they write and rehearse, so it is as if the audience is perpetually present. The audience is not something to be feared but something to draw strength and inspiration from. Listen to interviews with great rock musicians and you will hear them talk about their audiences in the same way some well-known novelists talk about theirs. A mutual loyalty is being described. Jazz musicians share to some degree the sense of audience, especially those who get a following in certain clubs, but they have the further cushion of improvisation. Improvisation is a very demanding enterprise, but it does give a kind of space that the strict notation of classical music does not.

There are some aspects of the ways music is heard in our culture that we take for granted much of the time, but which are nevertheless quite unusual and may contribute to the debilitating fear some musicians experience. An audience sitting in rows facing a stage with nothing else to think about is unusual in the world. In other cultures people wander in and out of the performance space, paying close attention when they like and peripheral attention at other times. The musicians are not watched so intently. Nowadays many people have CD's of the music being performed. Notes not written by the composer have been corrected on the CDs, and therefore people's ears are geared to a level of technical perfection that is unrealistic. Also, audience members may be comparing a university professor's performance to the performance of the finest concert musicians in the world. The comparison spoils what would otherwise be a profoundly enjoyable experience, and, to make matters worse, the performer may also be making the comparison, contributing to performance fear and dread. Some fine musicians perform infrequently, upping the ante on any one performance, like getting to play one or two poker hands a year.

And then there is the matter of envy. I will not write about envy in this essay because it has been discussed so brilliantly by James Jordan in The Musician's Soul, a book all musicians need to read and study because envy is a truly significant factor in performance fear and dread.
As is status. Musicians' status is our culture is described in one word: low.

Evidence: Joke

Three people appear at the pearly gates. The doctor is welcomed right in, likewise the lawyer. The musician is directed around to the back door.

Evidence: Cover Story in City Magazine

"How to Impress Your Friends This Year." Tip number ten: Buy season tickets to the symphony and never, never go.

Evidence: Musicians' Salaries at Universities

As compared with others who have spent decades of hard work in preparation for what they do.

Evidence: The Way Musicians Are Treated at the White House.

Rosalyn Carter made sure that musicians were greeted when they arrived and that they were served good food and had a comfortable place to change clothes and warm up and rest between performances, but other occupants of the White House have not followed her example.

Evidence: Lack of Elementary Safeguards for Musicians

The reluctance of symphony management to adopt and adhere to elementary safeguards for musicians and their instruments, like temperature control, reasonable schedules, and ear protection.

Evidence: The Failure of Universities to Credit Practice Time and Score Study as Work Hours

Many university musicians work a full work week in addition to their practice and study time. From a non-musician's point of view, this is cruel and counter productive, like asking a scientist to do research after hours, and it contributes to performance anxiety because the performing professor is tired and sometimes resentful.

I have been privileged to spend some time in a culture in which musicians are held in the highest esteem, revered, cared for, regarded as very, very special. Their status is in shocking contrast to that of musicians in American mainstream culture.

THE REMEDY FOR PERFORMANCE FEAR, TERROR, DREAD, and PANIC

I derive some linguistic pleasure from building the remedy on the letters in the word F-E-A-R, thus:

- F   Feel the fear
- E   Embody the fear
- A   Arrive
- R   Relate

The device also helps my students remember what to do. Feel the fear. Embody the fear. Truly arrive in the performance space. Truly relate to the space, the music, and the audience.

It sounds simple, but it is actually very mentally demanding, and the feeling and the embodying must be done over and over again throughout the preparation period whenever the episodes of fear occur, so it is a day by day commitment over a period of weeks or months, and it is particularly demanding at the time of performance because feeling and embodying must continue unabated while you at the same time truly arrive in the space and truly relate to it. Not simple. Not easy. Why do I recommend something so demanding as remedy? Because it's the only thing that works. Believe me, I've seen everything you can imagine tried to solve this problem and nothing but this demanding procedure really works. If you don't believe me, try all the others and then do this, hard as it is. No one ever said being a successful performer was going to be easy, only that is was going to be fulfilling and in keeping with our deepest humanity, so the reward is great.

So, here is how it's done, letter by letter.

F: Feel the Fear

Many people make the mistake of trying not to feel their fear, terror, dread, panic, or they try to diminish it, or they try to ignore it. This turns them into two people, the person who is feeling the fear and the one who is suppressing or ignoring it. You can't perform split. It just won't work. So, the first task in solving the problem of performance fear is to just agree to feel what you're feeling full out in every part of your body, not diminishing any tiny bit of it.

Now, understand that fear, terror, dread, panic only overwhelm if they are experienced in isolation from other sensations. So, your next *Feel* task is to feel also all the other emotions in your experience. You may think there are no others, but you will be wrong about this. If you go looking for them, you will find the others -- anger, perhaps; self-compassion, we hope; your love for the music you will be playing, your anticipation, yearning; hope for a fine performance; regard for the other musicians on your concert. The key here is to let all those other emotions live in your experience and come into relationship with the fear you feel. If you let them live there with the fear, the other emotions will cushion the fear, change its texture. Probably they will not diminish its intensity, but that's okay, really, because they will change the physical expression of the fear. Sweating and shaking will subside. Your body only produces these expressions of your fear if your fear is all you're feeling, if it's alone there in experience, all by itself. When you're feeling all your other emotions at the same time, the monochromatic response of shaking and sweating gives way to a rainbow of expression that also prevents the sensory distortions that compromise performance so seriously.

You may want to actively cultivate and enhance some of your other emotions. If you love music, right there in the presence of all your fear, expand and enhance that love. If you have some joyful anticipation of playing this marvelous music for people in the audience, enhance that. Don't stop feeling the fear, just give it good company. You are cultivating richness in your experience. If you allow it to, the music will help you as you practice it. Be sure you are making the fullest possible emotional response to the music you are practicing. You will need to make your entire nervous system available to the music, then it will provide you with the richest possible context for your fear. Music teaches you how to feel what it expresses. That is one of its glories, and it is how music helps you with your fear.

Now, remember, this is just the first step, and it will not work in isolation from the others to solve your performance fear problem, but neither can it be skipped or cheated. You will have to do this step consistently, day after day, in your practice and every single time you feel an episode of performance fear coming on.

E: Embody the Fear

Now you go the next step and give all your emotion a larger context. You need to put all your emotion in the company of all your other physical sensation. Just like fear never overwhelms when it is given the company of other emotion, so emotion never overwhelms when it is given the company of other sensation. We call this strategy embodying the fear.

First, put all your emotions in the context of your tactile experience, the feeling of your skin, your tactile sensation of your shoes, socks, floor, clothing, the temperature and movement of the air as perceived by your skin. Find it all and put your emotion firmly in relationship to it.

Then find all your kinesthetic sensation, that is, all your experience of your moving, of your position, of your size. You will be moving to perform, and you will need to feel your moving with great clarity in order to choose the best movement and in order to change your moving if it needs to be changed. So, in embodying your emotion, you are also availing yourself of information crucial for performance anyway, apart from its function as a primary cushion for fear.

As you become kinesthetically awake, you will feel overt movement and what is fashionably called micro-movement, all the inner hum of muscular and visceral activity. You will feel this all as related, like an orchestra of sensation, not isolated like orchestra members warming up.

You want to be sure you are feeling any other sensation that may be present. Pain, if it's there, hunger, thirst, pleasure, the whole richness of being. Then your fear is like a clarinet in the orchestra, just one element of a complex but unified whole. This reclaiming of experience requires intention, or will, but it is worth all the mental effort it takes to recover it.

To repeat, you must make this recovery every single time you feel the fear, terror, dread, panic, in the months coming up to performance. There is a discipline in this, a consistency. Every time.

A: Arrive

Then you have to put all this richness in the context of the actual performance situation. We are nesting experience here, you see, like those nested Russian dolls, one within another. Your fear is the littlest doll, which you put within all the others so that you have it in a safe context. You have to truly arrive in the space.

Now, this is the opposite of unsuccessful strategies like, "I try to pretend I'm still in my practice room." The pretending strategy is disastrous on two counts: it removes your from reality, and it ties up your imagination, which you need for performance.

Arrive. Come to the concert hall early. Walk out onto the stage. Get clear about where the walls are, the floors are, the seats are. Sense the space. Relate to the space. Claim the space. Be in the space. Get clear about the objects in the space, learning where the piano is, for instance, the music stands, the chairs, the lights. Watch in the wings as the audience filters in. Do this arriving in your dress rehearsals so you're used to it for performance.

You can also practice this by truly arriving in your practice space, using the same strategy for your practice you will use later for your performance.

In your practice space, even if it is very small, you will need claim a space for your moving that is at least as big as the space you will perform in, otherwise coming into the larger performance space will be a shock. Many successful musicians ordinarily claim a much larger space for their moving than a concert hall, but the size of the concert hall is the smallest that works. This does not mean that you imagine you are in the concert hall. No. Rather, you claim, own, move in, command, occupy a space in practice big enough for performance.

Arrive. An audience is coming into this space in which you will perform. Part of arriving is acknowledging the likely nature of that audience. If some of your audience is hostile, may write bad reviews, will be catty, you will need to arrive to that fact and really be present with it. There's no pretending they are other than they are. Hostile people, along with those who are kindly and truly interested in hearing the music, must be treated as audience. You are not responsible for how they behave, but you are responsible for how you behave, and it is your job to play or sing in good faith for all the members of your audience, including the hostile and the catty and the uppity. This is rich and complex experience, which is just how it is for an artist.

R: Relate

Which brings us to the final maneuver in eliminating performance fear as a problem. Fear remains, perhaps, as an emotion, but it is no longer a problem because you know how to handle it. You feel, you embody yourself and your feeling, you arrive, and you relate. You relate to the space; you relate to your audience, you relate to the music, you relate to your instrument.

Let's take each of those in turn. You relate to the space as I have described above, claiming the whole of it for your movement in performance. You do not go out on stage and play in a space the size of your practice room. If you do, we in the audience have to look into your space as through a window. We are not included in it and we feel left out, as though we were watching someone practice. If you do not relate to the space in performance, you do not get the advantages of perceiving its acoustical properties or its beauty or the spaciousness that might inform the quality of your moving. You do not get the benefit of its sheltering.

You relate to your audience, that is, they are in your awareness and you are playing for them. There is a mutuality. They enjoy your performance, and you feel their enjoyment and appreciation and that helps you in your performance. Performers who do not relate to their audiences do not get the benefit of the audience reaction for stamina and for pleasure in performing. It's a big, big loss to everyone.

You relate to the music, that it, you let the music benefit you as much as it is benefitting the audience. You make a full emotional response to the music, which carries and sustains your performance. You let the music sustain you.

You relate to your instrument. There is great security in this, for you will be able to feel your instrument clearly. It may seem that the instrument is warmed up, ready to go, that it is eager to perform, like a racehorse at the beginning of a race. This will help you. Your love for your instrument as well as your love for the music can be a source of stability and cushioning in the performance. This is especially true for singers, of course. If you are relating profoundly to your instrument as you perform, you will know when it needs some special care or some adjustment, as to a quirky reed or to a voice just recovering from a cold.

One result of feeling-embodying-arriving-relating is that time has a different flavor. There seems to be more of it. There is enough time to make choices. There is a temporal spaciousness that allows you to recover and renew your feeling-embodying-arriving-relating if it weakens. This all becomes second nature over time, as it is first nature for those who never lost it. The deliberateness falls away; the need for will falls away. Feeling-embodying-arriving-relating is no longer a discipline, but just what one does, naturally. Fear as a problem is a poignant memory.

BEST TIPS FOR ELIMINATING PERFORMANCE ANXIETY AMONG YOUR STUDENTS

1. Help your students see that their fear is not purely personal but is a shared, cultural phenomenon that requires a cultural change as well as a personal one, to which they may contribute.
2. Frequently remind your students that becoming a highly accomplished amateur is an option for them. Encourage your students to explore and enjoy all kinds of music and to see themselves as part of a community of musicians that includes all kinds of musicians.
3. Encourage your students to seek out performance opportunities, to perform in nursing homes, for instance, or at their own dinner parties.
4. Encourage your students to play or sing chamber music at every possible opportunity, just for the joy of it.

5. Cultivate a positive environment in your studio and set clear rules for how students treat each other. Always perform on your students' recitals, always. They need to see your preparation and they need your modeling.

6. Keep your own performance at a high level and perform frequently even if you primarily earn your living by teaching.

7. If a student comes to a lesson unprepared, practice for the student, talking to the student about what you're doing, e.g., "Notice that I repeated that passage because I changed my mind about how it goes." Or, offer to observe the student's practicing, coaching the student in good practice technique. Never, never just ignore or overlook the fact that the lesson is unprepared.

8. Play with your students.

9. Play for your students.

10. Face your students whenever possible. It's a great help for them to see what you're doing. They can't see you if they are on a stand with you. Help your students from the very first lesson to truly know their instruments. Many students are handicapped and fearful because they are playing fantasy instruments which differ greatly from the instruments they actually have (like a piano student listening to the keys instead of the strings; like a piano student imagining that the point of sound is at the key bed). Always let the students know the limitations of the instrument they are using so they don't feel bad because they can't make their student violin sound like your Strad.

11. Deal constructively with wrong notes. Much of the time you don't even need to point them out. Just play the piece again yourself, asking the student to listen carefully. If you feel its important to give feedback about the note, just say that the student played a note the composer didn't write and always play that note yourself. "You played this (you play B flat); the composer wrote this (you play B natural)." Give the student time to hear the difference and to play the difference, one and then the other, so that the correction can truly be assimilated. Put the correction in a musical context, asking, "Why did the composer choose B natural here instead of the B flat you played?" Sometimes the student will have played something that actually sounds better than what the composer wrote. Always acknowledge that when it is true.

12. Be very, very careful to give students age appropriate and skill appropriate music and not too much of it.

13. Keep the students at a skill level for a long time, letting them enjoy their success in coming to that level, so that year after year as they grow they get to experience real competence and musicality.

14. Never, never, never let a student perform unprepared. Just reschedule the student to the next recital.

15. Keep your young students out of competitions and seek opportunities for them to play for supportive, knowledgeable colleagues in non-competitive situations. Stay with them in those situations so you know they are being treated well and constructively.

16. Be as educated as you can be about the youth choirs and orchestras and the music camps in your area so that you can steer your students away from harsh circumstances and into nurturing, supportive circumstances.

17. Teach your students to improvise, right from the first. If you don't know how to improvise yourself, join Music for People and let David Darling and his certified improv teachers teach you how. Help your students build a genuine sense of having an audience. In the beginning it will be the parents and friends who come to the recitals. Refer frequently to the audience and to the pleasure the audience will take in the music. Make it clear that in your studio musicians are held in high esteem, consistent with the intelligence, humanity, and artistry it takes to do the job. Model for the students a very high level of self regard and self care.

18. Teach your older students how to treat auditioners and jurors as genuine audience.

Illustration Credits

Reprinted from *The Body Moveable* with kind permission from David Gorman: figures 2, 11–13, 31, 40, 54, 62–63, 65, 67, 72, 78–80.

Reprinted from *Eyebody; The Art of Integrating Eye, Brain and Body* with kind permission from Peter Grunwald: figure 81.

Reprinted from *How to Learn the Alexander Technique* with kind permission from Barbara Conable: figure 5.

Reprinted from *The Mind has a Body of its Own* with kind permission from Sandra and Matthew Blakeslee: figure 1.

Original illustrations by Tracy Dillon: figures 6, 9–10, 15, 20, 24–28, 30, 36, 41, 45–47, 57, 64, 74.

Reprinted from *What Every Musician Needs to Know about the Body* with kind permission from Barbara and Ben Conable: figures 3–4, 7–8, 14, 17–19, 21–23, 29, 32–35, 37–39, 42–44, 48–53, 55–56, 59–61, 66, 68–71, 73, 75–77.

❦

Conable, Barbara. *What Every Musician Needs to Know about the Body,* 2nd ed. Designed by Ben Conable. Chicago: GIA Publications, Inc. (dist.), 2000. ISBN 0-9622592-6-X. GIA Publications, Inc., 7404 S Mason Ave, Chicago, IL 60638.

Conable, Barbara H. and William Conable. *How to Learn the Alexander Technique,* 3rd ed. Chicago: GIA Publications, Inc. (dist.), 1995. ISBN 0-9622595-4-3. GIA Publications, Inc., 7404 S Mason Ave, Chicago, IL 60638.

Dillon, Tracy. tsdillon@nf.sympatico.ca.

Gorman, David. *The Body Moveable,* 5th ed. Toronto: LearningMethods Publications, 2002. ISBN 1-903518-15-6. LearningMethods Publications, 19 Stephen Drive, Toronto, Ontario, Canada M8Y 3M7.

Grunwald, Peter. *The Art of Integrating Eye, Brain and Body: Letting Go of Glasses Forever,* 2nd ed. Auckland: Condevis Publishing, 2008. ISBN 978-0-958289-92-1. Condevis Publishing, Box 46 325, Herne Bay 1147, Auckland, NZ. www.eyebody.com.

Endnotes

1. Nichols, Richard. "Scientific Basis of Body Mapping." www.bodymap.org.

2. Blakeslee, Matt. *The Body Has a Mind of Its Own.* New York: Random House, 2007, 19.

3. Nichols.

4. Nichols.

5. For an in-depth look at Inclusive Awareness for performers, see Appendix B: What to Do about Performance Anxiety by Barbara C. Conable.

6. In Body Mapping terms, *downward pull* is a series of misconceptions in the brain about how the bones are designed to meet each other at each of the major points of balance in the body.

7. Through many years of experimentation, F.M. Alexander discovered that the state of the *neck muscles* determines the state of the rest of the body—that the pattern of downward pull always begins in the tightening of the neck muscles, which then rotates the head "back and down" off of its perfectly balanced perch on top of the spine. Because the downward pull pattern *begins* in the neck muscles, Alexander named the relationship between the neck and head the "primary control." He discovered that when an individual's primary control is working relatively well, so that the neck muscles are only doing the work of moving a balanced head rather than trying to support it in an imbalanced position and then move it, the rest of the body can be led into a relatively balanced and unified state.

8. Jones, Frank Piere. *Body Awareness in Action: A Study of the Alexander Technique.* New York: Schocken Books, Inc, 1976, 132.

9. A common mis-mapping of the arm is that the thumb, or even worse, the palm, should be facing to the front when the arms are hanging at the sides. An arm hanging in a balanced neutral always has the back of the hand facing to the front, creating the feeling that there is plenty of space in the armpit. More on this in chapter 4.

10. "Color co-ordination." *The Strad,* June 2004.

11. Galamian, Ivan. *Principles of Violin Playing and Teaching.* Englewood Cliffs, NJ: Prentice-Hall, Inc., 1962, 38.

12. I have borrowed the terms *curl* and *curve* to differentiate between the flexed and neutral shape of the fingers from the pedagogy of Dorothy Taubmann.

13. *Heifetz & Piatigorsky: Historic Performance Film Footage.* Kultur Video, 2005.

14. Video-recording yourself rehearsing and wiring the live image through the television screen is a fantastically informative way to practice because you can watch your movement from virtually any angle desired by moving the camera around you. It prevents the added difficulties sometimes caused by using multiple mirrors to achieve the same result.

15. The word *torso* is used here to describe the portion of the body that lies between the base of the skull and the pelvic floor.

16. The idea of the collective ribs as shaped like a beehive is suggested by: Gilmore, Robin. *What Every Dancer Needs to Know about the Body.* Portland, OR: Andover Press, 2005, 50. www.bodymap.org

17. For an in-depth mapping of vision and to learn how some have successfully improved their eyesight and disposed of corrective lenses, see: Grunwald, Peter. *Eyebody: The Art of Integrating Eye, Brain and Body.* Auckland, New Zealand: Eyebody Press, 2004.

18. Originally titled "Origins and Theory of Mapping." Revised from a paper presented by William Conable at the Third International Alexander Congress in Engelberg, Switzerland, August, *1991.* Printed in its original form in the Congress papers, published by *Direction,* Bondi, Australia, *1992.*

19. 2004. http://bodymap.org/articles/artperformanceanxiety.html

About the Author

Jennifer Johnson is a certified Andover Educator and an active performer and teacher. During her twelve years as Principal Second Violin of the Newfoundland Symphony Orchestra and Second Violin of the Atlantic String Quartet, Jennifer performed regularly with artists of international acclaim, including Krystof Penderecki, Dennis Brott, Patrick Gallois, Rivka Golani, and Anton Kuerti.

In addition to her performing work she also has a well-established reputation as a pedagogue. Throughout her career she has been dedicated to the advancement of music education, specifically through the Suzuki Talent Education Program of St. John's, of which she served as Artistic Director from 1998–2002.

In 2004, a generous grant from the Canada Council for the Arts funded a seven-month Alexander Technique sabbatical for Jennifer which permitted her to study throughout Europe and the United States with many of the world's leading Alexander Technique teachers. Some of these teachers included Pedro de Alcantara, Walter Carrington, Marjorie Barlow, Joan and Alexander Murray, and Barbara Conable. Jennifer went on to train with Barbara Conable, and in 2005 became Canada's first certified Andover Educator.

She is now adjunct faculty at the Memorial University of Newfoundland Music School and presents Body Mapping workshops across North America, working with musicians who are interested in learning to enhance their musical ability and prevent injury through a clear understanding of how their bodies are designed to move. Jennifer lives in St. John's, Newfoundland, Canada with her husband and son.